total feng shui

total feng shui

Bring Health, Wealth, and Happiness Into Your Life

LILLIAN TOO

ILLUSTRATIONS BY JIM PILSTON, RAY MARTIN, AND NADINE FAY-JAMES

CHRONICLE BOOKS

SAN FRANCISCO

First published in the United States in 2005 by Chronicle Books.

Text and compilation copyright © 2004 Lillian Too
Book design and all illustrations copyright © 2004 The Bridgewater Book Company

The illustrations on pages 16, 21, 24, 30, 32, 40, 46, 47, 48, 78, 98, 99, 126, 128, 129, 133, and 150 were created by the Bridgewater Book Company and are their copyright 2004. However, the original diagrams and the information from which they were derived were created by Lillian Too and remain her copyright.

Library of Congress Cataloguing-in-Publication Data available.

ISBN 0-8118-4530-3

Manufactured in China.

Creative Director: Terry Jeavons
Art Director: Sarah Howerd
Managing Editor: Mark Truman
Designers: Frances Marr and Nicola Liddiard

Distributed in Canada by Raincoast Books
9050 Shaughnessy Street
Vancouver, British Columbia V6P 6E5

10 9 8 7 6 5 4 3 2 1

Chronicle Books LLC
85 Second Street
San Francisco, California 94105

www.chroniclebooks.com

CONTENTS

INTRODUCTION

✳ FENG SHUI IS FIRST AND FOREMOST A LIVING SKILL. IT OFFERS AN INTEGRATED SET OF GUIDELINES THAT CAN BE LEARNED AND PUT INTO PRACTICE. THE GUIDELINES TRANSCEND LIMITATIONS OF CULTURE AND RELIGION. FOR MANY YEARS, THIS WISDOM OF ANCIENT CHINESE SAGES WAS ACCESSIBLE ALMOST EXCLUSIVELY TO THE CHINESE PEOPLE (BARRING A FEW FOREIGN SCHOLARS) AND TO SOCIETIES THAT WERE HEAVILY INFLUENCED BY CHINESE CULTURAL PRACTICES, SUCH AS KOREA, JAPAN, TAIWAN, HONG KONG, AND SINGAPORE. HOWEVER, THIS SITUATION IS NOW CHANGING.

In today's age of incredible growth and global linkages, it is possible for virtually anyone to access the philosophy and practices of feng shui. Its complex fundamentals can now be distilled into easily understood and applied techniques.

Much of the mystique has been taken out of feng shui practice and it is gaining acceptance as the science of living space. However, feng shui is not a subject easily lent to logical analysis. It demands, at least initially, a degree of acceptance of the Chinese view of the universe, which includes the concept of the five elements, the symbolism of the trigrams, and the philosophy of the yin and yang of energy, to name three fundamental components.

Many people worldwide already accept and are committed to feng shui. They gain an advantage by integrating this commitment into the way they organize their living space and observe the timing of significant events in their lives. Those who use feng shui to organize their space also usually use feng shui to update the energy of their space, from year to year and from period to period. If you are receptive to feng shui's ideas, you stand to gain much by applying its ideas to your life and your environment.

✳ JUST WHAT IS FENG SHUI?

Feng shui is representative of Chinese science in the same manner that the electromagnetic spectrum is representative of Western science, in which terms of visible and invisible light emissions in the electromagnetic spectrum are used to define our surroundings.

The chi energy lines frequently referred to in feng shui underpin its whole practice. These can be compared to the invisible energy lines that form the spectrum of electromagnetic waves, perhaps better described as "earth currents" in the atmosphere.

In feng shui terms, chi consists of invisible lines of energy, picturesquely described as the "cosmic breath" of the celestial dragon. Surely chi is no different from the earth currents that modern scientific discoveries have shown us exist everywhere around us.

Computers have gone wireless. Messages, data, and even pictures are sent across the world through waves and radio energy. Surely it is possible that the chi lines referred to in feng shui are simply scientifically undiscovered dynamic forces that cause well-being or illness, good fortune or misfortune, thus having an impact on living people.

Feng shui's potency and visible effects are thus akin to the technological harnessing of electromagnetic energies seen in modern appliances such as microwave ovens, CD players, radios, and television sets.

Just as these emissions can be both productive and destructive, so too can chi and feng shui produce both beneficial and disastrous results—what the Chinese construe as good and bad luck!

To the non-Chinese reader, the prevalence of Chinese popular folklore, myths and beliefs, anecdotes, and grassroots interpretations is a source of added interest; and creative readers may well discover parallels in their own cultural milieu and folk wisdom.

This book can thus be viewed as a wonderful starting point on a journey into the boundless, assisting the reader in comprehending humankind's existence within the living space, and in the process coming to understand something of the enticing concepts of luck enhancement techniques.

✳ HOW CAN FENG SHUI IMPROVE MY LIFE?

Feng shui will not change your fate or destiny completely and it should not be practiced with this unrealistic expectation. It is also neither a pseudo-religious nor a spiritual practice. It is not magic nor shamanistic. It is a living skill requiring the acquisition of knowledge and practical experience and requiring an acceptance and understanding of the invisible energy forces that surround humankind.

Through the practice of feng shui, anyone can modify the severity of misfortunes encountered, thereby lessening their impact and making problems easier to bear. More excitingly, feng shui also promises the ability to enhance the magnitude of good times. In short, feng shui can be harnessed to enhance the highs and modify the lows of your life experience.

Applying feng shui principles to our lives will create an awareness of the energy forces that surround us and in the process help us come to terms with every vital moment of existence. In the simplicity of feng shui practice a profound awakening to the forces that influence our lives can be found.

Our lives are influenced by the quality of chi that pervades our living spaces. This affects how we vibrate in consonance with the rhythms of our environment. Wind and water, the literal components of feng shui, focus our awareness on this invisible energy that emanates from the natural environment—mountains, rivers, and landscapes that make up the earth. Understanding the intrinsic nature of chi and its variations, we learn to differentiate between auspicious chi and misfortune chi, between chi that brings vibrant good health and chi that brings sickness.

The living chi of the natural environment has the power to nurture us or to destroy us. When we succeed in blending harmoniously with it, we have succeeded in refining an approach to living that enhances our quality of life. This is the practice of feng shui—tapping into the good chi—the luck of the earth.

We can use feng shui in many ways and from different perspectives. It can be used to evaluate the external environment that surrounds homes and buildings and it can also be used to plan interior spaces. Feng shui gives us valuable expertise that can be put to good use in choosing, designing, and enhancing the spaces in which we live and work. Feng shui formulas also enable us to custom design our luck.

Feng shui offers practical guidelines that enable anyone to select good property—property whose chi is not afflicted by hostile hills and whose luck is not blocked by harmful structures and whose yang energy is vibrant and strong.

Depending on your life aspirations, you will find feng shui expertise has many solutions and suitable recommendations for you. Let this book open a valuable and comprehensive door into the fascinating world of feng shui....

PART ONE

GENERAL PRINCIPLES

THE PRACTICE OF **FENG SHUI** ALWAYS BEGINS WITH BASIC PRINCIPLES THAT

STRESS THE IMPORTANCE OF LOCATION. IF THE LOCATION OF YOUR HOME IS

AUSPICIOUS, ACCORDING TO FUNDAMENTAL FENG SHUI TENETS, YOU AND

YOUR FAMILY WILL BE ASSURED OF A GOOD LIFE AND EXCELLENT LUCK WILL

ACCOMPANY YOU IN YOUR ENDEAVORS. THE NATURAL ENVIRONMENT IS VERY

POWERFUL, SO EVEN IF YOUR HOME'S INTERIOR SUFFERS FROM **FENG SHUI**

MISTAKES, THE EFFECTS WILL BE OVERRIDDEN IF THE LOCATION OF YOUR

HOME ENJOYS GOOD CLASSICAL FORM SCHOOL **FENG SHUI**. FORM SCHOOL

FENG SHUI FOCUSES ON THE PHYSICAL SURROUNDINGS OF YOUR HOME

OR, IF YOU LIVE IN AN APARTMENT, THE BUILDING IN WHICH YOUR APARTMENT

IS SITUATED, TO DETERMINE IF THE LOCATION HAS GOOD **FENG SHUI**.

CHAPTER 1
FENG SHUI LOCATIONS

✳ LANDSCAPE FENG SHUI INVOLVES A STUDY OF THE NATURAL TERRAIN. THE ENVIRONMENT IS ALIVE WITH CHI, AND WHETHER THIS IS AUSPICIOUS OR NOT DEPENDS ON HOW THE WINDS AND WATERS HAVE SHAPED THE LANDSCAPE OVER TIME.

✳ TYPES OF LOCATIONS

There are many types of locations—some possess intrinsic good fortune that benefits all who live there, while others seem wreathed in bad luck, bringing misfortune to all who dwell in the vicinity.

Some neighborhoods have better feng shui than others—those who live there seem blessed with benevolent chi that brings success and serenity. Life is smooth and without major obstacles.

On the other hand, some locations cause residents to suffer many types of misfortune. These are places where the chi is afflicted, stagnant, or stale, and therefore harmful to residents.

The challenge for those who want to incorporate feng shui into their search for a good location is to acquire the knowledge of a set of guidelines upon which to base

their search—guidelines that quickly enable them to differentiate good from bad locations. This school of feng shui is known as Landscape Feng Shui and it involves a study of the natural terrain. Here the smell of the winds, the contours of the land and land masses, the quality of soils, vegetation, and waterways combine harmoniously or otherwise to create either good or bad feng shui. Feng shui is about living in harmony with the earth's environment and its energy, so balance is achieved.

The curving hills around this building, with its view of a meandering river, make its location truly auspicious.

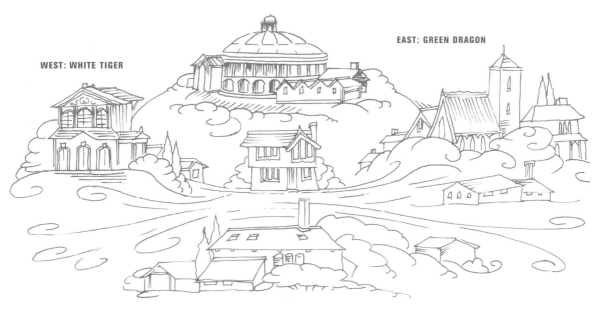

NORTH: BLACK TORTOISE

EAST: GREEN DRAGON

WEST: WHITE TIGER

SOUTH: CRIMSON PHOENIX

The central house is positioned auspiciously among the four celestial guardians. Note that in the modern city environments, buildings and houses take on the chi essence of the four celestial guardians.

✱ FOUR CELESTIAL GUARDIANS FORMATION

Auspicious locations are usually slightly elevated places where the Green Dragon of the East (*see* pages 181 and 241) nestles gently with the White Tiger of the West (*see* pages 181 and 281), their bodies curving gently toward one another to form a horseshoe or armchair shape.

This formation is at the same time protected from the North winds by a range of hills symbolizing the Black Tortoise (*see* pages 181 and 209), while in the South the presence of the Crimson Phoenix (*see* pages 181 and 219) considerably enhances the site. These four creatures are known as the four celestial guardians in feng shui lore. Represented by hills or land

formations, their presence in any location is the first sign of auspicious feng shui.

If, facing this wonderful configuration of celestial guardian hills, there is also a view of meandering or slow-moving water; and the vegetation in the area is green and lush, then a home built here is ensured of good feng shui and thus an abundance of good fortune, great comfort, and enormous wealth. This house will bring all these benefits to the household for many succeeding generations. Building a business's corporate headquarters here will ensure smooth and profitable growth for all its operations.

Since the celestial creatures are purely symbolic, dragons and tigers are not confined to hills and mountains, nor the

FOUR CELESTIAL GUARDIANS

BLACK TORTOISE The celestial creature of the North, it brings support, longevity, and protection from bad luck.

GREEN DRAGON The celestial creature of the East, the earth dragon is associated with hills and mountains, and is the ultimate symbol of good luck.

CRIMSON PHOENIX The celestial creature of the South, who can be represented by low-lying foothills or buildings in front of your home, or to the South.

WHITE TIGER The celestial creature of the West complements (but is subordinate to) the Green Dragon in the East and has a protective role towards the home.

tortoise and phoenix to undulating land. In a city environment, dragons and tigers are multilevel buildings and roads represent rivers. Tortoises and phoenixes are represented by smaller buildings.

Feng shui experts of the present century generally use the colors, shapes, and sizes of buildings to determine whether they are dragon or tiger buildings. For instance, a tall rectangular building that is predominantly green or blue in color could well be the Green Dragon, while a white lower-level building nearby could be the White Tiger.

For good feng shui, the dragon hill or building should be on your left (from the inside of the house looking out) and should be slightly higher than the tiger hill or

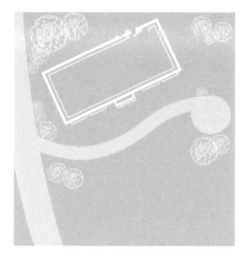

A wide open space in front of a building enables good chi to collect before entering. This is known as the bright hall effect (see page 211).

building (on your right). If it is not, the feng shui is deemed to be unbalanced.

Tortoise hills or buildings at the back should be rounded and wide to indicate support, while in the front any small building or sculpture can represent the Crimson Phoenix that brings opportunities for success. Ideally, there should be an expanse of open space in front to create the wonderfully lucky bright hall effect (*see* page 211).

When at least three of these formations are present, the location conforms to basic feng shui guidelines. This kind of location is deemed very auspicious indeed.

In terms of orientation, it does not matter if the dragon is not in the true East as measured by the compass. The dragon is always the range of hills or the big building on the left-hand side of the building or house (inside looking out). The tiger is always on the right.

LIFTING ENERGY

✳ **BRIGHT LIGHTS:** If the dragon side of your building is lower than the tiger side, shining a bright light on the dragon side will effectively "lift the energy" of the dragon.

SELECTING GOOD LOCATIONS AND PROPERTY

✳ WHETHER YOU ARE LOOKING FOR AN AUSPICIOUS PLOT ON WHICH TO BUILD A NEW HOUSE OR SEEKING A NEW READY-BUILT HOME, THERE ARE A NUMBER OF FACTORS TO BEAR IN MIND TO ENSURE GOOD FENG SHUI.

1 LOOK AT THE TERRAIN that surrounds the property. Be mindful of the way the roads are laid out. See if surrounding roads are pointing directly at any part of the land or building. As a general rule there should be nothing straight, sharp edged, or pointed aimed at the property or building. If there is, determine whether you can design your building to camouflage these potential "poison arrows." If these arrows are hard to dissolve, it is better to pass on the property.

RIVERSIDE LOCATION
A home on gentle sloping land, looking down over a slow-moving, unpolluted river or meandering stream, is very good feng shui and will bring good fortune.

2 LOOK FOR NATURAL WATER NEARBY
The cleaner the water, the better it will be in terms of bringing a flow of good fortune. The water should flow, not be stagnant. As a general rule, water at the front of the property is better than water at the back, although there are advanced feng shui formulas you can use to transform water behind you into a source of wealth luck. Usually, however, a flow of water behind your house indicates an inability to take advantage of opportunities that come your way.

3 CHECK TO SEE IF THE LAND IS LEVEL with surrounding roads or is higher or lower than these roads. Land that lies below road level is generally more difficult to develop and also less conducive to good feng shui. It is always better to build at a location higher than the road. At the same time, it is considered bad feng shui to be located at the very top of a hill or on a ridge where there are roads both at the back and front of the house. This suggests a severe lack of support and can lead to losses for the family living there.

4 LOOK AT THE RANGE OF LOCAL LANDSCAPES A field facing the building site is excellent feng shui as it represents the benign bright hall. Here good chi can settle and accumulate in front of the home, bringing good fortune. Facing a river that flows past the home, even from some

CLEAN WATER
Clean water near a building, whether natural or artificially created, is said to be an excellent source of chi, especially if it is flowing.

ROADS
Roads should not aim directly at a home. It is also best to avoid living near road junctions or intersections.

RAISED LAND
It is always preferable to live on land raised slightly above a road. Completely flat land is regarded as inauspicious.

BRIGHT HALL
A "bright hall" or open, unencumbered land in front of building is auspicious for the residents, especially if the vegetation is green and lush.

distance away, is always excellent. Facing a hostile building or hill, on the other hand, suggests obstacles and misfortunes.

5 ALWAYS CHECK THE COMPASS DIRECTIONS and then work out the orientations of the property you are considering to ensure that they harmonize with your personalized good fortune directions. When you check the orientations of a piece of land, you are preparing to incorporate compass feng shui applications

at a later stage. For this you will need to use the Kua Formula (*see* Chapter 14), which reveals the auspicious and inauspicious directions of every person based on dates of birth.

Personalized directions are part of the Eight Mansions formula (*see* Chapter 14), a powerful yet easy-to-apply formula, the effect of which can be felt almost immediately. Indeed, it is impossible to apply personalized good feng shui orientations without knowledge of this formula.

TIPS ON FINDING GOOD FENG SHUI LOCATIONS

WHEN LOOKING FOR LAND ON WHICH TO BUILD YOUR DREAM HOME, MAKE THE CHOICE OF ORIENTATIONS YOUR FIRST PRIORITY. BECOME FAMILIAR WITH COMPASS FORMULA FENG SHUI (*SEE* CHAPTER 13) IS MUCH EASIER TO PRACTICE (BEING LESS JUDGMENTAL AND MORE TECHNICAL) AND THEREFORE ALLOWS GREATER FLEXIBILITY IN TERMS OF OPTIONS AND IS A GREAT DEAL MORE DRAMATIC IN OFFERING QUICK RESULTS. BEFORE YOU HAVE THE SKILL NEEDED TO SELECT GOOD FENG SHUI LOCATIONS, YOU MUST FIRST LEARN THE METHOD AND UNDERSTAND HOW ORIENTATIONS AFFECT THE FENG SHUI OF ANY BUILDING. NOTE THAT IN CHINESE FENG SHUI PRACTICE, SPACE IS ALWAYS EXPRESSED IN TERMS OF COMPASS DIRECTIONS AND THESE DIRECTIONS ARE BASED ON A MAGNETIC COMPASS.

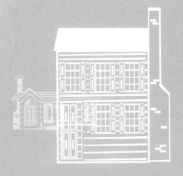

AVOID FACING HIGH BUILDINGS

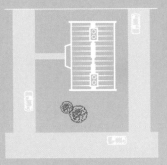

AVOID LAND BETWEEN TWO ROADS

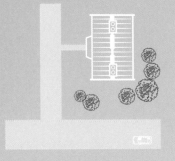

CHOOSE SECONDARY ROADS

✳ **HIGH BUILDINGS:** Avoid your building directly facing a building that is higher than yours, as this can cause obstacles to manifest.

✳ **ROAD LEVEL:** If your house is below road level, make sure your bedrooms are on the higher floor so as to be above the road. When the road is higher than your sleeping place, you will find it hard to advance in your chosen career.

✳ **UNDULATING LAND:** This is the best kind of land as it houses good earth energy.

✳ **LAND BETWEEN TWO ROADS:** Do not buy land located between two roads, especially if they are major highways. This situation suggests that any house you build there will be "hemmed in." The energy of such roads is too strong and can turn harmful, sending afflicting energy into key rooms of your home.

✳ **SEA PROXIMITY:** It is best to avoid living too near the sea but a view of the sea in the distance is good feng shui. Although sea winds may be benevolent, they are usually too strong and, unless you are planning a palace, it is better to live inland.

✳ **SECONDARY ROADS:** Try to select land that is on a secondary road rather than a primary one. Too much traffic will whiz your luck away.

✳ **SURROUNDING BUILDINGS:** Observe surrounding buildings and hill formations to ensure there is nothing around you that might be threatening. Physical afflictions in the form of sharp edges, triangular structures, and straight arrow-like protrusions can be harmful indeed and it is better to avoid them.

SHOULD YOU HIRE A FENG SHUI MASTER?

✳ WHEN YOU ARE NEW TO FENG SHUI, YOUR INITIAL ENTHUSIASM MAY LEAD YOU TO INVITE THE FIRST SELF-STYLED EXPERT YOU MEET INTO YOUR HOME. YOU COULD BE DISAPPOINTED. EVEN A FENG SHUI MASTER WHO HAS MANY YEARS OF EXPERIENCE IS NOT ALWAYS CORRECT OR ACCURATE IN HIS OR HER ASSESSMENT.

It is difficult to find an expert who will genuinely be able to use everything he or she knows based on a single consultation. It would simply take too long for anyone to investigate everything that needs to be investigated to come up with a truly comprehensive set of recommendations.

The few hours that are devoted to a commercial consultation are generally insufficient, because no outsider knows your home as well as you do, and a consultation cannot end at one sitting or with one onsite investigation. Follow-through and rethinking of options on remedies to feng shui afflictions almost always improve the application. And no matter how patient the consultant may be, she will not be able to answer all your questions at one meeting.

Remember that a professional feng shui consultant has many customers, and

the amount of time spent on you is very much a commercial proposition. When a consultant rushes through a job, careless mistakes can be made.

A feng shui master, no matter how good, can never be as good as you can be. When you are doing your own place, you are bound to be extra careful and fastidious. You also know yourself (and your aspirations) better than anyone else. Hence it is best to undertake your own feng shui analysis, and to do your own feng shui makeover and improvements. The purpose of this book is to show you how. Invest the time and effort to read, think through the principles, and then apply them to your space. Initially there may be some confusion, but the science of feng shui is not difficult and, if you persist, your investment will help you engineer vast improvements in your life and lifestyle.

CHAPTER 2
THE FENG SHUI OF HOUSES

❋ IT IS USEFUL TO REMEMBER THAT RESIDENTIAL HOUSES TODAY BEAR LITTLE OR NO RESEMBLANCE TO THE HOUSES OF HISTORIC CHINA. MANY OF TODAY'S ACCEPTED FENG SHUI GUIDELINES ARE A SYNTHESIS OF WHAT WAS PASSED DOWN BY WORD OF MOUTH FROM GENERATION TO GENERATION AND WHAT HAS BEEN GLEANED FROM ANCIENT BOOKS.

HONG KONG
Almost every high-rise building in Hong Kong incorporates design features based on good feng shui practices. This, together with its location around a harbor, has helped in the city's financial success.

Not all "authentic texts" contain correct information. In the early years of the Ming Dynasty, for instance, the founding emperor Chu Yuan Chuan was afraid feng shui might be used to overthrow him. Not only did he persecute and execute practitioners, he also disseminated fake feng shui books. During the Ming period, Taoist feng shui went underground. However, in the Ching Dynasty, feng shui enjoyed a revival and has been popular ever since.

Feng shui as it is practiced today can be traced to Taiwan, Hong Kong, and Singapore: three places that became the showcase of economic success during the final years of the last century—many say due to good feng shui. Overseas Chinese living in these countries incorporated feng shui into their homes and businesses, using combinations of methods. They often relied on experts to take care of their homes, provide correct orientations, and to update their feng shui each year to be protected from misfortune stars.

In designing their houses, they incorporated Form and Physical Feng Shui guidelines to ensure that offensive features such as improper door alignments, protruding corners, and stand-alone pillars were avoided. In decorating rooms and placing furniture, they relied on the use of decorative objects with powerful symbolic

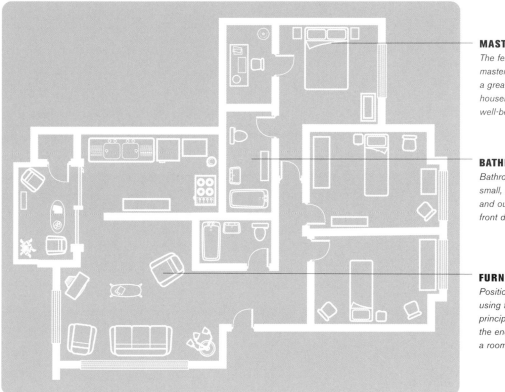

MASTER BEDROOM
The feng shui of the master bedroom has a great effect on a household's harmony, well-being, and finances.

BATHROOM
Bathrooms should be small, unobtrusive, and out of sight of the front door.

FURNITURE
Positioning furniture using feng shui principles can improve the energy flow within a room.

feng shui meaning. This tradition is based on the Five Elements Theory (*see* pages 40 and 282), which uses symbols as cures and remedies, and on the traditionally accepted symbols of good fortune used to enhance the chi of a corner or room, or as protectors for the home. At the same time all furniture would be arranged to facilitate the correct orientations personalized to benefit the two most important residents of the home—the patriarch and the matriarch. This combination of methods would not only ensure that the flow of chi through the

rooms of a home was benevolent and auspicious, but would also benefit the two most important people in the household.

This approach to practicing feng shui for the home is effective irrespective of the style of house. The essence of feng shui is far more important than its style, and as long as the guidelines to using each of the methods is adequately understood, anyone will be able to incorporate feng shui without too much difficulty. Before going deeper into different methods, familiarize yourself with the basics of household feng shui.

Furniture is oriented in the home to benefit the patriarch and matriarch of the family.

BASIC FENG SHUI FOR HOUSES

✳ THE FENG SHUI OF A HOUSE IS AFFECTED BY FACTORS SUCH AS: ITS POSITION RELATIVE TO LANDSCAPE FEATURES, ROADS, AND OTHER HOUSES; THE DIRECTION ITS FRONT DOOR FACES; THE REGULARITY OF ITS SHAPE; AND THE VIEW FROM ITS WINDOWS.

Houses halfway up a hill are preferable to those at the top or the bottom.

✳ Be alert to the contours of surroundings when investigating the feng shui of a house. When the road slopes, note that houses located halfway between the highest and lowest point are better than being at the very top or at the very bottom. The top exposes you to the elements, and the bottom suggests being at the starting point.

✳ If your land is below road level, build a two-level house with the upper level higher than the road and the bedrooms in the upper level. Orientate the home so that the left-side doors are more prominent than the right-side doors.

✳ A house that stands on stilts is unlucky, especially when viewed against an exposed hillside. This creates an empty space that symbolizes inadequate foundation. Close up the lower levels and place proper rooms there. Let your house hug the hillside, as this simulates the dragon's lair and can transform a potentially inauspicious home into an auspicious one.

✳ The main door should not face an oncoming straight road. The chi flowing toward you from the road is a poison arrow. Either move your main door or plant some trees to block the offending road from view.

HOUSE SHAPES

REGULAR-SHAPED HOUSES ARE BETTER THAN IRREGULARLY SHAPED HOMES. ANY BUILDING THAT IS A PERFECT SQUARE OR RECTANGLE, WHETHER IN TERMS OF ITS FLOORPLAN OR VERTICAL SHAPE, IS REGARDED AS LUCKY. IT IS EASY TO ENHANCE THE FENG SHUI OF SUCH BUILDINGS.

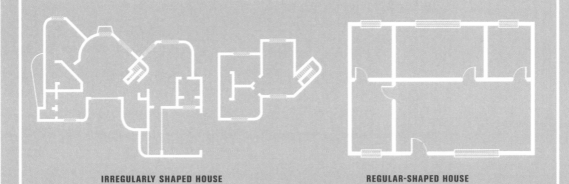

IRREGULARLY SHAPED HOUSE

REGULAR-SHAPED HOUSE

✱ Irregular shapes give rise to "missing corners" (*see* pages 24 and 248) and always create problems of one kind or another. The severity of the problem depends on which corner is missing, and this is expressed as one of the compass sectors.

If you divide your home layout into nine equal grids and check the compass direction of each of the grids, you can identify the compass direction of a missing corner. Whichever sector is affected will reveal a lack in the corresponding type of luck. For example, missing the Southeast corner will have a negative impact on your finances.

Missing corners can sometimes be corrected with wall mirrors or lights placed outside to extend the wall symbolically. But these cures are only partially effective; the best remedy is to add another room to restore the house to a regular shape.

✱ Square-shaped houses are best. The square signifies the earth element and offers the best potential for beneficial feng shui. The square shape lends itself easily to feng shui enhancements based on the compass formulas. Such houses are the most balanced, have all luck sectors intact, and represent one-third of the divine trinity of heaven, earth, and humankind. Therefore, they provide a particularly stable and firm foundation.

✱ Round-shaped structures suggest money luck. Round is the shape of money (that is, coins) and the circular shape is revered by the Chinese. However, round buildings can easily become excessively strong. Since the round shape signifies the chi of heaven, when used for a residential home, it can overwhelm the residents. Round shapes are better for large buildings such as banks, hotels, and convention centers.

INAUSPICIOUS HOUSE SHAPES

AUSPICIOUS HOUSE SHAPES

✳ It is vital to protect against Shar Chi (negative energy) that comes at you from any sharp edge, straight road, or triangular point emanating from a building across the road, a neighbor's roofline, or an oncoming elevated road. The hostile energy can be blocked from view, by trees, a wall or, in the case of the window, a curtain. It is more important to protect yourself from this type of Shar Chi than to focus on enhancing your Sheng Chi (positive energy). Even the most excellent feng shui features introduced into a home are powerless against the negative forces of severe Shar Chi. Any home that has been hit continuously by Shar Chi will begin to take on a drab appearance and eventually appear dilapidated. The cause of Shar Chi may not be immediately obvious, so be alert in your investigation of surroundings.

✳ Located on the inside of a curve with the road embracing your home, your house will have excellent feng shui. When it is situated on the other side of the curve, the road "attacks" the home. You will notice that homes hugged by roads tend to look more prosperous than homes on the outer edge. If your house is on the wrong side of the road, position a mirror to reflect the headlights of any oncoming traffic. This will protect your home effectively.

✳ If an elevated curving highway is built in front of your home, it is best to move to a less problematic neighborhood.

✳ Protruding corners strengthen the luck of the corner and the effect can be auspicious. When extensions are added to the home, the luck of the corner and that of the family member represented can be magnified. For example, an extension to the Southeast corner of any home strengthens the luck of the eldest daughter of the family. It also enhances wealth luck.

Right: Choose a house on the inner curve of a road, rather than the outer curve, for the best feng shui.

Far right: Building an extension in the Southeast corner of this house would improve the eldest daughter's luck and family finances.

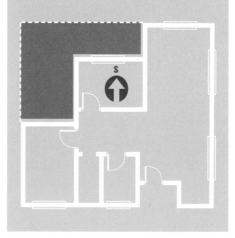

✳ Do not live at a dead end, because chi will stagnate in this location and when problems arise, there will be no way out. The remedy for living in a cul-de-sac is to keep the lights on at the gate as well as behind the house throughout the night. This simulates the presence of yang energy and prevents hostile chi from settling into your home.

✳ Your house should not be sandwiched between two buildings that dwarf it—this situation will keep you from benefiting from even a breath of good fortune wind. The solution in such an instance is to keep a bright light at the highest roof level of the house.

✳ Always activate the dragon side of your home, the East side, by placing an image of a dragon here. This can be a painting or a decorative carving made of wood or ceramic. The dragon is the most popular good fortune symbol.

✳ Keep the South side of the house properly lighted, especially at night, to reap the luck of recognition for residents of the household. This feng shui feature also ensures the good name of the family is preserved and protected. If your South side is allowed to become dark and dirty, the chi will get stale and yin spirit formation will result, causing afflictions against your family's good name.

If you live between two tall buildings, it is essential to keep a bright light shining at the highest roof level to ensure good fortune.

✳ The view from the house should never be blocked, especially directly in front of the main door. There should be no structure or hill for at least twice the length of the home. A small hump or elevation in the distance, or even a small rock on the lawn, represents the Crimson Phoenix, which is a good feng shui feature.

TIP

✳ SIGNS OF SUCCESS
Look for signs of prosperity in the neighborhood. Investigate the history and background of people already living there. Usually an area with good feng shui will look prosperous. Gardens will be thriving, homes will be well maintained, and streets will be clean. There is an air of prosperity that you can both feel and see.

CHAPTER 3
THE FENG SHUI OF BUILDINGS AND OFFICES

✳ WHEN INVESTIGATING THE FENG SHUI OF CITYSCAPES, REMEMBER THAT WE ARE EQUATING BUILDINGS WITH THE UNDULATIONS OF MOUNTAIN TERRAIN. BE AWARE, HOWEVER, THAT CITY BUILDINGS EMANATE A GREAT MANY MORE POISON ARROWS THAT SEND SHAR CHI IN ALL DIRECTIONS.

The increased Shar Chi of cities may partly explain the higher rate of crime and misfortune inside cities than in the countryside. This is due to there being more high buildings, sharp edges, and pointed structures that send out the negative chi of secret poison arrows.

✳ THE FENG SHUI OF LARGE BUILDINGS

The feng shui of large buildings is always harder to control than the feng shui of houses and interiors. When applying feng shui to the design of large buildings, the methods and formulas used are exactly the same as those used for houses. Use the same protective safeguards (such as watching for hidden poison arrows) and the correct positioning of surrounding buildings (ideally reflecting the armchair formation of the four celestial creatures) for the greatest benefit.

Buildings should always face the direction that corresponds to the wealth sector of its largest shareholder, chairman, or CEO, depending on whom you wish the building to benefit. The shapes and colors of buildings must also be determined with care. Buildings that reflect incorrect feng shui may cause company and individual cash flows to decrease.

CASE HISTORY 1: THE SHOPPING MALL

A successful tycoon decided to build the largest shopping mall in the city. He hired the best architects and used the sharpest consultants, but he forgot to incorporate correct feng shui into his planning. The mall was designed to face the Northwest direction. In feng shui, this means the building would "sit" in the Southeast, thereby making it a wood element building. According to the cycle of elements, this building would benefit from either a green dominant color or, better still, a blue water-tone color, since water produces wood.

Unfortunately, the owner liked red tiles and he wanted his shopping mall to reflect the fire element because he thought (mistakenly) that this was the best color for overcoming the harmful chi energy coming from the land next door. The land next to his plot formerly housed a prison, and he believed that if his building were all red, its yang energy would subdue the yin energy of the former prison.

He forgot to consider that his mall was a wood element building and the fire element exhausts wood. If he had wanted a red building, he should have had the building face North, thereby making it a fire element building (sitting South). It is not surprising that almost from the first day, his proposed shopping mall ate into his cash flow. Month after month as the building grew higher and higher, its fire energy consumed more and more cash from the tycoon until he fell into serious financial difficulties. In the meantime, his shopping mall was finally completed, but responses to it were lukewarm.

CASE HISTORY 2: SHAR CHI AFFLICTION

One building contained moving escalators that created a gigantic X directly facing the grand entrance of another building across the road. The company across the road was badly hit by the emanating Shar Chi, and its sales performance was immediately affected in a negative way. The sales manager reportedly consulted a feng shui expert who recommended the use of a cannon pointed at the offending X escalators. An antique cannon was positioned as recommended. Sales recovered immediately, but then performance of the company "hit" by the cannon suffered. They too consulted a feng shui master who recommended the use of a mirror to reflect back the cannon. The mirror was not strong enough and the building was eventually sold. The new owner displayed the company logo—a lion—that proved to be a match for the cannon. The feng shui of both sides seems to be afflicted no longer.

CASE HISTORY 3: POISON ARROW AFFLICTION

An even more dramatic example is a tall, sharp, angular building, its façade covered with large crosses. It looked exactly like a sharp poison arrow and its sides seemed deadly indeed. Each side of the building seemed to point directly at the Governor's mansion. Not surprisingly, the Governor suffered from bad feng shui throughout his tenure. When he left, the new Governor never moved into the mansion. The new Governor enjoyed such excellent feng shui that despite being unpopular and ineffective, he was seemingly unassailable.

COLORS AND SHAPES OF BUILDINGS

✳ THE EASIEST AND MOST EFFECTIVE WAY TO DETERMINE THE BEST COLORS AND SHAPES FOR BUILDINGS IS TO DETERMINE THE SITTING ELEMENT OF THE BUILDING. THIS IS BASED ON ITS SITTING DIRECTION, WHICH IS THE EXACT OPPOSITE OF THE FACING DIRECTION.

HOW TO DETERMINE THE SITTING DIRECTION OF A BUILDING

1 First determine the front of the building; this is usually where the main entrance is located. Then use a compass to determine the facing direction of the building.

2 The sitting direction is the exact opposite of the facing direction. Thus, if the facing direction is East, the sitting direction is West, and if facing is Southwest, then sitting is Northeast (and vice versa and so on).

3 Once you have determined the sitting direction of a building, you can identify its sitting element (*see* opposite), from which you can determine the best color and shape as well as the most harmful.

When the sitting direction is South, it is a fire element building. The best shape is triangular. The best dominant colors are red or green.

When the sitting direction is North, it is a water element building. The best shapes are circular and modular. The best dominant colors are black and blue or white.

When the sitting direction is Southwest or Northeast, it is an earth element building. The best shape is square, although rectangular shapes are also good. The best dominant colors are yellow or red.

When the sitting direction is East or Southeast, it is a wood element building. The best shape is rectangular. The best dominant colors are green or blue.

When the sitting direction is West or Northwest, it is a metal element building. The best shape is circular, although rectangular shapes are also good. The best dominant colors are white or yellow.

SITTING DIRECTION MEANINGS

	ELEMENT	BEST SHAPES	BEST COLORS	WORST COLORS
SOUTH	FIRE			
NORTH	WATER			
SOUTHWEST/NORTHEAST	EARTH			
EAST/SOUTHEAST	WOOD			
WEST/NORTHWEST	METAL			

AVOIDING SHAR CHI IN THE OFFICE

SHAR CHI, OR BAD LUCK, CAN BE PRODUCED IN THE WORKPLACE BY INCORRECT POSITIONING OF YOUR DESK WITHIN AN OFFICE AND ITS RELATIONSHIP TO OTHER ITEMS OF FURNITURE CAN SUBJECT YOU TO THE SHAR CHI OF POISON ARROWS (SEE PAGE 266). INSIDE THE OFFICE, YOU SHOULD WATCH OUT FOR THE FOLLOWING:

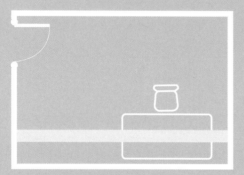

✳ Sitting under an exposed overhead beam—if you are, move out of the way and look for another place to sit. When you sit under a beam, it presses down on your luck and negatively impacts your health.

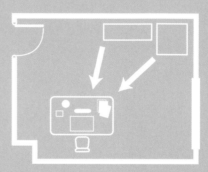

✳ Being "hit" by the sharp edge of a square pillar or protruding corner sends Shar Chi toward you and the effect is one of continuous bad luck. Place a plant between you and the sharp edge. Also be wary of the sharp edges of furniture such as bookcases, file cabinets, and tabletops. While not as serious as the edges of pillars, these still require modification.

✳ Sitting at the end of a long corridor puts you in the "firing line" of harmful chi. Slow down the chi coming at you by placing paintings or plants along the corridor. Anyone sitting in the office at the end of the long corridor will suffer from bad feng shui. They should move their desk to the opposite side of the room or move the door to the room.

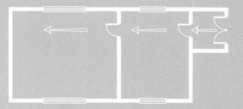

✳ Three doors in a straight line in the office—in this case, it is a good idea to place something in front of the second door. Three doors in a row introduce bad chi into the office. If you are directly hit by the long straight energy you will experience problems in your work.

ENHANCING SHENG CHI IN THE OFFICE

FOR THE PROFESSIONAL OR ENTREPRENEUR, FENG SHUI CAN BE USED INSIDE THE OFFICE TO INCREASE SUCCESS AT WORK, TO IMPROVE CAREER PROSPECTS, AND TO ENHANCE BUSINESS LUCK. HERE ARE SOME IMPORTANT TIPS THAT WILL BRING YOU AND YOUR COLLEAGUES BETTER LUCK IN THE WORKPLACE AND IN YOUR CAREERS.

* Sit facing the door into the office. The best location for the desk is diagonal to the door. Avoid having a corner behind you, but if unavoidable (as here) put a painting of a mountain behind you.

* Sit side by side if it is necessary to be seated near your colleagues. It is better not to sit in a confrontational way as this creates hostility chi that can strain your friendship.

* Cover bookshelves with sliding doors. Exposed bookshelves, either in front of or behind you, are like having blades coming at you, bringing Shar Chi.

* Hang a picture of a phoenix, or another kind of bird—better still, a painting with a hundred birds—at the entrance into your office to open many potentially beneficial opportunities.

* A rooster image on your desk or worktable can help guard against office politics.

* Place a sailing ship filled with gold ingots in your office. If the ship appears to be sailing in from one of your good fortune directions, it will bring success and increased income.

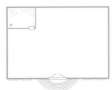

* The corner diagonal to the entrance and deepest inside the building is the power spot. If you are the CEO of your company, your office should be located in the Northwest corner. This is the place of the leader.

* Always sit facing one of your four best directions while working. The office is one place where the application of the Eight Mansions formula of personalized directions can work real magic.

CHAPTER 4
THE FENG SHUI OF APARTMENTS AND CONDOMINIUMS

＊ IT IS GENERALLY MORE DIFFICULT TO MAXIMIZE FENG SHUI IN APARTMENTS, AS THERE ARE FEWER OPTIONS FOR IMPROVEMENTS. HERE FENG SHUI CAN BE INCORPORATED INTO LAYOUT ARRANGEMENTS AND FURNITURE PLACEMENT AS WELL AS THE USE OF DECORATIVE SYMBOLS THAT ACTIVATE AND ATTRACT GOOD CHI.

DETERMINING THE FACING DIRECTION OF APARTMENTS

DISTANT HILLS
PICTURE WINDOW
POND
APARTMENT A
APARTMENT C
CITY
APARTMENT B
MAIN ENTRANCE
PICTURE WINDOW

＊ **APARTMENT A:** Apartments on the ninth floor and above with picture windows and/or large balconies may vary in their facing and sitting directions from those of the main building. Apartment A's large picture window with view of distant hills determines its directions.

＊ **APARTMENT B:** This apartment is a studio apartment with no picture windows, so, whatever floor it is on, its facing and sitting directions are the same as those of the whole building.

＊ **APARTMENT C:** This apartment has a large picture window with views of the city. If it is on the ninth floor or above, the facing direction of this picture window would determine its facing and sitting directions, rather than the main entrance of the whole building.

The best approach is to focus on the application of methods that use the compass, because these formula methods can be applied in small, tight spaces and depend less on the bigger environmental picture that takes into account mountains, buildings, and external structures, which are beyond your control. In apartment feng shui, the practical approach is to focus on matters that are within your control.

Several important points are useful to bear in mind when applying feng shui principles to apartments.

Generally, you should consider your apartment as part of the whole apartment building unless you are on the ninth floor or above. First take into account the facing and sitting directions of the building itself. When an apartment building is afflicted by harmful physical structures that send Shar Chi toward the building, the residents will feel the negative impact.

The entrance into the building as well as landscaping of gardens and pool are also important considerations. When the surroundings of the apartment building are conducive to good feng shui, everyone living in the building will benefit. As a single apartment owner, it may be hard for you to correct any afflictions unless you are able to convince your neighbors to agree to any necessary changes.

When the Flying Star Feng Shui formula is applied (*see* Chapter 15) , the facing direction of the whole building will determine the chart that is relevant to the building and also in general terms to the individual apartments. It is important not to use the facing direction of entrance doors going into individual apartments.

Flying Star Feng Shui is a potent feng shui method of demarcating the luck sectors within buildings and within individual units inside the buildings. It incorporates the time dimension into feng shui practice and offers valuable input into diagnosing afflictions and putting remedies into place.

This is the best kind of feng shui because it offers methods for preventing the occurrence of illness and misfortune as well as accidents.

Note that for apartments located above the ninth floor, the facing direction is no longer considered the facing direction of the entrance into the building. Instead, the facing direction is taken looking out from the balcony or large picture window of the apartment. The apartment is thereby deemed to be facing maximum yang energy, which is created by the panoramic view of the surrounding scene.

One compass method that is very useful in apartments is the method for determining your personalized auspicious orientations—the Eight Mansions formula. This method will allow you to arrange your furniture so that your family can sleep and sit facing their most auspicious directions. Details of this formula are contained in Chapter 14. This formula can be used with equal success in workplaces and houses.

DECORATE FOR GOOD CHI

IT IS POSSIBLE TO DECORATE SECTORS OF YOUR APARTMENT IN WAYS THAT WILL MINIMIZE ANY NEGATIVE CHI ENERGIES AND MAXIMIZE POSITIVE CHI ENERGIES.

Auspicious decorative symbols, colors, shapes, and images can be used to activate the different corners of the apartment so that good energy flows from room to room. Apply the Pa Kua Eight Aspirations method (*see* Chapter 13), which offers specific guidelines on how the element and trigram attributes of each corner can be enhanced to bring specific types of good fortune luck. This method of feng shui is best practiced in combination with symbolic feng shui.

SMALL TAI CHI AND BIG TAI CHI

✳ A FENG SHUI CONCEPT THAT IS PARTICULARLY USEFUL IN APARTMENT AND HOUSE INTERIORS IS THAT OF BIG AND SMALL TAI CHI, WHICH EXPRESSES THE YIN AND YANG OF SPACE.

Chi energy is expressed in the Tai Chi symbol, shown as a circle with a black and a white embryonic symbol. The white signifies yang chi while the black signifies yin chi. Note that there is some yin within the yang and vice versa.

The feng shui practitioner defines the space, which can be just a small room, as the Tai Chi. Or you can be planning to feng shui the whole apartment, in which case the Tai Chi symbol is superimposed onto the entire floor plan. This is the concept of small Tai Chi and big Tai Chi, in which the room becomes the small Tai Chi and the whole apartment becomes the big Tai Chi.

Once you understand this way of looking at a space, it becomes much easier to apply and use the different formulas of feng shui. This is because the concept of small Tai Chi and big Tai Chi applies to all the formulas of feng shui.

One practical implication of this concept is that you can superimpose any feng shui chart—be it a Pa Kua aspirations chart (*see* Chapter 13), an Eight Directions or Mansions chart (*see* Chapter 14), or a Flying Star chart (*see* Chapter 15)—over any space.

The space can be individual rooms or it can be the whole house. It can even refer to an entire city, a whole country, or even an entire continent. There are no limits to the universality of space. Understanding this concept will make it easier to feng shui your home.

The Pa Kua is used in the Compass School of Feng Shui and incorporates the eight trigrams and the Tai Chi (yin–yang) symbol.

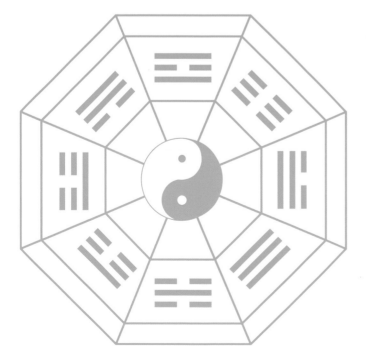

HOW TO ACTIVATE SMALL TAI CHI AND BIG TAI CHI

For instance, if you want to activate the Southwest corner for romance luck but the Southwest corner is missing because of your apartment's irregular shape, you cannot activate the big Tai Chi Southwest. So, instead, choose a regular-shaped, frequently used room, such as the living room, and identify the Southwest of that room. Then you will be able to activate the small Tai Chi of the living room. If you often occupy this room, then you will definitely benefit from the enhanced and activated Southwest corner and consequently from its romance luck.

In the same way, you can successfully activate any corner of any room (including the bedroom) simply by using the concept of the small Tai Chi.

If you stop to think about this principle, you will realize that it opens up fabulous pathways to the application potential of feng shui formulas.

Illustrated in the box on the right are examples of how you can apply the principles of small Tai Chi and big Tai Chi to the Pa Kua Eight Aspirations method of feng shui whereby each of the eight sides of the Pa Kua stands for different aspirations (*see* Chapter 13).

You will of course need a proper compass to establish the orientations of the Pa Kua and superimpose it onto your floor space correctly but will soon learn how to apply this useful formula to your apartment or condominium.

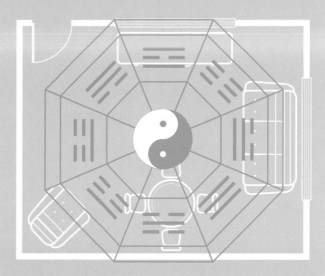

✳ **SMALL TAI CHI:** To activate the small Tai Chi in this example, the Pa Kua is superimposed on the living room space only and not on the whole apartment.

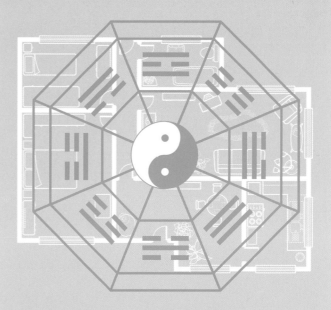

✳ **BIG TAI CHI:** In this apartment the Pa Kua is superimposed on the whole apartment. Here the big Tai Chi is being activated.

PART TWO

PRACTICAL TECHNIQUES

FENG SHUI IS A LIVING SKILL THAT CAN BE LEARNED. IT IS NEITHER

RELIGIOUS NOR SPIRITUAL AND ITS PRACTICES ARE NO LONGER MYSTERIOUS.

FENG SHUI COMPRISES DIFFERENT TECHNIQUES OF APPLYING GUIDELINES

AND FORMULAS THAT FOCUS ON THE OPTIMUM BALANCING OF CHI ENERGY

IN LIVING AREAS AND WORKSPACES. THESE TECHNIQUES EMPHASIZE

PROTECTING OUR HOMES AND OFFICES AND ENHANCING AND ACTIVATING

GOOD FORTUNE. WHEN THE METHODS ARE CORRECTLY APPLIED, RESULTS

ARE ACHIEVED QUICKLY. HISTORICALLY, THE PRACTICE OF **FENG SHUI** WAS A

HIGHLY RESPECTED PROFESSION AND MOST EXPERTS WERE FAMILIAR WITH

THE VARIOUS WAYS OF USING THE TRADITIONAL COMPASS AND OTHER TOOLS.

CHAPTER 5
FENG SHUI PROTECTING AND ENHANCING TECHNIQUES

✱ THE PRACTICE OF FENG SHUI REQUIRES KNOWLEDGE OF ITS DIFFERENT FORMULAS AND GENERAL GUIDELINES. THESE ARE COLLECTIVELY USED TO PROTECT AND IMPROVE THE LUCK OF LIVING SPACES. STUDYING THE DIFFERENT FORMULAS, HOWEVER, IS ONLY THE FIRST STEP.

Before you are able to use these formulas on a practical basis, you need a good understanding of the basic concepts that underpin the practice. These concepts are the basis of formulated remedies and they also support the strategic placement of symbolic enhancers within a living area or workspace. We have already seen the importance of a good location, which is the first important concept. The other fundamental concepts include:

It is better for chi to meander (below, right) than to hurry unimpeded through constricted spaces (below).

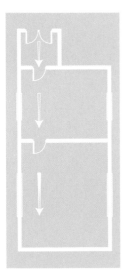

1 CREATING A GOOD FLOW OF CHI Chi is described as the "dragon's cosmic breath"—the intrinsic energy that brings good

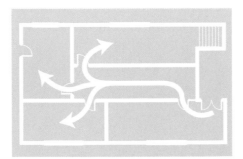

fortune. Every feng shui recommendation is rooted in the need to capture this auspicious energy, which is present in the environment when the elements are in balance and yin and yang are in harmony.

Good fortune chi is generally referred to as Sheng Chi, which can be roughly translated to mean growth and expanding energy. It is present when breezes blow and energy is vibrant and healthy; it is generally more yang than yin. It scatters and dissipates when winds blow too fast or hard. It settles and expands where breezes are gentle. Sheng Chi evaporates when caught in a raging river, but slows down when the flow of water is gentle and meandering.

Sheng Chi transforms into negative energy when forced to move too quickly or in a straight line. Constricted spaces such as long and narrow corridors generate harmful chi. Sheng Chi stays benevolent when allowed to meander. The correct flow of chi brings immense good fortune and wherever it has a chance to amass and collect abundance is magnified.

Every aspect of every structure affects the flow of chi in any living space. In the external environment, chi is affected by the shape, contours, and elevation of land as well as by the orientation of mountains and rivers, and also by manmade structures.

When these structures blend with the natural environment without there being anything to create negative energy (such as sharp edges, straight roads, and triangular elevations) there is an auspicious flow of chi. When discordant notes are created the flow of chi turns malevolent, thus bringing misfortunes. Inside buildings and homes the flow of chi is determined by the flow that is naturally created as a result of the way walls, rooms, and also the furniture are placed. When these are smooth, allowing the chi to meander and flow unimpeded, good feng shui gets created, but when the flow is blocked or afflicted, it creates both obstacles and misfortune for those living or working within that space.

CHI FLOW AND FURNITURE ARRANGEMENT

BAD ARRANGEMENT

GOOD ARRANGEMENT

BAD CHI FLOW: A scattered arrangement (top) will not generate good chi. Furniture in an L-shape arrangement forms a poison arrow (above).

GOOD CHI FLOW: A careful arrangement of furniture allows chi to flow at a good pace (top). The room division means chi will meander (above).

2 DEFLECTING THE HARMFUL BREATH OF SHAR CHI Much feng shui practice has to do with deflecting, dissolving, and dispersing harmful chi also known as Shar Chi. It is more important to guard against the buildup of Shar Chi before enhancing feng shui. Even the most excellent feng shui features introduced into the home or office are powerless against severe Shar Chi. This is why experienced feng shui practitioners always start by looking at the big picture to determine what is harming a residence or office and setting it right before moving on to enhancing techniques.

3 CREATING HARMONY WITH THE FIVE ELEMENTS The premise of most cures and spatial enhancers in feng shui is based on the theory of the five elements—wood, fire, earth, metal, and water. According to the Chinese view of the universe, everything in the world—physical as well as abstract—can be categorized as one of these five elements, and all five relate mutually to one another. The nature of the interactions between the five elements creates harmony or disharmony in any area.

To use the theory of the elements in feng shui, it is necessary to understand the

THE FIVE ELEMENTS

EVERYTHING IN THE WORLD COMPRISES ONE OF THE FIVE ELEMENTS. HOW THE ELEMENTS RELATE TO EACH OTHER CAN PRODUCE AUSPICIOUS OR INAUSPICIOUS ENERGY. THERE ARE TWO DIFFERENT CIRCULAR FLOWS BETWEEN THE ELEMENTS: THE PRODUCTIVE CYCLE AND THE DESTRUCTIVE CYCLE. FENG SHUI USES AN APPRECIATION OF THESE CYCLES TO DISPEL DISHARMONY AND PROMOTE HARMONY.

1 FIRE is associated with the South. Its color is red. It produces and thus enhances earth; and is in turn produced by and thus exhausts metal. Water destroys fire and is destroyed by earth.

2 WATER is associated with the North. Its color is blue or black. It produces and thus enhances wood; and is in turn produced by, and thus exhausts metal. Water destroys fire and is destroyed by earth.

3 EARTH is associated with the Southwest, the Northeast, and the center. Its color is yellow. It produces and thus enhances metal; and is in turn produced by and thus exhausts fire. Earth destroys water and is destroyed by wood.

4 METAL is associated with the West and Northwest. Its color is white or metallic. It produces and thus enhances water; and is in turn produced by and thus exhausts earth. Metal destroys wood and is destroyed by fire.

5 WOOD is associated with the Southeast and east. Its color is green. It produces and thus enhances fire; and is in turn produced by and thus exhausts water. Wood destroys earth and is destroyed by metal.

attributes associated with each of the five elements and the three interactive relationships between them.

4 BALANCING YIN AND YANG All the energies of the earth are either yin or yang. Yin is the dark, cold, female passive aspect of life; yang is the light, warm, male, active aspect of life. For good feng shui these two complementary but opposing energies must be in balance.

The relative strength of the two forces must be finely tuned according to the usage of rooms and buildings, and, because we are dealing with houses of the living, there must always be a dominance of yang chi. However, an excess of yang energy causes yin energy to be obliterated; when this happens misfortune sets in, because if yin is diminished into non-existence, yang also disappears—the two energies are mutually dependent.

When there is yin spirit formation (that is, a state in which yin totally dominates), the results may be severe illness and perhaps even death.

A large part of feng shui skill is developing the experience and the vision to gauge the balance of yin and yang within any living space and to make corrections where necessary. For instance, when a home is too dark and yin energy starts to build up, merely lighting up the space can correct the imbalance, thereby improving the feng shui.

CAUSES OF SHAR CHI

MANY THINGS IN THE ENVIRONMENT CAN CAUSE SHAR CHI, IN THE GUISE OF POISON ARROWS THAT CAUSE MISFORTUNES AND BAD LUCK.

✳ An imposing building

✳ A neighbor's wall

✳ A transmission tower

✳ A cross

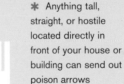

✳ Anything tall, straight, or hostile located directly in front of your house or building can send out poison arrows

✳ A straight road or an elevated highway can also send harmful chi your way

The remedy for overcoming the effect of these harmful structures is to create a barrier to deflect or block it from view. Different methods for warding off Shar Chi are based on the theory of the five elements (*see* opposite and page 282).

The hexagram Ta Yu (Abundance) is based on the trigrams for Fire and Heaven, which feature in the common feng shui tool, the Pa Kua.

5 APPRECIATING THE SYMBOLISM OF FENG SHUI The language of feng shui is symbolic, and its source book, the wonderful *I Ching*, comprises a set of sixty-four six-line combinations of broken and unbroken lines (known as hexagrams: *see* page 243) with every one of these representing a powerful symbolic message. Each of the lines is yin (broken lines) or yang (unbroken lines) and provides a great deal of information in combination with the others. There is also the eight-sided Pa Kua symbol, wherein each side comprises attributes of different symbols and elements. The nine-grid Lo Shu Square (*see* pages 48 and 255) of numbers and the symbolism of the four celestial creatures (dragon, phoenix, tortoise, and tiger) have all become interpretative tools of feng shui.

6 UNDERSTANDING THE SIGNIFICANCE OF COMPASS DIRECTIONS In feng shui, all space is expressed in terms of the eight compass directions, and in advanced

The compass is an essential tool in feng shui practice. Its twenty-four directions are referred to as the "twenty-four mountains."

formulas these are further subdivided into twenty-four directions, which are referred to as the "twenty-four mountains." Auspicious and inauspicious manners of sitting, sleeping, working, and so forth are always expressed as directions. It is useful to understand these definitions before proceeding to study the formulas, which are always expressed as such.

In addition, it is also important to understand to which directions various sectors refer. Sectors generally refer to the different corners of a home or a room and are usually expressed as a compass direction, for example, North sector or South sector. To demarcate the sectors of a room, stand in the middle of the room with your compass and divide the space into nine equal grids (eight sectors plus the center). Then, when a recommendation to "activate the North sector with water" is given, you will know exactly where in the room to place this feature.

Because compass directions play such a central role in the practice of feng shui, it is necessary to invest in a reliable and well-made compass. Although the Luo Pan is the feng shui compass used by most professional practitioners, a standard Western compass that references magnetic North will do just as well. All the formulas given in this book apply equally to the northern and southern hemispheres. When we refer to directions we are referring to directions bearing from the magnetic North.

COMPASS DIRECTIONS

FRONT DOOR

SE WOOD	**S** FIRE	**SW** EARTH
E WOOD		**W** METAL
NE EARTH	**N** WATER	**NW** METAL

USING YOUR COMPASS

Once you have used your compass to establish the direction of your front door (from inside looking out), you can create a Lo Shu square (*see* pages 48 and 255) and superimpose it on a drawing of the layout of your home. Each sector is associated with an element, as shown here, which is important in terms of how you go about activating the good luck in that sector.

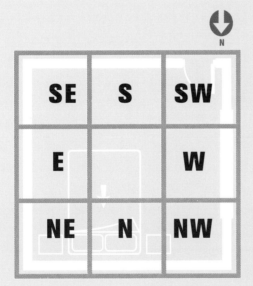

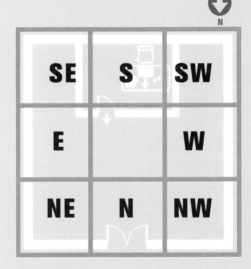

SLEEPING DIRECTION

If you work out your Kua Number (*see* page 114) it will tell you which is the most auspicious part of your home to have your bedroom.

If your bedroom is not in the most auspicious place for you, then position your bed so that your head is pointing toward your best direction while you sleep.

WORKING DIRECTION

The direction you face and where in a room you choose to locate your desk are important feng shui factors. You can improve your general luck and career prospects by sitting in your most auspicious sector and facing your best direction and avoiding your least auspicious direction (*see* pages 120–121).

7 THE TIME DIMENSION OF FENG SHUI In addition to spatial concepts and influences in feng shui, it is also vitally important to understand the time dimension of feng shui and that the quality of space changes according to changes in time periods.

The time dimension is part of Flying Star Feng Shui (*see* Chapter 15), which divides time into cycles that last 180 years each. These are further subdivided into nine periods of twenty years, with each period defined by a number.

Period Seven lasted from February 4, 1984 through February 4, 2004; so the world's feng shui is now in Period Eight. This change of period means that all houses and buildings built in the previous periods will lose energy and must be revitalized using special methods to reactivate the heaven, earth, and humankind chi of the buildings. By making certain changes, you can modify your Period Seven house into a Period Eight house (*see* page 137). This will ensure that the chi within the home does not stagnate.

Because of the change in period, 2004 witnessed changes in direction within companies, governments, and most of all in people's attitudes. Period Seven was the era of wealth creation and prominent Western direction.

During Period Eight, the direction is the Northeast. For example, if we consider the United States, we can see that Period Seven favored the West and its element, metal (Californians struck it rich with computers). In Period Eight the Northeast will rise in prominence (New York, Boston, Washington…). In 2004 many countries of the world changed governments.

Flying Star Feng Shui also offers methods for analyzing the charts of each New Year, as well as for each month of the year. Like a horoscope, it provides valuable warnings against annual and monthly afflictions.

There are also prescribed remedies to guard against illness, quarrels, legal troubles, and other misfortunes. Remember that Flying Star updates do not rely on the Chinese Yhue Li (lunar calendar). Instead, they use the Chinese Hsia Li (solar calendar), upon which all time-dimension feng shui is based.

TIME PERIODS

PERIOD 7	**PERIOD 8**
February 4, 1984 to February 4, 2004	February 4, 2004 to February 4, 2024
Direction: West	**Direction:** Northeast

SAMPLE FLYING STAR CHARTS

FLYING STAR CHARTS HERE ARE EXAMPLES OF A PERIOD SEVEN CHART AND A PERIOD EIGHT CHART. THE NUMBERS CONTAINED WITHIN EACH SECTOR OF THE GRID OFFER CLUES TO THE CHI QUALITY OF THAT SECTOR OF THE HOME.

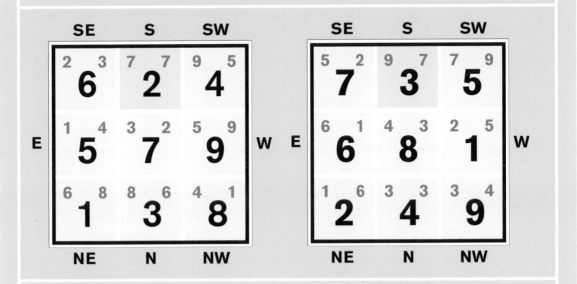

PERIOD SEVEN CHART Most buildings today are Period Seven, that is, they were built or renovated between February 4, 1984, and February 4, 2004. To select the chart appropriate to your home, *see* pages 138–141. During Period Seven, houses with their front door in the auspicious 'double seven' sector enjoyed enhanced wealth luck.

PERIOD EIGHT CHART Houses built or renovated after February 4, 2004 belong to Period Eight which lasts until February 4, 2024. The number eight is already a lucky number in Chinese numerology, and in Period Eight it is especially lucky and will bring good fortune to those who tap into its potency. To select the chart appropriate to your home, *see* pages 142–145.

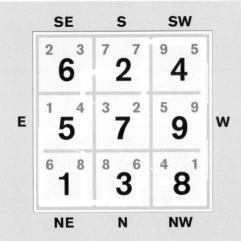

SUPERIMPOSING THE FLYING STAR CHART
Selecting the correct Flying Star chart for your home involves first determining the facing direction of your house (*see* pages 128–129). Then you can superimpose the chart on a layout of your home and analyze the numbers to discover what action needs to be taken to enhance good chi and minimize bad chi.

CHAPTER 6
FENG SHUI TOOLS

THE FIVE IMPORTANT TOOLS OF FENG SHUI ARE:

1 THE PA KUA SYMBOL FOR ANALYSIS AND USE IN VARIOUS FORMULAS

2 THE EIGHT TRIGRAMS AND THEIR MEANINGS FOR UNDERSTANDING SECTORS

3 THE LUO PAN, THE FENG SHUI REFERENCE, FOR ANALYSIS

4 THE LO SHU SQUARE AND ITS ARRANGEMENT OF NUMBERS FOR ANALYSIS

5 THE FENG SHUI RULER FOR MEASURING AUSPICIOUS DIMENSIONS

THE PA KUA

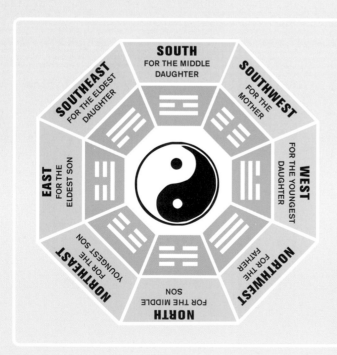

THE PA KUA IS AN EIGHT-SIDED SYMBOL AND EACH KUA, OR SIDE, REPRESENTS ONE OF THE EIGHT DIRECTIONS OF THE COMPASS.

The eight trigrams are arranged round these sides of the Pa Kua to give it meaning. The Yin Pa Kua has the trigrams arranged around it according to the Early Heaven arrangement and is used mainly as an aggressive protective tool to ward off secret poison arrows and overcome Shar Chi. The Yang Pa Kua has the trigrams arranged according to the Later Heaven arrangement and is used to analyze and practice yang feng shui in the houses of the living. The Yang Pa Kua is of greater significance to us.

THE EIGHT TRIGRAMS

THE EIGHT TRIGRAMS PLACED ROUND THE PA KUA OFFER ATTRIBUTES TO THEIR CORRESPONDING DIRECTIONS. THE TRIGRAMS, ROOT SYMBOLS OF THE I CHING, REFLECT THE PATTERNS OF CHANGE OVER TIME ON THE LUCK OF EACH DIRECTION. THE RULING TRIGRAM OF THE PRESENT PERIOD EIGHT IS KEN, THE MOUNTAIN, WHICH HERALDS AN AGE IN WHICH RESEARCH AND KNOWLEDGE BECOME RESPECTED. KEN ALSO STANDS FOR A GREATER EMPHASIS ON RELATIONSHIPS THAN ON WEALTH.

Trigram	Name	Direction	Characteristic	Family Member	Nature
	Chien	Northwest	Creative	Father	Heaven
	Kun	Southwest	Receptive	Mother	Earth
	Chen	East	Arousing	Eldest son	Thunder
	Tui	West	Joyous	Youngest daughter	Lake
	Sun	Southeast	Gentle	Eldest daughter	Wind
	Li	South	Clinging	Middle daughter	Fire
	Kan	North	Abysmal	Middle son	Water
	Ken	Northeast	Mountain	Youngest son	Mountain

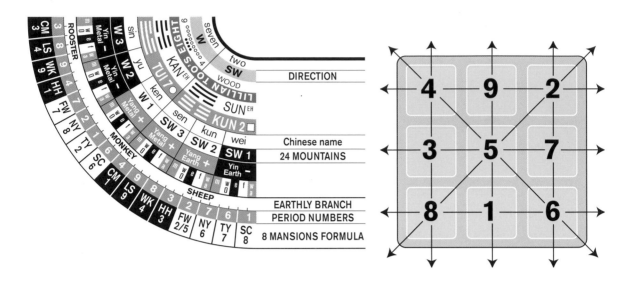

This anglicised version of the traditional Chinese Luo Pan (right) has thirteen rings: some versions have as many as thirty-six rings. Each ring contains a code for a feng shui formula.

The Lo Shu Square (above, right) has five as its center number; any three horizontal or vertical numbers add up to fifteen, the number of days of one cycle of the waxing or waning moon. Hence, the Square is a very significant tool in time dimension feng shui.

The feng shui ruler (far right) can be used to reveal the auspicious dimensions of everyday objects, such as furniture and doors.

✳ THE LUO PAN

This was and continues to be the basic reference tool used by feng shui professionals. Usually made of wood and painted red, it contains concentric rings of Chinese words indicating references required for feng shui analysis. It is not a necessary tool for amateur practitioners and an ordinary compass will suffice.

✳ THE LO SHU SQUARE

The Lo Shu Square is the nine-sector grid of numbers that are arranged in such a way that the numbers directly across from each other add up to ten. The center number is five, and any three numbers horizontally, vertically, or diagonally add up to fifteen, which is the number of days it takes for the moon to wax or wane. The Lo Shu Square is generally regarded as the key that unlocks the secrets of time.

The Lo Shu Square contains many other secrets, especially those pertaining to the numerology of feng shui, but for our purposes it is sufficient to note the number arrangement around the nine squares.

The corresponding compass sectors of the numbers offer important clues for analysis. Each number has a corresponding compass direction and element: North is water; Northeast and Southwest are earth; East and Southeast are wood; South is Fire and West and Northwest are metal. The numbers indicate the numerical energy of the eight sectors. For example, the number for North is one and the celestial creature of the North is the tortoise, so keeping a single tortoise in the North sector is beneficial. In the same way, the number of the East is three, and this sector has the element of wood, so keeping three plants here will produce good feng shui.

THE FENG SHUI RULER

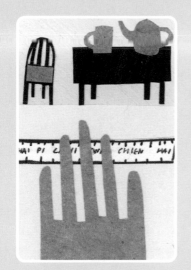

A FENG SHUI RULER OR TAPE MEASURE CAN BE USED TO MEASURE WINDOWS, DOORS, AND FURNITURE TO ENSURE THAT ONLY AUSPICIOUS DIMENSIONS ARE INTEGRATED IN YOUR ENVIRONMENT. THE RULER HAS EIGHT CYCLES OF DIMENSIONS, FOUR OF WHICH ARE AUSPICIOUS AND FOUR OF WHICH ARE INAUSPICIOUS. EACH CYCLE MEASURES THE EQUIVALENT OF 17 INCHES OR 43 CENTIMETERS. EACH CYCLE IS FURTHER BROKEN DOWN INTO EIGHT SEGMENTS. THIS CYCLE OF LUCKY AND UNLUCKY DIMENSIONS IS REPEATED TO INFINITY.

Each of the auspicious and inauspicious measurements is subdivided into four further measurements of about $\frac{1}{2}$ inch (1 cm), which have their own feng shui significance.

THE AUSPICIOUS DIMENSIONS

Chai (abundance)—between 0 and $2\frac{1}{8}$ inches or 0 and 5.4 cm. The four subdivisions are: money luck; a safe filled with jewels; six types of good luck; abundance.

Yi (excellent children luck)—between $6\frac{3}{8}$ and $8\frac{1}{2}$ inches or 16.2 and 21.5 cm. The four subdivisions are: excellent children luck; unexpected added income; successful son; excellent good fortune.

Kwan (high honors)—between $8\frac{1}{2}$ and $10\frac{5}{8}$ inches or 21.5 and 27 cm. The four subdivisions are: exam success; speculative luck; improved income; high honors.

Pun (prosperity)—between $14\frac{6}{8}$ and 17 inches or 37.5 and 43.2 cm. The four subdivisions are: money luck; exam success; abundance of jewelry; abundant prosperity.

THE INAUSPICIOUS DIRECTIONS

Pi (jail or death)—between $2\frac{1}{8}$ and $4\frac{2}{8}$ inches or 5.4 and 10.8 cm. The four subdivisions are: warning of money retreating; potential legal problems; bad luck, possibly even going to jail; death of a spouse.

Li (burglary)—between $4\frac{2}{8}$ and $6\frac{3}{8}$ inches or 10.8 and 16.2 cm. The four subdivisions are: store of bad luck; losing money; meeting unscrupulous people; theft or burglary.

Chieh (loss of money) – between $10\frac{5}{8}$ and $12\frac{6}{8}$ inches or 27 and 32.4 cm. The four subdivisions are: death or departure; disappearance of needed items/loss of livelihood; you could be chased from your home in disgrace; severe money loss.

Hai (quarrels) – between $12\frac{6}{8}$ and $14\frac{6}{8}$ inches or 32.4 and 37.5 cm. The four subdivisions are: disasters; death; sickness and ill-health; scandal and quarrels.

CM   INCHES

C H A I

P I

L I

CHAI YI

PART THREE

IMPROVING THE QUALITY OF YOUR LIFE

FENG SHUI'S POTENTIAL FOR IMPROVING YOUR LIFE AND LIFESTYLE IS TRULY AWESOME. IF YOU APPROACH THE SUBJECT WITH AN OPEN MIND AND CAN RELATE TO THE NOTION OF POSITIVE AND NEGATIVE ENERGY, YOU WILL FIND IT EASY TO RESONATE WITH THE PRECEPTS OF **FENG SHUI**. IT IS EXCITING THAT SO MANY OF THE METHODS AND FORMULAS HAVE SURVIVED INTACT AND THAT SO MUCH OF **FENG SHUI** CONTINUES TO BE RELEVANT IN TODAY'S WORLD.

FENG SHUI CAN IMPROVE THE QUALITY OF YOUR LIFE AS YOU FOCUS ON THE KEY AREAS AND ASPIRATIONS THAT MAKE YOU HAPPY, HEALTHY, AND FULFILLED, FROM WORK TO RELATIONSHIPS TO FINANCIAL SUCCESS.

CHAPTER 7
SUCCESS, RECOGNITION, AND PROMOTION

✳ YOU CAN ARRANGE YOUR HOME AND OFFICE INTERIORS TO MAXIMIZE GOOD FORTUNE IN YOUR WORKING LIFE AND TO MANIFEST CAREER SUCCESS, UPWARD MOBILITY, RECOGNITION, AND APPRECIATION OF YOUR CONTRIBUTIONS.

A picture of a mountain behind you acts in a protective way like the Black Tortoise.

Work out your Kua number to help you decide which is the best sitting direction to increase your luck.

When your feng shui is good, your efforts will be acknowledged. You can and will be rewarded with promotion and expanded responsibility. Even when everyday tasks increase and the scope of your work is broadened, you will continue to benefit from good feng shui. There is no limit to what the correct practice of feng shui can bring to you. No matter how clever and successful you may be, remember that you always need the element of luck for your life to move smoothly forward.

When the chi energy around you is becoming benevolent Sheng Chi, no matter how high you climb you will be able to meet the challenges of your job. This is the meaning of career success. To enjoy a successful career on a sustained basis, be sure to do the following:

✳ Sit correctly, facing your most auspicious direction and making sure that no poison arrows are able to strike you. Check your Kua number and see what direction suits you best (*see* Chapter 14).

Arrange your desk at work, as well as your desk at home, so that you can sit facing your best direction.

✳ If you are unable to face your best direction, try to face at least one of your good directions. Never sit facing one of your four bad directions, as this will cause you to lose energy or, worse, have an adverse effect on your work and on your luck. Facing your total loss direction can also get you fired from your job.

✳ Position your desk at work in a way that will prevent betrayal by seemingly well-meaning colleagues. When you sit with a window behind you on one of the higher levels of a multilevel building, the "hole" behind you indicates that no one is there to support you should you ever have a career crisis. When you are at the office, it is important to "watch your back." If you work from home, this arrangement is not such a bad feature as there are no adversaries in the home.

✱ Install a mirror to counter the bad luck being produced by having a door located behind you. If there is a door behind you and you simply cannot move your desk, try installing a long mirror in front of you toward your right side (this is your tiger side). The mirror should not be directly facing you; instead it should reflect your back and put it on your tiger side to invoke the protective energy of the White Tiger. You can also shine a light toward your back as an extra precaution, but make certain that it is not brighter behind you than the front of you.

✱ Hang a picture of a mountain if a window is behind you. Similarly, if you cannot do anything about a window behind you, hang a large painting or photograph of a mountain or mountains. A mountain behind you simulates the tortoise hill and gives you protection, as well as ensuring support for your ideas and projects. If you are a career person, you will discover that support from the top is vital to success. If you find it hard to place a mountain image, then look for a dragon tortoise, that is, a tortoise with a dragon head. This is a powerful symbol to have near you.

DESK PLACEMENT

POSITION YOUR DESK AT WORK SO THAT YOU ARE FACING ONE OF YOUR BEST DIRECTIONS (SEE CHAPTER 14) AND IN A WAY THAT MINIMIZES POISON ARROWS.

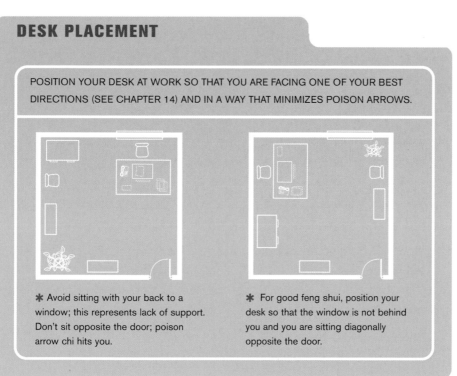

✱ Avoid sitting with your back to a window; this represents lack of support. Don't sit opposite the door; poison arrow chi hits you.

✱ For good feng shui, position your desk so that the window is not behind you and you are sitting diagonally opposite the door.

NORTH CORNER ACTIVATION

✳ ACTIVATE YOUR NORTH CORNER WITH GOOD FENG SHUI. THIS CORNER GOVERNS CAREER SUCCESS, SO PLACING APPROPRIATE IMAGES, PAINTINGS, OR DECORATIVE ITEMS HERE IS ESSENTIAL.

Hanging an image of water in the North sector of your office will increase your Sheng Chi and help to give your career a boost. This image, showing the Dragon Gate when the carp becomes a dragon, is a symbol associated with examination luck but it can also be used for jumpstarting your career luck.

✳ Ensure that you do not inadvertently place crystals or crystal spheres in the North corner of your office or of your living room at home. The earth chi of crystals directly conflicts with the water chi of the North to cause an imbalance, which translates into bad feng shui. Wood elements are also not good for the North corner, so plants (whether real or artificial) are not recommended.

✳ Get an aquarium for the North. The best thing to activate your North corner is a well-lit and clean aquarium filled with plenty of small fish such as goldfish or colorful guppies. The fish must be happy, so the water needs to be carefully maintained. This is a cardinal principle, for when the fish tank gets dirty or the fish die from improper maintenance, you will experience severe bad luck and your career prospects will dim. Always remember that energized water and happy lively fish bring enormous good fortune. It is important that you yourself exude happy positive energy, which will be picked up by both the fish and the water.

✳ Hang a painting of water in the North. This excellent feng shui energizer enhances the intrinsic chi of this corner. In feng shui, water can mean "small water" as in a real water feature, or it can be "big water," as depicted by a painting or photograph of a lake, the sea, or a small mountain waterfall—something that blends harmoniously with your room. Do not hang an image of the Niagara Falls in your office as the chi will be too strong. Nor should there be a waterfall

NORTH CORNER: GOOD CHI ENHANCERS

Auspicious fish for your aquarium include goldfish and guppies. The fish should experience a clean and happy environment if they are to bring you career luck.

PLACE AN AQUARIUM IN THE NORTH SECTOR OF YOUR OFFICE

PLACE A WEALTH BOAT IN THE NORTH AREA OF YOUR DESK

The sailing ship is one of the most auspicious symbols you can have in the office as it represents wealth brought to you by the winds and waters (see pages 168–169 and 271).

with water appearing to flow out of your room. Be sensitive to these small observations. Do not hang water images if the North is behind you, and never hang a waterfall at your back. These placements will cause water to harm you.

✱ Activate the North corner of your desk. Either leave this corner empty, or place a small decorative item such as a golden ship sailing toward you. The metal chi of the gold ship (filled with ingots) will give your career a big boost.

✱ Do not place conflicting elements on your desk. A vase of flowers, crystal spheres, or any other decorative crystal items on the North corner of your desk will inevitably cause the intrinsic chi of the North to become afflicted. The effect will be felt in your work and career prospects can get blocked.

NORTH CORNER: INAUSPICIOUS PLACEMENTS

TO AVOID BAD FENG SHUI IN THE OFFICE, IT IS IMPORTANT TO APPRECIATE THE CORRECT AND INCORRECT PLACEMENT OF CRYSTALS, PLANTS, FLOWERS AND WATER IMAGES. HERE ARE SOME GUIDELINES ON PLACEMENTS TO BE AVOIDED.

✳ **CRYSTALS:** Don't place crystals in the north area of your office

✳ **CRYSTALS:** Don't place crystals in the north area of your desk

✳ **PLANTS:** Don't place plants in the north area of your desk

✳ **FLOWERS:** Don't place flowers or plants in the north area of your office

✳ **WATERFALL:** Don't place a waterfall image behind your desk

SOUTH CORNER ACTIVATION

✳ ACTIVATE YOUR SOUTH CORNER WITH GOOD FENG SHUI. THIS CORNER BRINGS RECOGNITION AND ACKNOWLEDGEMENT OF YOUR EFFORTS. IF IT IS AFFLICTED, YOUR SUGGESTIONS WILL BE IGNORED.

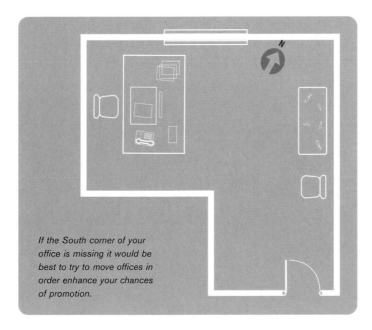

If the South corner of your office is missing it would be best to try to move offices in order enhance your chances of promotion.

If the South corner of your home or office is missing or afflicted, then you can forget about being selected for higher office. Promotion prospects will be blocked and you will find that high-level appointments will be an uphill battle.

The South corner is afflicted when elements that clash with or exhaust the fire chi are present. Anything that suggests the water element will cause problems as water destroys fire. The exception to this rule is when the Water Star here is auspicious according to the Flying Star formula (*see* Chapter 15). When the Water Star indicates potential wealth luck, it overrides the intrinsic fire energy of the South.

✳ Earth exhausts fire, so you must not place crystal spheres or raw crystals in this corner of your office. When you exhaust the fire energy, you will not receive any recognition at work. Your good name could also be compromised.

✳ Place bright lights in the South. When the South sectors of your office and of your living room at home are well lit, massive quantities of yang chi enhance your chances of gaining widespread respect. Keep the lights turned on through the night so the chi energy always works in your favor.

✳ Place images of horses in the South. The energy of the horse will help you move more swiftly than your competitors. When you place the victory horse in the South—this is the running horse always depicted with a swallow flying beside it—you will

SOUTH CORNER: GOOD CHI ENHANCERS

YOU CAN ADVANCE YOUR CAREER PROSPECTS BY PAYING CAREFUL ATTENTION TO THE USE OF LIGHTS AND THE WISE PLACEMENT OF AUSPICIOUS PAINTINGS OR OTHER IMAGES AND FIGURES IN THE SOUTH CORNER OF YOUR OFFICE.

✳ **LIGHTS:** Use bright lights in south corner of your office and desk to increase the respect your colleagues and boss have for you.

✳ **PHOENIX:** Place a painting of a Phoenix in the south corner of your office to help you to advance professionally.

✳ **BIRDS:** Decorative images of birds placed in your south corner will bring enormous benefits and opportunities your way.

✳ **HORSES:** Place images of horses, such as the tribute horse (left) and the victory horse (right), to enable you to outpace your competition.

easily emerge the victor in any race to the top. If you want extra income and prosperity to accompany your rise to prominence, you should also place the tribute horse—a horse loaded with gold and ingots—in the South. Horses in the South always bring the respect of a good name to the family.

✳ Place decorative images of birds in the South. Bird images will bring enormous benefits and opportunities, as well as spreading your good name far and wide, so birds are also excellent for those who desire fame. Place a variety of birds in all colors in the South, perhaps the famous Chinese painting of "a hundred birds" to bring great good fortune. The most important bird is the phoenix, and when you invite this lovely king of birds into your office, you will be amazed at your sudden professional advancement.

✳ A rooster in the South overcomes office politics. Taoist feng shui practitioners consider the red comb on its head all-powerful. Its claws signify an ability to wipe out backbiting and partisan politicking in a work environment. The image of a cockerel is equally effective as that of rooster.

SOUTH CORNER: INAUSPICIOUS PLACEMENTS

THE INCORRECT PLACEMENT OF CRYSTAL AND WATER FEATURES COULD PRODUCE AN ELEMENTAL CLASH THAT SPELLS BAD FENG SHUI IN YOUR WORKPLACE. HERE ARE SOME TIPS:

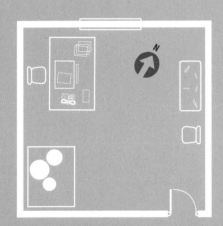

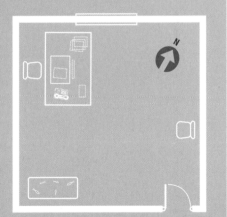

✳ **CRYSTALS:** Don't place crystal spheres or crystals in the South corner; they will clash the Fire chi.

✳ **WATER:** Don't place water features in the South corner; they will destroy the Fire chi.

CHAPTER 8
SUCCESSFUL RELATIONSHIPS

✱ FENG SHUI IS EXCEPTIONALLY POWERFUL IN SMOOTHING RELATIONSHIPS AND CREATING BENEFICIAL INTERPERSONAL BEHAVIOR BETWEEN PEOPLE WHO LIVE OR WORK TOGETHER. THERE ARE SEVERAL WAYS TO ENSURE THAT AGGRAVATIONS ARE KEPT TO A MINIMUM AND THAT DIPLOMACY AND A CLIMATE OF TOLERANCE PREVAILS.

A work environment can be arranged in a manner that is conducive to creating smooth working relationships between co-workers, bosses and employees, and also between business partners and associates. Good feng shui can help to engender goodwill between friends, colleagues, and partners.

In the home, the living space can be arranged to ensure warm and nurturing rather than hostile and argumentative relationships between spouses and between siblings. For example, you could arrange the chairs and sofas in your living room into an auspicious Pa Kua shape.

Peace in the household is the key to marital happiness.

Contentious relationships between family members are not uncommon, but, with the help of feng shui, contentious behavior can be significantly reduced. The level of goodwill and tolerance achieved is often extended to friends and associates outside the family circle.

THE SOUTHWEST CORNER

In the home the southwest corner is the matriarchal corner and creates nurturing luck. It is also the corner that attracts:

- love, romance, and faithfulness
- the loving energy of caring for the family.

When this energy is not afflicted either by the presence of sharp and hostile physical structures or by the intangible energy of bad Flying Stars in the annual or monthly charts (*see* Chapters 15 and 16), all residents living or working within will get along well with each other.

FURNITURE ARRANGEMENT
Arrange furniture to ensure a warm and nurturing environment; one way is to place chairs and sofas in a Pa Kua shape around a central table.

ENHANCING RELATIONSHIP LUCK

THE FOLLOWING METHODS WILL CREATE GOOD RELATIONSHIP LUCK AT WORK AND AT HOME:

PROTECT YOUR SOUTHWEST CORNER

In the home, the Southwest corner represents the matriarch and creates nurturing luck. At the office it represents the foundation of teamwork and is conducive to fostering a family atmosphere. Bathrooms, storerooms, and kitchens placed here are inadvisable, as they will lock up all the goodwill and love that should be flowing through the home or office.

MEETING OR LIVING ROOM

Meeting rooms and living rooms in the Southwest corner work well to foster harmony.

BATHROOM

Avoid putting bathrooms, storerooms or kitchens in the Southwest corner.

ACTIVATE THE SOUTHWEST

The best way to do this is to place earth element items here. Good examples are crystal spheres, which will engender a mood of tolerance and goodwill. Crystals also represent the element of Period Eight. The presence of fire element in the form of lights, candles, and anything red in color is also excellent for the Southwest corner.

PLACE WATER IN THE SOUTHWEST

Water in the Southwest brings wealth luck to your relationships. During the twenty years of Period Eight, the Southwest direction is the place of the "indirect spirit," which is always energized by the presence of water. Do not make your water feature too large. A small Zen-like bubbling water feature is just right. Do not use this water feature in the bedroom since water in the bedroom can cause loss, but note that it is ideal for the office.

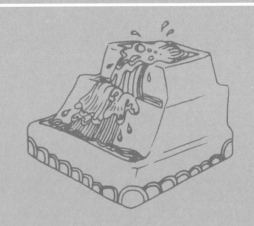

TIPS FOR MARITAL BLISS

AVOIDING BAD FENG SHUI IS THE KEY TO A HARMONIOUS HOME AND RELATIONSHIP. ENHANCE YOUR MARRIAGE WITH THESE IMPORTANT FENG SHUI GUIDELINES.

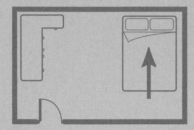

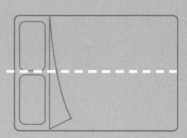

✷ SLEEPING DIRECTION: Ensure that your sleeping direction is auspicious and does not bring bad luck (see page 65). Sleeping direction refers to the direction toward which the heads of the sleeping couple point. If husband and wife have differing good directions, choose the direction that benefits the main breadwinner. Meanwhile, watch out for these taboos in the bedroom that could cause a rift between husband and wife: Position your bed so that your head points in an auspicious direction (see page 65), but if this means your feet pointing at the door, adjust the bed slightly so they do not point this way.

✷ MATTRESSES: Avoid using two mattresses to create one bed; use one large mattress to make the relationship harmonious. In other words, do not place two separate mattresses on one box spring or frame. Doing so creates an invisible split between the couple, possibly creating one of them to move out of the marital home. Change to one large mattress if you are in this situation. The presence of an overhead beam creating a strong energy field aligned between the couple has the same effect, so you should either move the bed from under the beam or cover the beam with a fake plaster ceiling.

✷ MIRRORS: Avoid mirrors directly reflecting the bed as they can cause unwelcome third-party involvement in the marriage, leading to infidelity and unhappiness. Mirrors are truly bad news in the bedroom and it is advisable to either cover or remove them. Television screens and computers should also be avoided for the same reason. Avoid sharp corners pointing at the bed and being open to rushing chi from the door as both bring bad chi.

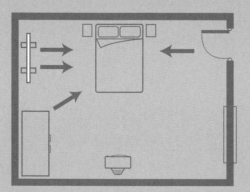

✷ FLOWERS: Do not place fresh flowers in the bedroom of a happily married couple as this can cause sudden misunderstandings and quarrels to flare up, especially when the flowers are roses with thorns, or are red in color. It is also a good idea to keep fake flowers out of the bedroom.

ASTROLOGICAL ALLIES

CARRY IMAGES OF YOUR SECRET ALLY AND ASTROLOGICAL FRIENDS. THIS RECOMMENDATION MARRIES CHINESE ASTROLOGY WITH FENG SHUI AND IS ONE OF THE MOST POWERFUL METHODS OF ATTRACTING RELIABLE RELATIONSHIPS INTO YOUR LIFE. WHEN YOU CARRY THESE IMAGES INSIDE YOUR POCKETBOOK OR WEAR THEM ON YOUR BODY AS DECORATIVE JEWELRY, YOU WILL EXPERIENCE GOOD WILL IN YOUR LIFE BECAUSE YOU WILL BE CREATING "TRIANGLES OF AFFINITY" AROUND YOU. CHINESE ASTROLOGY ASSIGNS EVERYONE ONE OF THE TWELVE ANIMAL SIGNS BASED ON BIRTH YEAR (SEE CHINESE CALENDAR, PAGES 284–285) AND EACH PERSON HAS A SECRET ALLY AND TWO ASTROLOGICAL FRIENDS. THERE ARE FOUR GROUPS OF ASTROLOGICAL FRIENDS AND SIX PAIRS OF SECRET ALLIES.

| RAT | ROOSTER | DOG | SNAKE | TIGER | OX |
| HORSE | SHEEP | MONKEY | PIG | RABBIT | DRAGON |

ASTROLOGICAL FRIENDS	SECRET ALLIES
RAT, DRAGON, AND MONKEY	ROOSTER AND DRAGON
OX, SNAKE, AND ROOSTER	MONKEY AND SNAKE
HORSE, DOG, AND TIGER	SHEEP AND HORSE
SHEEP, PIG, AND RABBIT	RABBIT AND DOG
	TIGER AND PIG
	OX AND RAT

When you marry your astrological friend or your secret ally, it is likely the relationship will be beneficial and more than cordial. When children and parents belong to the same affinity triangle or have an ally relationship, there is harmony between them. When you have good affinity with your business partner or an important colleague based on this method of analysis, chances are good that the relationship will be long-lasting. To determine your relationships, please refer to the lists above. For example, if your astrological sign is the Dragon, your astrological friends are Rat and Monkey and your secret ally is Rooster.

AFFINITIES BASED ON KUA NUMBER COMBINATIONS

 ANOTHER WAY TO DETERMINE GOOD AFFINITY BETWEEN INDIVIDUALS IS TO USE THE EIGHT MANSIONS KUA FORMULA.

The Kua number is calculated by adding the last two digits of your year of birth, then adding those numbers again if necessary, so that the sum is reduced to a single-digit number. Next, if you are male, deduct that number from 10 and, if female, add 5 to that number—reduce to a single digit again, if necessary. The result is your Kua number. Everyone with Kua numbers 2, 5, 6, 7, and 8 belong to the West group and tend to have

CALCULATING YOUR KUA NUMBER

TO CALCULATE YOUR PERSONAL KUA NUMBER AND DISCOVER WHETHER YOU ARE AN EAST OR WEST GROUP PERSON FOLLOW THIS EXAMPLE (SEE ALSO CHAPTER 14):

EXAMPLE: MALE

If you are born in 1947, then
4 + 7 = 11
1 + 1 = **2**, when reduced to a single digit.

If you are male,
10 − **2** = 8,
so your Kua number is 8

EXAMPLE: FEMALE

If you are born in 1947, then
4 + 7 = 11
1 + 1 = **2**, when reduced to a single digit.

If you are female,
2 + **5** = 7
so your Kua number is 7

1 3 4 9

E

2 5 6 7 8

W

affinity with one another in terms of having similar thought processes and attitudes. Those with Kua numbers 1, 3, 4, and 9 belong to the East group and have the same kind of affinity with each other. When people of the same group marry, it is easier to feng shui their homes, as the same sets of directions are good or bad for both.

This does not mean that West group people should not marry East group people—there are certain combinations of numbers that may create a special chemistry between them, thereby causing the relationship to be beneficial. Thus, Kua numbers that add up to 10 are referred to as the "Sum of Ten" combination, which is

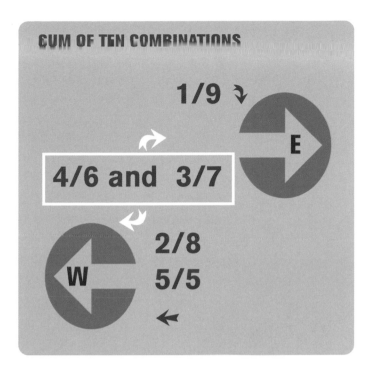

SUM OF TEN COMBINATIONS

1/9

E

4/6 and 3/7

W

2/8
5/5

YOUR KUA NUMBER AND YOUR MARRIAGE DIRECTION

BED PLACEMENT: FOR MARRIAGE LUCK, SLEEP WITH YOUR HEAD POINTING IN YOUR MARRIAGE DIRECTION AND THE BED IN AN AUSPICIOUS POSITION. TO GET YOUR MOST AUSPICIOUS DIRECTION FIRST DETERMINE YOUR KUA NUMBER (SEE OPPOSITE). THEN USE THE TABLE BELOW TO FIND YOUR MARRIAGE DIRECTION.

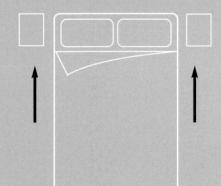

KUA NUMBER	MARRIAGE DIRECTION
1	South for both males and females
2	Northwest for both males and females
3	Southwest for both males and females
4	East for both males and females
5	Northwest for males and west for females
6	Southwest for both males and females
7	Northwest for both males and females
8	West for both males and females
9	North for both males and females

most auspicious and suggests that the two parties are mutually benefiting each other. This is an excellent method of checking if someone who wants to marry you or go into partnership with you will be beneficial to you. Sum of Ten pairings belonging to the West group are 2/8 and 5/5, while a pairing of 1/9 belongs to the East group. The other Sum of Ten pairings, 4/6 and 3/7, are pairings of both groups.

HO TU NUMBERS

FOUR MORE SETS OF NUMBERS ARE ESPECIALLY BENEFICIAL WHEN THEY ARE PAIRED AND THESE REFLECT THE HO TU COMBINATIONS OF NUMBERS. THESE COMBINATIONS ARE SAID TO BE AS GOOD AS, IF NOT BETTER THAN, THE SUM OF TEN COMBINATION.

1 AND 6 (EAST AND WEST GROUP)

As siblings, this combination ensures there will be little or no jealousy—and the support that one gives to the other is both material and crucial. It is an excellent relationship. When paired in a marriage or a partnership this combination will bring power and excellent working luck to the couple. There will be plenty of mutual respect and tolerance between these two. The pairing has a long shelf life.

2 AND 7 (WEST GROUP)

When paired in a marriage this combination will produce many children who will bring honor and glory to the family. If the relationship is a business partnership, the two will succeed in building a large company with many subsidiaries and a great deal of success luck in business. When this pairing is of siblings or close friends, they will generate a great many workable ideas and solutions. They work extremely well together and will bring out the best in each other.

3 AND 8 (EAST AND WEST GROUP)

When paired in a marriage this combination will produce a very powerful son. The couple will also create a solid foundation for making a mark in the world. Achievements will probably be in the academic or scholastic field. In a business relationship, the good fortune manifests when the partners are involved in a business that involves communications and research. In siblings, this combination will ensure that they rise above any differences they may have. It will also help them overcome their personal differences to achieve great things together.

4 AND 9 (EAST GROUP)

If this is a business relationship, the pairing will be extremely successful. When paired as siblings, the two will succeed in partnership. When paired in a marriage, this couple will enjoy fame, recognition, and great love for each other. This is a happy relationship—a rare coming together of minds that will grow with the years.

FIRMING UP FRIENDSHIPS

✳ APPLES AND CRYSTAL SPHERES PROVIDE AN EASY WAY TO ENSURE THAT RELATIONSHIPS ARE GOING TO BE CORDIAL, FRIENDLY, AND ALWAYS INVOKING GOODWILL.

Place six crystal or glass spheres in the center of any common room, such as the living room or dining room. At least one of these spheres should be of rock or quartz crystal, but other spheres placed nearby to complement it can be made of glass. Souvenir "snow balls" collected from different cities of the world contain the essence of success chi so they contain a great deal of yang chi. You can also use glass balls that contain auspicious hand-painted images.

Place the spheres in the center of the room to ground the earth energy. You will find that their presence inside the home will soothe frazzled nerves. You may simply pick up the quartz crystal sphere, cradling it with both hands, and gaze into it for several seconds. This will instantly create a soothing feeling of calm.

Another valuable enhancing agent for ensuring peace and goodwill in the home is the crystal apple in any color. The Chinese word for "apple" sounds like the word *ping*, or peace, and placing an apple fashioned out of raw crystal or glass invokes the peaceful calmness of earth element energy. Crystal vases serve the same function.

Glass or crystal apples placed in a common room in your home will help foster peace.

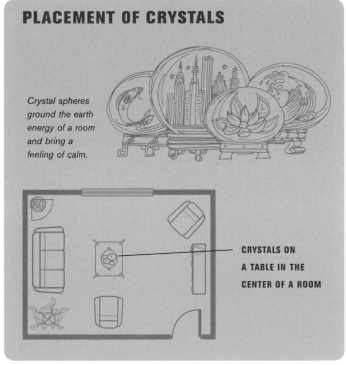

PLACEMENT OF CRYSTALS

Crystal spheres ground the earth energy of a room and bring a feeling of calm.

CRYSTALS ON A TABLE IN THE CENTER OF A ROOM

CHAPTER 9

LOVE, FAMILY, AND HAPPY MARRIAGES

✳ FENG SHUI IS NOT JUST ABOUT ATTAINING SUCCESS OR ACQUIRING WEALTH; IT CAN ALSO HELP ANYONE INVOKE THEIR CHI ENERGIES TO ATTRACT LOVE, MARRIAGE, AND REAL HAPPINESS INTO THEIR LIVES. USED CAREFULLY FENG SHUI TECHNIQUES CAN ALSO ENHANCE ROMANCE.

The Chinese often use the dragon–phoenix symbol at wedding banquets; together they symbolize marriage luck and conjugal happiness.

Using various feng shui methods, it is possible to create energy vibrations within the home that are conducive to finding love and marriage for those who are still single; for helping those who are childless to have children, and for bringing a new lease of life to those whose marriage has suffered from neglect or bad feng shui. Used properly, feng shui is a powerful tool that can generate wonderful family happiness.

Singles seeking love and romance should first understand the natural polarities of yin and yang forces. Yin naturally complements yang and vice versa. In their living spaces they must ensure that this balance is present. Women looking for a husband should bring the essence of male yang chi into their living space. Similarly, men who are looking for a wife should also bring female energy into their homes and bedrooms. The most obvious approach is to display pictures symbolizing the desired partner, but better yet is to display images of happy couples. Birds are excellent energizers for love—they are said to be the messengers of the God of Marriage who resides in the moon. The best bird image is that of the phoenix. In fact, the dragon and phoenix image is one of the most powerful symbols of marriage, but you can also display a pair of phoenixes, male and female. It is also good to display images of lovebirds or mandarin ducks in pairs to signify undying love and fidelity.

ATTRACTING ROMANCE

IN ADDITION TO MAKING YOUR PERSONAL SPACE CONDUCIVE TO ATTRACTING ROMANCE, FOLLOW THESE ADDITIONAL GUIDELINES THAT HAVE PROVED SUCCESSFUL:

✳ SLEEPING DIRECTION: Sleep with your head to your Nien Yen, or personal love, direction (*see* page 121 to determine your direction). It is best to sleep in this orientation with a solid wall behind you to support you.

✳ LAMP: Introduce a red or yellow lamp into the Southwest of your bedroom. This will activate the powerful chi of this corner. The Southwest is always a corner to focus on when it concerns the desire to attract relationship luck.

✳ CRYSTALS: Place an earth element object in the Southwest to strengthen the influence of this element. Placing crystals here will have a positive effect. The best crystals are amethyst and rose quartz, which are highly effective in creating an ambience of happiness. You may also wear them as jewelry to manifest their attributes.

✳ DOUBLE-HAPPINESS SYMBOL: If possible, wear the double-happiness motif on your body or carry it with you. The best enhancer is a double-happiness ring made of gold and diamonds and worn on your ring finger. The double-happiness sign is the ultimate symbol of marriage and has helped many singles find lasting love.

DESCENDANTS' LUCK

✳   CHILDLESS COUPLES WHO DESIRE CHILDREN CAN USE FENG SHUI TO BRING THE HAPPINESS OF DESCENDANTS' LUCK. THERE ARE SEVERAL WAYS TO BRING THIS LUCK INTO YOUR LIFE.

1 SLEEPING DIRECTION The couple wishing to start a family should sleep with their heads toward the husband's Nien Yen direction (*see* page 121). This arrangement must be achieved without inadvertently being hit by afflictions or poison arrows.

2 ACTIVATING THE WEST SECTOR Activate the West side of your home, your living room, your bedroom, or all three. The West side of the home greatly influences and directly impacts the luck of the children of the household. When there are no children yet, it is possible to activate this corner to conceive and bear a child.

Hang a picture of a baby or a young child that resembles you or your spouse in this corner. If you are hoping for a boy, hang a picture of a baby boy or a picture of a baby girl if you are hoping for a girl. Install bright lights that shine directly onto the picture. You may wish to place five lamps in five colors to create a complement of elements.

Improve conception luck by placing a pair of elephant statues in the bedroom.

3 SYMBOLS OF FERTILITY Incorporate these symbols—especially pomegranates, which need not be real but which can be beautifully made of crystals or gemstones. Pomegranates should be placed in the couple's bedroom. Another symbol of fertility is the powerful elephant. A pair of benign elephants (with the trunk down) placed in the bedroom invokes energy for the couple to conceive. Many tourists visit the Ming tombs—gigantic elephants flank the driveway en route. Rumor has it that local women who want to conceive visit daily to experience the chi of the elephants.

4 ONE HUNDRED CHILDREN Hang an image or a screen depicting a hundred children. There is something magical about the number 100—to invoke a particular emblem or symbol, the Chinese always depict the image not once or twice, but a full one hundred times. If having children is at the top of your agenda, then you should look for vases, crystal balls, furniture, screens, and so forth, which are decorated with a painting of the hundred children.

ATTRACTING DESCENDANTS' LUCK

IN ADDITION TO MAKING YOUR PERSONAL SPACE CONDUCIVE TO ATTRACTING ROMANCE, FOLLOW THESE ADDITIONAL GUIDELINES THAT HAVE PROVED SUCCESSFUL.

❋ **SLEEPING DIRECTION:** Sleep with the husband's head towards his Nien Yen direction (see Chapter 14 to determine your direction). This brings good luck in marriage and will also enhance descendants' luck.

HUSBAND'S NIEN YEN DIRECTION

❋ **FERTILITY SYMBOLS:** Place symbols of fertility in the couple's bedroom:
• Pomegranates
• Paper lanterns with auspicious characters
• Elephants

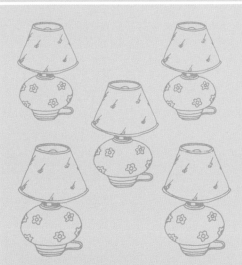

❋ **BRIGHT LIGHTS:** Activate the West sector of your home, living room, bedroom or all three using bright lights, and images of babies. Place five lamps in five colors in this area. Lava lamps show liquid energy moving slowly and the water and bright lamps combine to activate the corner effectively.

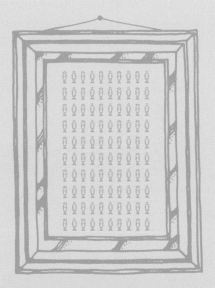

❋ **ONE HUNDRED CHILDREN:** Hang an image or object depicting a hundred children. Place this image in the Northeast for a son and place it in the West for a daughter.

MARRIAGE RESCUE

✳   FENG SHUI CAN PLAY A PART IN REVITALIZING A STALE MARRIAGE. IT CAN BRING HAPPINESS BACK TO A RELATIONSHIP THAT IS FLOUNDERING OR ENDING.

When love between married couples becomes stale or turns ugly, the cause can often be traced to their bedroom feng shui or to the front door of their home, afflicted by some negative Flying Star.

Many things can cause a marriage to go sour, not the least of which is when the couple moves into a home that is hit by poison arrows caused by physical structures in the surrounding environment. Even the way furniture has been arranged inside the home can cause problems.

It is always a good idea to ensure that all beams, corners, edges, and so forth are neutralized with feng shui remedies. Blocking these sources of bad chi is not difficult, and absorbing or dispersing bad chi is essential.

CHECK YOUR FLYING STAR CHARTS

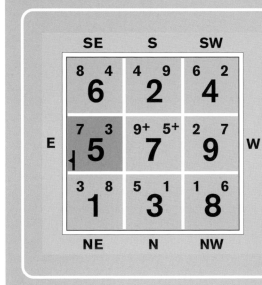

Flying Star charts reveal the good and bad luck sectors of your home. If you are having marital problems, check that your bedroom is not in an inauspicious sector (see Chapter 15).

AVOIDING MARRIAGE DIFFICULTIES

ONE OF THE MAIN CAUSES OF MARRIAGE DIFFICULTIES OCCURS WHEN A THIRD PARTY ENTERS THE PICTURE. AT AN EARLY STAGE, BEFORE AN ILLICIT RELATIONSHIP IS ENTERED INTO, MARRIED PEOPLE SHOULD NOTE THE FOLLOWING POINTS OF ADVICE:

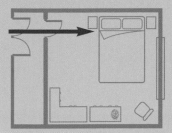

✴ **POISON ARROWS:** Poison arrows pointing at a house or marriage bed can cause disharmony between couples. Move the bed out of the way of the door, or place a divider between it and the door.

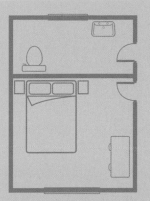

✴ **TOILET:** Placing a bed against a toilet wall will flush away your marriage happiness. A toilet in the Southwest of the house is also bad for the marriage.

✴ **TOTAL LOSS DIRECTION:** Ensure that the husband does not sleep with his head toward a total loss direction (or any other bad luck direction based on the Kua formula; *see* page 121).

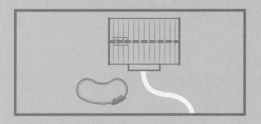

✴ **PONDS AND SWIMMING POOLS:** No water features should be placed on the right-hand side of the main door (inside looking out).

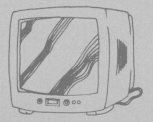

✴ **REFLECTIVE SURFACES:** No mirrors or other reflective surfaces should be allowed to directly face the marital bed. This includes televisions and computer screens.

✴ **WATER FEATURES:** Do not place water features (fountains or aquariums) inside the bedroom, as doing so can cause loss.

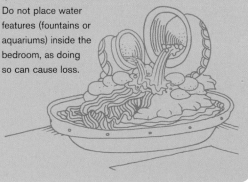

ENHANCING RELATIONSHIP CHI

✳ THERE ARE MANY WAYS OF ENCOURAGING LOVING CHI TO ENTER YOUR HOME USING SYMBOLIC FENG SHUI IMAGES AND SYMBOLS. HERE ARE A FEW GUIDELINES THAT WILL BENEFIT YOUR ROMANTIC RELATIONSHIPS.

The peony is regarded as the most supreme of all flowers, creating loving energy between couples, especially in the first ten years of marriage.

✳ TO IMPROVE A MARRIAGE

To improve a marriage that has begun to turn sour, place seven crystal spheres in the Southwest of the bedroom. This will create powerful nurturing chi inside the bedroom and cause both sides to be less hostile and more tolerant of one another. Repeat this in the center of the living room with six crystal spheres on a coffee table. At least one of the spheres must be rock or quartz crystal.

✳ TO SAFEGUARD AGAINST INFIDELITY

Place a raw amethyst geode tied with red string under the foot of the bed, on the wife's side if the husband tends to have a roving eye, and on the husband's side if it is the wife who is vulnerable. Amethysts are excellent safeguards against infidelity. To strengthen the chi energy, Taoists recommend that the amethyst be tied to the bedpost. It can be tied to either one of the bottom bedposts to safeguard both the husband and the wife. Install a small red light near the vicinity of the bed and keep it turned on through the night to more closely bond the couple. You can also place a red lantern inside the bedroom.

AMETHYST GEODE

✳ TO ENHANCE ATTRACTION

Place a beautiful painting of blooming peonies (the Mou Tan flower) inside the bedroom. These flowers create the luck of loving energy and are particularly effective during a couple's first ten years of marriage. If the couple is already middle aged, placing peonies inside the bedroom could cause the husband to develop an interest in younger women. If you can find fresh peonies, place these in the living room rather than in the bedroom.

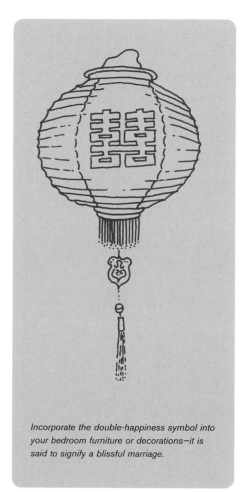

Incorporate the double-happiness symbol into your bedroom furniture or decorations—it is said to signify a blissful marriage.

✳ TO NURTURE LOVING CHI

The couple should be sure to sleep on the correct side of the bed. The husband should sleep on the left-hand side (determined when lying on your back) and the woman should sleep on the right-hand side to ensure that the correct balance of yin and yang chi is maintained in the marital bed.

✳ USING SYMBOLS OF TOGETHERNESS

Place good fortune symbols that enhance loving energy between you and your loved one. The double-happiness symbol should always be present in the bedroom to create togetherness chi.

Other auspicious symbols such as mandarin ducks and dragon–phoenix images inside the bedroom also benefit the marriage enormously. Remember, however, not to overdo it—only display one pair of ducks, or one double-happiness symbol, as two signify two marriages. Paintings and works of art that suggest romance are also beneficial to the couple's relationship.

A pair of mandarin ducks symbolizes young married love, and love that has a happy ending.

✳ WEDDING PORTRAITS

It is not a good idea to place wedding portraits inside the bedroom, especially facing the bed. Wedding portraits are best placed in common areas. Place pictures of children in the bedroom instead, as this not only enhances the correct type of yang chi in the bedroom, but also enhances the couple's descendants' luck.

CHAPTER 10
BUSINESS SUCCESS AND WEALTH

✳ PROBABLY THE MOST ENTICING ASPECT OF FENG SHUI'S POPULARITY IS RELATED TO ITS AMAZING IMPACT ON MONEY LUCK. WHEN THE HOUSE, THE WORKPLACE, OR THE OFFICE IS ORIENTED TO BRING GOOD FENG SHUI, INCOMES USUALLY RISE.

For businesses, this translates into higher sales and profits and smooth business growth. Business relationships between associates and workers are positive and productivity is significantly improved. Businesses that have good feng shui usually find it easier to attract good staff and maintain teamwork and goodwill in the office.

Feng shui can be designed to focus on wealth creation, prosperity, and abundance. Activating good feng shui for commercial offices is much easier and shows much faster results than applying feng shui to residential homes. At work, the emphasis can be specifically focused on enhancing wealth-creating energies without being worried about other aspects of the happiness equation. However, before you proceed to activate for wealth, first focus on protection against loss and against obstacles that create loss. A defensive attitude in the practice of feng shui will pay dividends.

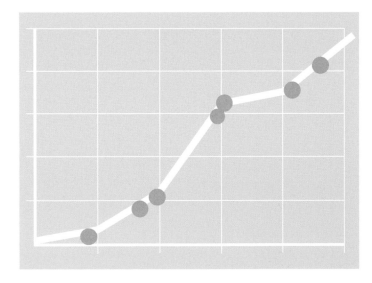

Companies that use feng shui measures to increase good chi can expect to see their profits rise.

ACTIVATING GOOD OFFICE FENG SHUI

ACTIVATE GOOD FENG SHUI IN YOUR OFFICE BY MAKING SURE EMPLOYEES FACE THEIR AUSPICIOUS DIRECTIONS. THE CHIEF EXECUTIVE OFFICER'S (CEO'S) OFFICE SHOULD BE IN THE NORTHWEST CORNER. OFFICE LAYOUT IS BEST WHEN DESIGNED TO MAXIMIZE THE FLOOR AREA ACCORDING TO FENG SHUI. USE ANY ONE OF THE FORMULAS TO IDENTIFY THE MOST IMPORTANT SPOT FOR THE MOST SENIOR PERSON IN THE OFFICE. USE CURVED WALKWAYS AND DISARM ALL POISON ARROWS WITH PLANTS AND HANGING CRYSTALS. THESE ACTIONS WILL ENSURE MAXIMUM PRODUCTIVITY, LEADING TO GOOD PROFITS.

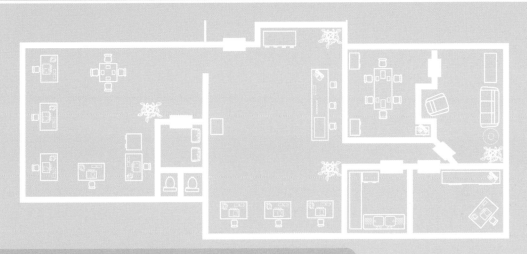

WHAT CAN GO WRONG

WHEN YOU ARE IN BUSINESS ON YOUR OWN, YOUR MONEY IS ALWAYS AT RISK SO IT MAKES SENSE TO USE SOME FENG SHUI HELP TO PROTECT AGAINST ANYTHING THAT CAN POSSIBLY GO WRONG. BUSINESS RISKS ARE FINANCIAL AS WELL AS COMMERCIAL. BUSINESS PEOPLE CAN LOSE MONEY IN MANY DIFFERENT WAYS:

✳ Being cheated by associates or employees

✳ Losing money through delays caused by unexpected obstacles

✳ Bad sales and turnover leading to losses

✳ Galloping expenses due to unforeseen mishaps

✳ Mismanagement

✳ Miscalculations

PROTECTIVE FENG SHUI FOR BUSINESS

✳ THERE ARE MANY AUSPICIOUS WAYS OF INCREASING YOUR GOOD FORTUNE IN BUSINESS. HERE ARE JUST A FEW.

✳ PROTECTIVE GUARDIANS

Place a pair of protective guardians outside the office, flanking the main door. Large corporations that have a designated building should place a pair of Fu dogs or lions at their entrance.

Fu dogs, placed either side of the main entrance, are believed to give protection against every kind of bad luck.

It is unnecessary to use only Chinese-type celestial guardians. Both the Hong Kong Bank and London's Trafalgar Square boast a pair of classic stone lions.

✳ CORPORATE LOGO

Design a corporate logo that is auspicious and place it high above a doorway or on the building. Always ensure that your corporate logo signifies strength, stability, and vigor.

Here is the World of Feng Shui dragon. It looks fat and happy and has brought amazing good fortune.

THE CEO'S OFFICE

IT IS IMPORTANT TO PROTECT THE CEO'S OFFICE, BECAUSE IF THE CEO'S
OFFICE SUFFERS FROM BAD FENG SHUI, IT USUALLY AFFECTS THE HEALTH
OF THE WHOLE COMPANY.

It is vital that the CEO's office
is not hit by poison arrows or
facing the CEO's total loss
direction according to the
Eight Directions (or Mansions)
Kua Formula (*see* Chapter 14).
This can happen without the
CEO's awareness, unless he
or she has some knowledge
of feng shui.

N

CEO'S OFFICE

✳ FLYING STAR

The list of things that can go wrong and
negatively impact your business is very long.
Always protect your business with Flying
Star safeguards.

In Chapter 15, you will learn about
auspicious mountain stars and water stars.
You will learn how to locate these
auspicious stars in your office and, when
you do, it is an excellent idea to ensure that
these crucial stars are not missing or
afflicted in any way. If they are, the company
fortunes will be adversely affected.

Since timing plays such an important
role in company performance, take note
of annual updates in feng shui. You will
discover that there will be years when your
office is affected by negative Flying Stars

that will bring loss, obstacles, illness,
disharmony, quarrels, law suits, and so on—
all the things that have a negative impact
on your business—and it is absolutely vital
to guard against these stars and their
negative chi (*see* Chapter 16). When you
learn about annual and monthly Flying Stars
you will be able to determine whether your
office is affected, and, if so, how to remedy
the afflictions.

The good news is that there are
specific "cures" for all Flying Star feng shui
afflictions—the key is to find out where bad
luck stars are located every year. Usually
when the entrance into the office is
negatively affected, or when the CEO's
office houses a negative star, the company
will be most afflicted by bad luck.

EXCELLENT ENHANCERS FOR BUSINESS

✳ ONCE YOU HAVE ASCERTAINED WHAT NEEDS TO BE DONE TO SAFEGUARD THE FENG SHUI OF YOUR BUSINESS, YOU CAN THEN PROCEED TO ENHANCE THE LUCK OF THE COMPANY. USE THE THREE-STEP APPROACH OUTLINED BELOW.

A water feature, correctly placed using Flying Star feng shui, will ensure the flow of wealth into the business.

1 USE THE EIGHT DIRECTIONS (or Mansions) Formula (*see* Chapter 14) to ensure the important personnel within the company sit facing at least one of their good luck directions. Work with the Human Resources department to place managers according to their Kua numbers and auspicious directions (*see* pages 64–65 to calculate your Kua number and opposite to find your best facing direction and avoid your worst directions). This will ensure that everyone works facing good luck. It will make a huge difference in performance and productivity.

2 USE THE PRINCIPLES OF FLYING STAR FENG SHUI to allocate good fortune sectors to key members of your management team (*see* Chapter 15). The CEO, operating supervisors, and strategic financial people should all be located in sectors of the office that are blessed by good Flying Stars.

In addition, this method of feng shui will help you to locate the auspicious Water Star in the office. Place a water feature in this sector to bring increased profits. This method also enables you to locate the auspicious Mountain Star. When this

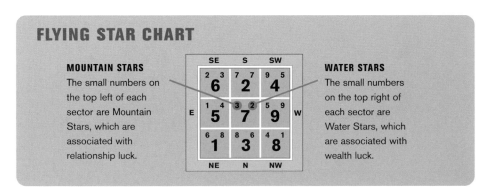

FLYING STAR CHART

MOUNTAIN STARS
The small numbers on the top left of each sector are Mountain Stars, which are associated with relationship luck.

	SE	S	SW	
	2 3 **6**	7 7 **2**	9 5 **4**	
E	1 4 **5**	3 2 **7**	5 9 **9**	W
	6 8 **1**	8 6 **3**	4 1 **8**	
	NE	N	NW	

WATER STARS
The small numbers on the top right of each sector are Water Stars, which are associated with wealth luck.

EAST GROUP KUA NUMBERS: FACING DIRECTIONS

KUA NUMBER	1	3	4	9
SHENG CHI: WEALTH	Southeast	South	North	East
FU WEI: PERSONAL GROWTH	North	East	Southeast	South
HO HAI: BAD LUCK	West	Southwest	Northwest	Northeast
WU KWEI: FIVE GHOSTS	Northeast	Northwest	Southwest	West
LUI SHAR: SIX KILLINGS	Northwest	Northeast	West	Southwest
CHUEH MING: TOTAL LOSS	Southwest	West	Northeast	Northwest

WEST GROUP KUA NUMBERS: FACING DIRECTIONS

KUA NUMBER	5 (MALE)	5 (FEMALE)	2 (ALL)	6 (ALL)	7 (ALL)	8 (ALL)
SHENG CHI: WEALTH	Northeast	Southwest	Northeast	West	Northwest	Southwest
FU WEI: PERSONAL GROWTH	Southwest	Northeast	Southwest	Northwest	West	Northeast
HO HAI: BAD LUCK	East	South	East	Southeast	North	South
WU KWEI: FIVE GHOSTS	Southeast	North	Southeast	East	South	North
LUI SHAR: SIX KILLINGS	South	East	South	North	Southeast	East
CHUEH MING: TOTAL LOSS	North	Southeast	North	South	East	Southeast

location is activated with a mountain feature, such as a block of crystal, it will ensure excellent staff cooperation and teamwork within the company.

3 ENHANCE YOUR OFFICE WITH GOOD FORTUNE SYMBOLS specifically intended for those in business (*see* table, overleaf). When combined with the Pa Kua Eight Aspirations method (*see* Chapter 13) in which each sector of any space enhances a specific type of luck, these symbols work especially well. In the case of creating wealth, the Southeast sector requires activating with lights, water, or sounds. Saturating the Southeast of the office with these types of yang essence ensures that money continues to flow into the business.

GOOD FORTUNE SYMBOLS

SYMBOLS OF GOOD FORTUNE PLAY A POWERFUL ROLE IN ENHANCING THE CHI IN THE OFFICE ENVIRONMENT. WEALTH CREATION IS PARTICULARLY FAVORED WHEN THESE SYMBOLS ARE USED IN CONJUNCTION WITH THE PA KUA EIGHT ASPIRATIONS METHOD (SEE CHAPTER 13) TO DETERMINE WHICH SECTOR OF A BUILDING OR AN OFFICE WOULD BE BEST FOR THE DISPLAY OF IMAGES OF GOOD FORTUNE TO ACTIVATE A PARTICULAR KIND OF LUCK.

TYPES OF GOOD LUCK ENHANCERS YOU MAY WISH TO ACQUIRE AND DISPLAY IN YOUR OFFICE INCLUDE THE FOLLOWING:

SYMBOL			
 **SAILING SHIP**	 **GOD OF WEALTH**	 **HORSES**	 **BIRDS**
CHARACTERISTICS Make sure the sailing ship has no nails and no hidden poison arrows such as small cannons, then load the ship with ingots, real money from countries you do business with, and other precious items. Every additional ship signifies another source of income for the company.	The Indians, the Tibetans, and the Chinese all have their own wealth gods. You can choose the wealth god according to your cultural preference. The Chinese wealth gods that particularly favor businesses are Tsai Shen Yeh and Kuan Kung.	Horses bring the company recognition. There are three types. The tribute horse suggests abundance and prosperity brought by business associates. The celebration horse ensures success against obstacles or setbacks. The victory horse enables you to outpace the competition.	Birds always suggest good news coming in and when you have a hundred birds even a thousand birds—for instance in a painting—the favorable impact is amazing.
PLACEMENT Place a sailing ship near the entrance of your office, preferably in the foyer. Position it on a low coffee table, making certain the sails are placed to indicate the ship is sailing inward (if possible sailing in from the owner or CEO's Sheng Chi direction).	Place the image of a wealth god deep inside the office, preferably in the CEO's office.	Place horse images in the South corner of the office.	Place bird images near the entrance. The more images you use, the better. Be sure to place an image of the celestial phoenix to welcome beneficial opportunities.

WATER FEATURE	CRYSTAL GEODE	CRYSTAL LOTUS	SINGING BELL
	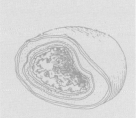		
Water features bring increased sales and profits. The deeper the water, the greater the wealth luck created. It can be an aquarium or a large bowl of water activated by a small fountain. A fountain featuring a rolling crystal ball suggests an increase in turnover.*	The "mountain" can be calcite, quartz, or rock crystal, or any kind of natural stone that catches your fancy. It brings good health for the staff and enhances relationship luck, thereby bringing improvements in the company's productivity.	This excellent Taoist feng shui activator will radiate yang energy outward and when it moves in a clockwise direction sales will register a significant increase. However, a negative movement (counterclockwise) will cause sales to decline.	Use a metal singing bell*** to increase the number of customers patronizing your retail business or restaurant. It is made from seven different types of metals to signify the seven planets and the seven major chakras of the human body.
Place the water feature in the corner where the Water Star Eight is located. *You may also hang a painting of water to suggest the presence of water.	Put a crystal geode where the Mountain Star Eight** is located to simulate powerful earth energy. **The Mountain Star Eight is particularly auspicious during the current Period Eight, when its chi is said to be at its peak.	Place a pink crystal lotus on a small rotating stand inside a display showcase.	Ring the bell several times in the morning just after you open to create the energy required for attracting customers. ***Alternatively, use a metal abacus. Shaking the abacus will drum up more business for the store.

CHAPTER 11

EDUCATION AND GROWTH

✳ FENG SHUI CAN GENERATE AN ENERGY FIELD OF WELL-BEING TO ENHANCE YOUR PERSONAL GOOD FEELINGS. PERSONAL GROWTH IS OFTEN MORE IMPORTANT THAN THE PURSUIT OF MATERIAL WEALTH. IN THIS RESPECT, THE FOCUS IS AS MUCH ON DEVELOPING YOUR MIND—WHICH SUGGESTS AN ACQUISITION OF KNOWLEDGE INVOLVING BOTH EDUCATION AND SCHOLARSHIP—AS ON EXPANDING YOUR SPIRIT AND NURTURING YOUR SPIRITUAL WELL-BEING.

When it comes to expanding your knowledge, feng shui can help facilitate the growth path. Those in the early first trimester of life can improve their education luck by increasing their concentration and desire to achieve goals, thus contributing toward nurturing their minds and their hearts. When the chi of education feng shui is activated in the correct corners of the home, the acquisition of knowledge becomes an easy and enjoyable process. Moreover, with regard to any tests or examinations, feng shui can help in the luck of attaining success in examinations.

✳ THE NORTHEAST DIRECTION
The most important direction in the pursuit of education is Northeast—the location occupied by the trigram Ken, or mountain, which denotes a repository of wisdom and knowledge. Ken deals with the scholarship of the mind and the pursuit of education. Ken is also the ruling trigram of Period Eight, which means that for the next twenty years, the focus will shift toward the acquisition of wisdom and knowledge rather than the acquisition of wealth. The Northeast should be enhanced by a mountain symbol such as a crystal geode, a large boulder, or a decorative stone. These powerful earth element items will create excellent scholarship luck.

MOUNTAIN OF WISDOM
The trigram Ken stands for patience and a time of preparation and study. It signifies the mountain or earth element.

✳ PERSONAL GROWTH DIRECTIONS

Ensure that your child sits according to his or her personal growth direction—the Fu Wei direction of the Eight Directions or Mansions Kua Formula (*see* Chapter 14). As the child works or studies, every time she looks up, she should be facing her personalized auspicious direction.

When using the Eight Mansions Formula, many amateur practitioners make the mistake of arranging the sitting directions of their children in accordance with their children's Sheng Chi direction, which is basically a wealth direction.

At such a young age, the Sheng Chi direction is of little consequence. Instead practitioners should use the Fu Wei (personal growth) direction to expand their children's horizons and help them become hungry for knowledge and experience. If your child cannot face this auspicious direction, it is imperative that another auspicious direction be selected rather than allowing the child to face one of the four negative directions.

Select the correct personal growth directions to help your children expand their horizons.

FU WEI: PERSONAL GROWTH DIRECTION

KUA NUMBER	FU WEI: BEST DIRECTION FOR PERSONAL GROWTH
1	North
2	Southwest
3	East
4	Southeast
5	Southwest/Northeast
6	Northwest
7	West
8	Northeast
9	South

If your child's Kua number is 3 the best direction to face for study luck is East.

AVOIDING POISON ARROWS IN CHILDREN'S BEDROOMS

IT IS IMPORTANT TO ARRANGE YOUR CHILD'S DESK AND BED SO THAT HE OR SHE IS FACING THE MOST AUSPICIOUS SITTING AND SLEEPING DIRECTIONS (TAPPING INTO THE CHILD'S FU WEI DIRECTION). THE FENG SHUI OF THE ROOM SHOULD BE DIRECTED AT ENSURING GOOD HEALTH AND STUDY LUCK AND AT AVOIDING POISON ARROWS THAT CAN BE CREATED BY SHARP FURNITURE AND BAD CHI.

AUSPICIOUS

AUSPICIOUS ROOM LAYOUTS

The child should avoid sitting with his or her back to the door. Here the desk's diagonal position is good feng shui.

Exam success is enhanced when the sleeping direction is Fu Wei and the headboard is set against a solid wall.

Avoid poison arrows pointing at the desk by placing no furniture with sharp edges or open shelving next to the desk.

INAUSPICIOUS

INAUSPICIOUS ROOM LAYOUTS

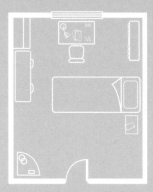 

BOOKSHELVES

Sitting with your back to the door is bad feng shui. The chi will cut straight through the bed and be lost through the window.

Open bookshelves pointing directly toward the desk act as poison arrows and should be avoided if possible.

✳ ACTIVATE THE DRAGON GATE IMAGE

A popular Chinese legend tells of the humble carp transforming into a mighty dragon when it successfully jumps over the Gate of Eternal Learning. Known as the Dragon Gate, this image represents the successful completion of the Imperial examinations, which, for many centuries, have been the premier method used by emperors to recruit officials and ministers to the court. Since the time of the Sung and Tang periods, the Dragon Gate has symbolized the aspirations of a nation's young men. The Imperial exams were seen as the passport to fame, wealth, and glory. Those serving the emperor became members of the aristocracy and outranked everyone else in the land.

When you hang a Dragon Gate at the door of your child's room, or even above the main door, then each morning as your child steps outside, he instantly "becomes the dragon" for he has effectively stepped through the Dragon Gate. A decorative image of the Dragon Gate or three carp fish poised to jump the gate is most auspicious. Your child will pass examinations with honors, cross the Dragon Gate, and eventually land a good job with good prospects.

✳ A CRYSTAL GLOBE

One of the most effective ways to activate luck for examinations and scholarships in your young child's bedroom is to place a crystal etched as a world globe on a small table in the Northeast corner. The globe need not be very large—even 1 inch (2.5 cm) in diameter will do nicely. Do not place this globe on the ground level. It should sit on a table and, if possible, on the desk or worktable itself if it is in the Northeast corner.

A geographic globe can enhance the attainment of knowledge. If it is twirled daily, it creates a movement that stirs up auspicious chi.

DRAGON GATE
This image portrays the Chinese legend of the carp that swam upstream against the current and then leaped across the dragon gate to become the dragon.

CHAPTER 12

HEALTH AND LONGEVITY

✳ ONE OF THE MOST IMPORTANT ASPECTS OF GOOD FORTUNE IS A HEALTHY AND LONG LIFE. PREVENTION OF ILLNESS BY PLACING POWERFUL SYMBOLS OF LONGEVITY WITHIN THE HOME IS THUS A SIGNIFICANT PART OF FENG SHUI PRACTICE. THESE SYMBOLS WILL CREATE THE CHI OF LONG LIFE WITHIN THE HOME.

One of the most popular words rendered in Chinese calligraphy and in stylized renditions thereof is longevity.

Long life does not just mean living for many years—it also means enjoying a healthy life without physiological problems caused by chi blockage within the body. Longevity also means protection from fatal injuries and physical accidents.

Health issues in feng shui are usually preventive, thus the proliferation of protective symbols as part of the practice. Most importantly, feng shui warns against the afflictions of "illness stars" that bring illness during specific months or years by way of an afflicted entrance door.

Knowing how to determine the location of these illness stars in your home from year to year is extremely beneficial. This knowledge makes it possible for you to safeguard the residents of the home against the illness stars through various feng shui remedies.

✳ ILLNESS STARS IN THE HOME

Illness stars of time dimension feng shui can affect you when either the period illness star or the annual and monthly illness stars fly into your bedroom. Illness star afflictions can be discerned using Flying Star Feng Shui (*see* Chapter 15). This advanced formula method of feng shui reveals how illness moves from one part of a building to another over the passage of time, whether a twenty-year period or an annual or monthly time frame.

The illness affliction becomes very powerful when, for example, three illness stars—the period illness star, the annual

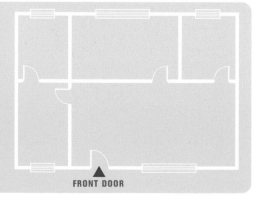

ILLNESS STAR
When the illness star is located in the same sector as the front door, the whole household may be affected.

FRONT DOOR

illness star, and the monthly illness star—enter your bedroom within any given month. However, the bedroom usually becomes afflicted even when only the annual illness star is located there, so it is useful to understand feng shui annual updates (*see* Chapter 16). When the illness star afflicts your bedroom, you should temporarily move to another bedroom or place strong metal cures such as the six-rod all-metal windchimes to exhaust the star.

ILLNESS STAR LOCATION

THE LOCATION OF THE ILLNESS STAR FOR A PERIOD OF SIX YEARS IS OUTLINED BELOW:

YEAR	SECTOR AFFECTED BY THE ILLNESS STAR
2004	Southwest
2005	East
2006	Southeast
2007	Center
2008	Northwest
2009	West

PERIOD ILLNESS STARS

THE LOCATION OF THE ILLNESS STAR FOR YOUR HOME DEPENDS ON THE FACING DIRECTION AND THE PERIOD YOUR HOUSE WAS BUILT (*SEE* PAGES 126–129).

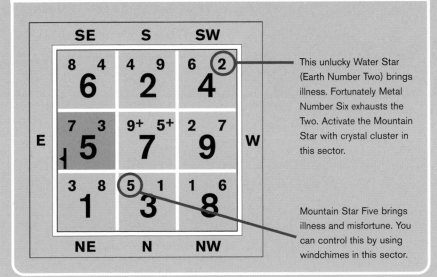

This unlucky Water Star (Earth Number Two) brings illness. Fortunately Metal Number Six exhausts the Two. Activate the Mountain Star with crystal cluster in this sector.

Mountain Star Five brings illness and misfortune. You can control this by using windchimes in this sector.

A crystal cluster can act as a useful feng shui remedy against unlucky Water Stars.

Illness can strike the whole household when the illness star hits the main door of the home. When this happens, opening and closing the door will activate the illness star, making it even more powerful. Once again, the illness star can be controlled only by placing windchimes near the front door.

✳ HELP FROM THE HEAVENLY DOCTOR

If you are ill, sleep with your head toward your Tien Yi direction to aid your recovery.

If you or any member of your family is ill, you can use the Eight Mansions formula to activate the direction of the "heavenly doctor" (*see* Chapter 14). According to this formula, if you sit facing your Tien Yi direction and sleep with your head toward your Tien Yi direction, then you will receive the chi of the "heavenly doctor" direction. This is one of the four auspicious directions and it promises that those prone to illness will be cured and not experience recurring bouts of illness.

The Tien Yi direction is excellent for the elderly residents of your home, as well as being suitable for those recuperating from illness.

TIEN YI DIRECTION

KUA NUMBER	TIEN YI DIRECTION FOR HEALTH
1	East
2	West
3	North
4	South
5	West (male)
5	Northwest (female)
6	Northeast
7	Southwest
8	Northwest
9	Southeast

TIEN YI DIRECTION

TIEN YI DIRECTION

If your Kua number is 9, sleep with your head pointing Southeast to protect yourself from the illness stars, and sit facing Southeast to receive the chi of the "heavenly doctor."

HANGING WINDCHIMES

BE CAREFUL ABOUT ALL HANGING OBJECTS IN YOUR HOME, SINCE EVERY ITEM HAS SOME FENG SHUI SIGNIFICANCE. METAL WINDCHIMES ARE ONE OF THE MOST USEFUL FENG SHUI TOOLS. BOTH THE FIVE-ROD AND SIX-ROD WINDCHIMES ARE EXCELLENT CURES, ALTHOUGH THE SIX-RODS ARE FAR MORE POWERFUL.

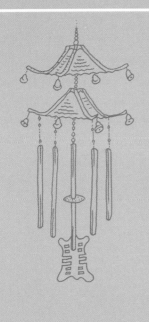

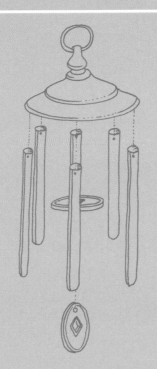

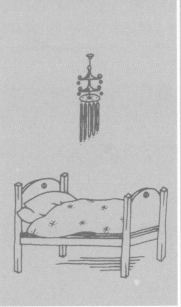

✳ Some designs incorporate other powerful symbols such as the Wu Luo, the Eight Trigrams, Twelve Animals, coins, and so forth, which add remedy chi to the windchimes. Do not use windchimes made of wood or ceramic as they are completely ineffective. Mobiles are likewise of little use in feng shui.

✳ Store some all-metal six-rod windchimes in the home and hang them in the appropriate corner each year. Remember to update from year to year, as windchimes are not necessarily beneficial in every corner. For instance, windchimes could prove to be harmful in the East or Southeast unless they have been put there to counter that year's illness star.

✳ Do not hang the windchimes high above your head. Windchimes that hang directly above your head as you sit or sleep will cause you great harm. Instead, windchimes should be hung about three feet above the ground, preferably against a wall, and not directly affecting anyone physically.

EXCELLENT ENHANCERS FOR LONGEVITY AND GOOD HEALTH

✳ ONCE YOU HAVE SAFEGUARDED YOURSELF FROM THE ILLNESS STARS OF FLYING STAR FENG SHUI AND GARNERED ASSISTANCE FROM THE HEAVENLY DOCTOR USING YOUR AUSPICIOUS TIEN YI DIRECTION, THE NEXT STEP IS TO ENHANCE YOUR HEALTH LUCK BY STRATEGICALLY PLACING LONGEVITY SYMBOLS INSIDE THE HOME. MANY OF THESE SYMBOLS ARE DEPICTED ON CONTAINERS, FURNITURE, AND CERAMIC TABLEWARE.

✳ SAU

Sau, the God of Longevity, is an old man with a long forehead, often depicted with deer and holding a staff with the Wu Luo gourd hanging from it. When shown in a painting, there is usually a pine tree in the background and Sau may be holding a peach. These symbols are themselves representative of longevity. The peach is a popular symbol, and placing peaches made of gemstones or ceramic in the dining room area will bring long life and good health. If you find an image of Sau that you like, invite him into your home and give him a place inside your bedroom or prominently facing the main door. Sau can be made of ceramic or carved in wood. If you are already displaying Fuk Luk Sau, note that the last named Sau is one and the same God of Longevity for he is one of the Three Star Gods (*see* pages 171 and 237).

✳ WU LUO

The Wu Luo is the bitter gourd container, said to be the best cure for those who are ill. Placing a metal Wu Luo by your bedside will ensure that illness chi is kept away. During Period Eight, the Wu Luo that contains the images of the Eight Immortals will be especially powerful in overcoming illness chi. The most effective Wu Luos are made of brass or other metals. Ceramic or wooden Wu Luos are less effective.

✳ PEACH TREE

The peach tree can be a decorative tree made from different colored jadeite. A small tree will have five ripe peaches to signify the five elements made friendly. A larger tree will have nine peaches, which signify good health through the entire time cycle of feng shui periods. The decorative peach tree is best placed in the East. If you live in a temperate climate and can plant a real peach tree in your garden, plant it in the East sector of the garden where its good effects will be optimized.

THE EIGHT IMMORTALS

THE EIGHT IMMORTALS ARE TAOIST DEITIES WHO ATE OF THE FRUIT OF IMMORTALITY WHEN THEY DINED AT THE QUEEN OF THE WEST'S PARADISE REALM. EACH OF THEM SIGNIFIES AN ASPECT OF LIFE'S ASPIRATIONS. WHEN INVITED INTO YOUR HOME EITHER AS A DECORATIVE CERAMIC PIECE OR A CHINESE PAINTING, THEY WILL BRING YOU EIGHT TYPES OF LUCK, ONE OF WHICH WILL BE A LONG AND HEALTHY LIFE. IT IS PARTICULARLY AUSPICIOUS TO HAVE THEM IN THE HOME DURING PERIOD EIGHT. ONE RENDITION OF THE EIGHT IMMORTALS SHOWS THEM IN DISCUSSION IN THE GARDEN OF THE QUEEN OF HEAVEN. THIS IMAGE IS SUITABLE FOR THOSE WHO ARE OLDER, PERHAPS RETIRED, AND TO WHOM GOOD HEALTH IS OF THE MOST UTMOST IMPORTANCE (SEE PAGES 227–229).

LAN TSAI HO

HO HSIEN KU

LI TIEH KUAI

TSAO KUO CHIU

CHANG KUO LAO

CHUNG LI CHUAN

HAN HSIANG TZU

XLU TUNG PIN

REMOVING BLOCKAGES FROM THE HOME

✱   ONE OF THE EASIEST WAYS TO ENSURE GOOD HEALTH IN THE HOME IS TO CLEAR ALL OBSTRUCTIONS AND STRUCTURES THAT SEEM TO BLOCK THE FLOW OF CHI. THIS PRINCIPLE OF CLUTTER CLEARANCE APPLIES NOT ONLY TO THE PLACEMENT OF FURNITURE IN THE HOME, BUT ALSO TO ELEMENTS OF THE GARDEN.

✳ CLUTTER

Clutter can block chi, as can too many pieces of furniture in a room or furniture that has been haphazardly placed. These physical impediments can also cause the flow of chi within our bodies to get blocked and then illness can strike.

Check your drains and your waste extraction systems regularly to make sure they never get blocked. If they do, not only will you get sick, as plumbing represents the arteries of the home, but you will also experience other blockages in your life. When this happens, examine your

Right: This disorganized and haphazard arrangement of furniture will slow down the flow of good chi.

Far right: This organized arrangement of furniture allows for an auspicious flow of good chi.

CUT DOWN ROTTING TREES

If there is a rotting tree in any part of your garden—indeed, even if the tree is just sickly and has not yet begun to rot—you should have it cut down and removed. The energy of old and decaying trees is certain to pass on to residents whose chi levels are low. Rotting trees also cause yin spirit formation, which almost always causes sickness to strike.

house to determine what may have caused the blockages. Usually the culprit is the inevitable buildup of clutter in the home.

At least once a year, if not more often, clear out old newspapers, unwanted clothes, and other objects whose energy has become stale.

You may not realize it, but stale energy has a significant negative effect on your immune system. When the home is clean and free of dirt, it is also free of stale and stagnant energy.

Apply the antidotes of cleanliness, white paint, and lights to cramped, dark areas in your home. White is the best colour for painting dark corners; it is a strong yang color that will instantly improve the chi of the home. Installing soft warm lights will further improve the energy flow.

A good spring clean—whatever the time of year—will bring good chi to your home and your health.

FRESH FLOWERS

WILTING FLOWERS ARE ANOTHER SOURCE OF YIN SPIRIT FORMATION, SO IF YOU LOVE FRESH FLOWERS, MAKE CERTAIN THEY ARE ALWAYS FRESH AND ARE THROWN AWAY AS SOON AS THEY FADE.

PART FOUR

THE SECRET FORMULAS

FENG SHUI IS NEITHER RELIGIOUS NOR SPIRITUAL. **FENG SHUI** CAN IN

FACT BE QUITE TECHNICAL AND IS BEST VIEWED AS A LIVING SKILL REQUIRING

AN UNDERSTANDING AND ACCEPTANCE OF THE CONCEPTS THAT UNDERPIN ITS

PRACTICE. THESE ARE ALMOST EXCLUSIVELY CHINESE–THE FIVE ELEMENTS,

THE THEORY OF THE TAI CHI'S YIN AND YANG, THE CONCEPT OF CHI, AND SO

ON. BUT AS A LIVING SKILL, **FENG SHUI** CAN BE LEARNED. WITH TIME AND

EFFORT, IT IS EASY ENOUGH TO LEARN THE DIFFERENT FORMULAS, SO THAT

ANYONE WISHING TO BENEFIT FROM IT CAN DO SO. WHEN YOU GET IT RIGHT,

FENG SHUI WILL QUICKLY SURPRISE YOU WITH POSITIVE RESULTS. ANYONE

CAN USE THESE SIMPLIFIED FORMULAS TO MAXIMUM BENEFIT. THEY TAKE THE

UNCERTAINTY AND GUESSWORK OUT OF **FENG SHUI** PRACTICE–YOU SIMPLY

HAVE TO BE FOCUSED WHEN APPLYING THE FORMULAS TO AVOID MISTAKES.

CHAPTER 13
PA KUA OF EIGHT ASPIRATIONS THEORY

✳ THIS METHOD OF FENG SHUI USES THE HIDDEN MEANINGS OF THE EIGHT-SIDED PA KUA SYMBOL, WHICH LIE AT THE HEART OF FENG SHUI PRACTICE. THE PA KUA IS EMPOWERED BY ITS TRIGRAMS, THE THREE-LINED SYMBOLS (MADE UP OF BROKEN AND/OR UNBROKEN LINES) THAT SIGNIFY THE ASPIRATIONS OF HUMANKIND. THEIR PLACEMENT AROUND THE PA KUA IS BASED ON TWO ARRANGEMENTS, WHICH ARE REFERRED TO AS THE EARLY HEAVEN AND THE LATER HEAVEN ARRANGEMENTS.

YIN PA KUA

THIS IS USED for protection against poison arrows and evil chi caused by hostile structures in the environment. It has the power to deflect or dissolve bad energy, and is used only as a last resort.

Feng shui is the skill of deciphering the meanings of the arrangements of trigrams under different situations. The Pa Kua Eight Aspirations method makes use of the Later Heaven arrangement of trigrams, which indicates the type of luck each side or direction stands for.

Use a proper compass to identify the direction of the sector or corner to be activated. The corner you choose to activate depends on the kind of aspiration or luck you desire.

You may activate all eight sectors of your home or of specific rooms. In the example opposite, you can see how the Pa Kua has been fitted into the living room. Each of the eight red arrows points to the respective corner that stands for career (North), education (Northeast), health (East), wealth (Southeast), fame (South), romance (Southwest), children (West), or patrons' or mentors' (Northwest) luck.

YANG PA KUA

THIS IS USED for analyzing the feng shui of houses, apartments, and buildings. It is based on the Later Heaven arrangement of trigrams. Each of the compass sectors stands for a particular type of luck.

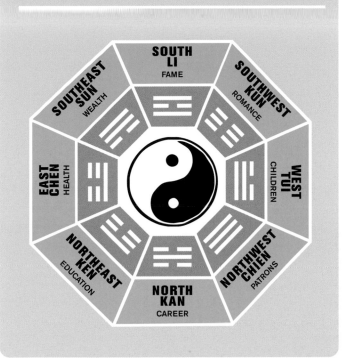

In the diagram below, the Pa Kua has been placed in the living room. When activating a specific room, remember that these luck sectors are based on compass directions— not on the location of the main door.

PA KUA IN THE LIVING ROOM

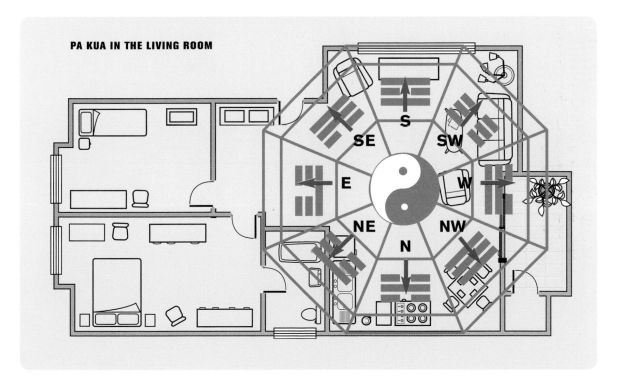

APPLYING THE FIVE-ELEMENT THEORY

✳ IN FENG SHUI, KNOWLEDGE OF THE FIVE ELEMENTS AND ITS THREE CYCLES—PRODUCTIVE, EXHAUSTIVE, AND DESTRUCTIVE—OFFER INVALUABLE INSIGHTS INTO CURES, REMEDIES, AND ENERGIZERS.

It is a good idea to commit the three cycles of the five elements to memory, because applying the five-element concept to the Eight Aspirations method is especially potent.

The five elements are fire, wood, water, metal, and earth, and everything in the universe, tangible as well as intangible, belongs to one of these five elements. These elements have three types of relationship to one another that give rise to three cycles: productive, exhaustive, and destructive. They are explained in the diagram opposite.

TWO DEMARCATION OPTIONS

There are two ways to demarcate space or superimpose the Eight Aspirations Pa Kua onto any space. You can use either the pie chart method or the grid method.

THE PIE CHART METHOD requires superimposing the circular compass onto a space and demarcating that space as though it is radiating outward from a center point. This way suggests that distribution of chi comes from a center point in the room or the home. Each sector is shaped as a triangular slice. This method of demarcation is widely used by the Cantonese feng shui masters of Hong Kong. They base their preference for this method on their belief that chi revolves around the compass.

THE LO SHU GRID METHOD relies on the compass to read the orientation and on the Lo Shu grid to separate the space into nine sectors, made up of eight outer sectors and a center sector. Note that both methods require a compass to define the directions. The difference lies in defining the space that falls into each direction sector. The grid method may be easier to work since it is laid out in a regular square or rectangular shape. Once you have defined your favored aspiration and can locate the eight different sectors of your home and the important rooms within it, you are ready to begin.

FIVE-ELEMENT CYCLE

TO ACTIVATE THE APPROPRIATE SECTOR IN YOUR ROOM OR HOME, USE THE FOLLOWING GUIDE: FOR WOOD USE PLANTS, FLOWERS, AND GREEN; FOR FIRE, USE LIGHTS, CANDLES, RED; FOR EARTH, USE CRYSTALS AND ROCKS; FOR METAL, USE BELLS, WINDCHIMES, AND WHITE; FOR WATER, USE WATER FEATURES SUCH AS FISH BOWLS, AQUARIUMS, AND MINIATURE FOUNTAINS.

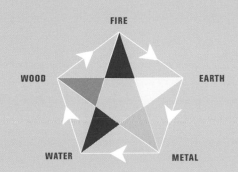

✳ PRODUCTIVE CYCLE
—used to enhance and activate corners

• WOOD PRODUCES FIRE
• FIRE PRODUCES EARTH
• EARTH PRODUCES METAL
• METAL PRODUCES WATER
• WATER PRODUCES WOOD

✳ EXHAUSTIVE CYCLE
—used to install remedies for afflicted chi

• FIRE EXHAUSTS WOOD
• WOOD EXHAUSTS WATER
• WATER EXHAUSTS METAL
• METAL EXHAUSTS EARTH
• EARTH EXHAUSTS FIRE

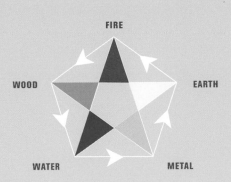

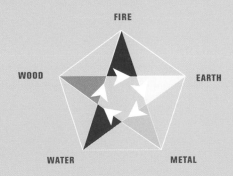

✳ DESTRUCTIVE CYCLE
—used for overcoming negative chi

• FIRE DESTROYS METAL
• METAL DESTROYS WOOD
• WOOD DESTROYS EARTH
• EARTH DESTROYS WATER
• WATER DESTROYS FIRE

1 THE SOUTH: RECOGNITION LUCK

✱   NOTE THAT THE SOUTH SECTOR OF YOUR HOME, OFFICE, OR ANY PARTICULAR ROOM STANDS FOR THE LUCK THAT BRINGS RECOGNITION, FAME, AND A GOOD NAME. THIS CORNER ALSO BRINGS PROMOTIONS AND UPWARD MOBILITY IN CAREERS. THOSE IN THE ENTERTAINMENT INDUSTRY, PUBLIC RELATIONS, WRITING, AND POLITICS WILL BENEFIT GREATLY FROM PROPER FENG SHUI IN THE SOUTH SECTORS.

The South sector belongs to the fire element, so anything symbolizing Fire, such as the color red, bright lights, and candles, placed here will be beneficial. The South is also an excellent location for two powerful symbols that bring victory, success, and opportunities: the horse and the phoenix.

HORSES IN THE SOUTH

There are three types of horse you can place here—the tribute horse, the victory horse, and the celebration horse. The tribute horse brings elevation in society and attracts excellent luck for those in the political arena. This horse is loaded with gold and jewels and is often white in color. The horse is usually depicted being led into the South corner of your house by the Wealth God. Make sure that the horse is looking into the house. The living room area is an excellent place for the tribute horse. The victory horse brings the luck that enables you to beat the competition. If you are in a competitive business or sport, or taking examinations and you want to succeed, activate the South sector of the room with a victory horse. Remember to shine a light at the horse. The celebration horse is depicted rearing up in triumph and this brings the luck of great success in all the things you do. Horses can be made of wood or ceramic. You can also acquire horses fashioned from cloisonné or metal.

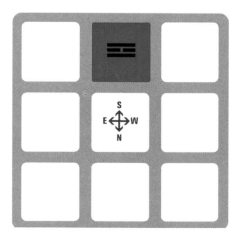

PHOENIXES IN THE SOUTH

The other excellent symbol of the South is the celestial phoenix. A pair of phoenixes here will attract amazing opportunities into your life. Phoenixes are the kings of birds and, since birds are already so powerful as feng shui enhancers, when you place even a single phoenix in the South corner, it activates supreme recognition luck.

You may also place images of other birds in the South since almost all birds are auspicious. Lovebirds such as parrots bring excellent relationships. Owls are said to bring wisdom, while roosters help you overcome negative chi energy. Mandarin ducks and swans bring love and romance, while cranes bring longevity and good health. Bird images inside your home or office send out all your good intentions and aspirations.

CAUTION!

✳ IT IS GENERALLY NOT A GOOD IDEA to place too many earth element decorations or the color yellow in the South because Earth exhausts Fire.

SYMBOLS OF SUCCESS

PLACED IN THE SOUTH SECTOR, THESE SYMBOLS BRING SUCCESS: PAIR OF PHOENIXES, PAIR OF MANDARIN DUCKS, TRIBUTE HORSE, PAIR OF CRANES, ROOSTER.

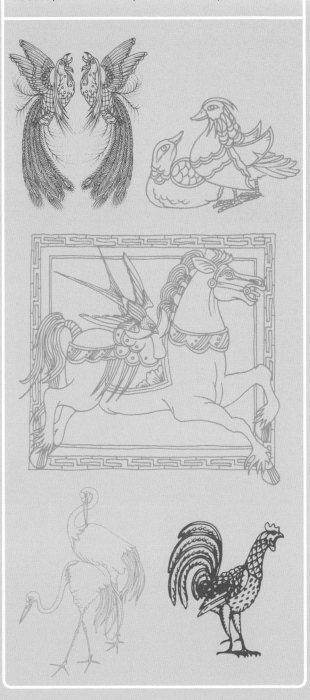

2 THE NORTH: CAREER LUCK

✳ USE WATER TO ACTIVATE THE NORTH AND YOU WILL GAIN QUICK RESULTS IN YOUR CAREER. USE A COMPASS TO DETERMINE NORTH IN YOUR HOUSE OR FAVORITE ROOM AND ACTIVATE THAT SECTOR WITH A WATER FEATURE, SUCH AS AN AQUARIUM OR INDOOR FOUNTAIN, OR A SYMBOL OR PICTURE OF A WATER SCENE.

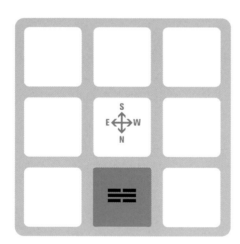

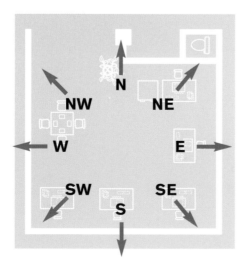

To enhance career luck, activate the North part of your home or office.

If you choose to place a landscaped water feature outside in the garden, there must be a door, or at least some windows, from the house into the landscaped area. Only by having an opening can the water-drenched chi enter the home and bring luck to the household. Since water stands for wealth, its strategic placement around the home or office is always important.

Place smaller water features to energize the North sectors of individual rooms. The dining and living rooms can be activated with paintings depicting water or with an aquarium of live fish.

If you decide to keep goldfish, which are considered lucky, place nine of them in an aquarium. Of the nine, eight should be gold and one black. The black fish will absorb any bad luck that inadvertently enters the home or office.

Alternatively, paint the North wall blue (or deep purple) to signify water. Do not use black, as it is too yin.

You can also use metal energy in the North, so the North wall of the room can be painted in white, silver, or gold, or decorated with curtains and carpets in these colors. Metallic stereo systems work well here.

Be as creative as you wish, and remember that in order to benefit from your efforts you must use the rooms that you energize.

When using feng shui to activate luck at work, bear in mind that advancement may bring with it a larger workload, although it will also protect you against being betrayed at work and getting fired. Activating career luck ensures that you gain at work; it is about gaining power and influence, rather than money, though prosperity is implicit.

CAUTION!

✱ IT IS NOT GOOD to have too many plants in the North, as they will exhaust the chi of the corner.

WEALTH ACTIVATORS

ENERGIZE THE NORTH PART OF YOUR HOME WITH A WATER FEATURE. KEEPING GOLDFISH, EIGHT GOLD AND ONE BLACK, IN THE NORTH SECTOR OF A ROOM IS AN EXCELLENT WAY TO IMPROVE YOUR FINANCE LUCK, ALTHOUGH THEY SHOULD NEVER BE KEPT IN THE BEDROOM. IF YOU CANNOT PLACE A REAL WATER FEATURE, HANG A PAINTING OF A WATER SCENE.

3 THE EAST: HEALTH AND WEALTH LUCK

✳ THE ELEMENT OF THE EAST IS WOOD AND THE TRIGRAM IS
CHEN, WHICH REPRESENTS THE ELDEST SON. EAST ALSO DENOTES
THE SECTOR OF HEALTH AND WEALTH. THIS DIRECTION IS FILLED WITH
THE MOST SHENG CHI, OR GROWTH CHI, AND SO IS THE IDEAL PART
OF THE HOME FOR THE CHILDREN OF THE FAMILY.

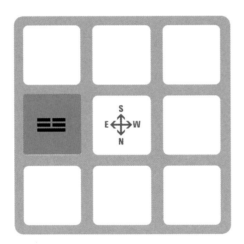

Since East is the place of the celestial dragon, always activate this sector with the image of the dragon. One of the best images is one that shows the dragon holding a rotating pearl and spouting water. To generate maximum luck for the family, you may have as many dragons as you wish, but make sure you have the karma to carry the number of dragons you display.

Not everyone can sustain the powerful yang energy of nine dragons. Even though dragons bring a great deal of good fortune and excellent health, it is better not to be too greedy. A single celestial creature—one that is neither too large nor too small—is usually sufficient.

If you were born in the year of the dragon, or already hold a high position such as a minister or company president, you may wish to place as many as five dragons. Be sure to place your dragon image near or inside water.

Activating the East brings good health, longevity, and descendants' luck. It also creates the luck for accumulation of wealth assets. Wood element energy grows upward and outward, sending many branches into the sky to symbolize amazing good fortune, as long as you place the symbols correctly. Make free use of plants. Live young plants with broad leaves are excellent for accumulating wealth chi.

Wealth trees made of semiprecious stones such as citrine and aventurines are also auspicious in the East. Choose trees

AUSPICIOUS ACTIVATORS

PLACED IN THE EAST SECTOR, THE DRAGON BRINGS GOOD FORTUNE AND GOOD HEALTH, WHILE A BROAD-LEAVED POTTED PLANT, OR A TREE MADE OF SEMIPRECIOUS STONES, BRINGS WEALTH.

with a solid trunk to ensure a firm foundation. Tie special coins with red or gold ribbon to simulate the money tree. Placed in the East of your living room, these crystal trees bring excellent feng shui energy into the home. Ensure that the citrines are genuine and not made of plastic. You can energize such trees with empowering mantras if you wish.

CAUTION!

✴ IT IS NOT GOOD to have too many lights in the East, as they exhaust the chi of the corner.

4 THE WEST: DESCENDANTS' LUCK

✳ IN TRADITIONAL FENG SHUI LORE, THE WEST HAS ALWAYS BEEN IDENTIFIED AS THE PLACE OF THE WHITE TIGER, WHICH IS ALSO THE SYMBOL OF PROTECTION. IN THE LATER HEAVEN ARRANGEMENT OF THE TRIGRAMS, THE WEST IS HOME TO THE TRIGRAM OF JOYOUSNESS—TUI—ALSO KNOWN AS THE RIVER OR LAKE TRIGRAM.

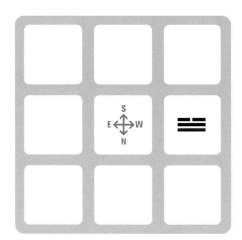

The West is the space where happiness arises as a result of a happy family. When the chi in the West part of the home is protected and energized, the family stays together and is both healthy and strong. All the older members of the family will live a long life. Both the patriarch and the matriarch whose luck theoretically resides on both sides of the West direction (the Northwest and Southwest, respectively) will enjoy increasing happiness and good fortune as the years pass. Always keep the West side chi smooth and harmonious.

The West represents children's luck. If you are unable to conceive and there is no physical cause, activating the West is a powerful feng shui tool that may help. To enhance child-bearing luck, place any of the following images in the West part of the home. Remember to shine a bright light on the auspicious object, as light is one of the most powerful energizers.

CAUTION!

✳ **IT IS NOT GOOD** to have water in the West, as this exhausts the chi of the corner.

✳ A screen, wealth jar, painting, or crystal sphere depicting one hundred children. A crystal sphere with a colorful image of the one hundred children hand-painted inside, placed in the West beneath a bright light will activate the yang chi perfectly.

✳ Images of the fertility fruit, pomegranates. Beautiful pomegranates made of crystal or wood, when activated with a bright or red light, will facilitate the conception of children.

✳ An elephant image in the bedroom symbolizes successful conception, provided that the elephant's trunk is benevolently down. Elephants with the trunk raised represent victory and celebration.

The element of the West sector is metal. The color is white. The best activators of chi for the West are a variety of gold coins. China and Taiwan now manufacture copies of many of the ancient coins of the golden ages of past dynasties.

Old Chinese coins, with their square holes in the middle, can be used as feng shui coins.

SYMBOLS OF FERTILITY

PLACE IMAGES OF ELEPHANTS OR POMEGRANATES IN THE WEST SECTOR OF YOUR BEDROOM TO IMPROVE YOUR CHANCES OF CONCEPTION. ANOTHER POWERFUL ACTIVATOR IS A CRYSTAL SPHERE DEPICTING ONE HUNDRED CHILDREN.

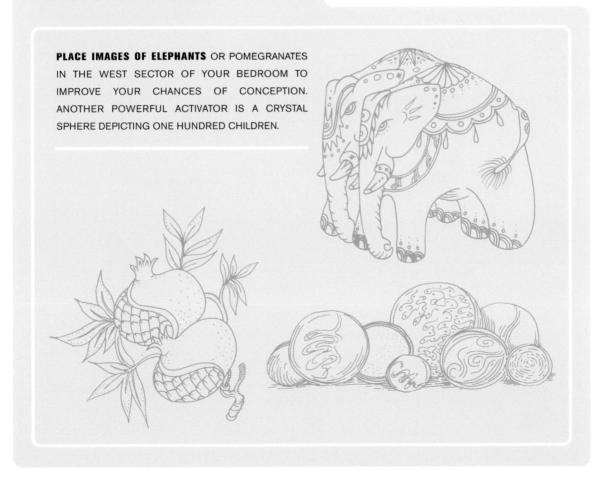

5　THE SOUTHWEST: LOVE AND MARRIAGE

✳ THE SOUTHWEST IS THE PLACE OF KUN, THE MATRIARCHAL
TRIGRAM THAT ENHANCES THE LUCK OF RELATIONSHIPS AND BRINGS
ROMANCE, LOVE, AND THE START OF A NEW PHASE IN THE LIVES
OF SINGLE PEOPLE.

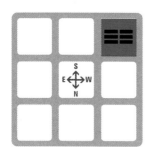

The Chinese celebrate three "happy occasions" in life, referred to as hei see. Of these three (a birth, a marriage, and a longevity birthday) marriage is regarded as the most significant. The Chinese word for "double happiness" has come to symbolize the marriage union. Placing this symbol in the Southwest is a powerful talisman for creating marriage luck. If there are children of marriageable age in the household, there should not be too many plants in the Southwest since the wood element destroys the earth element. It is particularly bad if the Southwest corner is missing, for then the nurturing auspiciousness of maternal energy is lacking. This can cause a complete absence of marriage prospects for the daughters and sons of the home.

The best way to activate Southwest is with bright lights. Keep lights turned on for three hours each night. A bright red light burning continuously in the Southwest

Use the image of a matriarch to enhance love luck.

corner of your bedroom brings romance into your life. You can also place any of the love symbols here so they will also be activated by the light.

Another excellent energizer for the Southwest is an image of a matriarch. The Chinese have always had high respect for their matriarchs, and an image of the matriarch enhances the trigram, and thus the luck, of this area.

CAUTION!

✳ **IT IS NOT GOOD** to have metallic objects in the Southwest, as they exhaust the chi of the corner.

6 THE NORTHWEST: PATRONAGE LUCK

✳ THE NORTHWEST IS THE PLACE OF THE PATRIARCH. HERE THE TRIGRAM IS CHIEN, WHICH SIGNIFIES THE LUCK OF INFLUENTIAL BENEFACTORS AND PATRONS. IF YOU WANT HELP FROM YOUR BOSS, YOUR FATHER, OR AN UNCLE, ACTIVATE THIS CORNER.

If you want your patriarch to become prosperous (this can be your husband or your father) then this is the corner in which to focus your Feng Shui. Hang a portrait of a smiling patriarch here.

The element of this corner is metal, which signifies gold. The Northwest is the source of a family's wealth—the kind that lasts many generations. If you make a wealth vase, keep it hidden in the Northwest corner to benefit the patriarch. If you bury a symbolic wealth box in the Northwest of your garden, this too will benefit the patriarch. Ingots and coins are perennial favorites and cloisonné objets d'art, such as the nine-dragon screen, are also potent. Anything made of gold or plated in gold will activate this corner. Golden windchimes are especially auspicious, since the sound of gold is beneficial. Bells and singing bowls made from seven types of metal—including gold and silver—symbolize the energy of the sun and the moon.

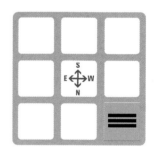

CAUTION!

✳ **IT IS NOT GOOD** to have water in the Northwest, as this exhausts the chi of the corner.

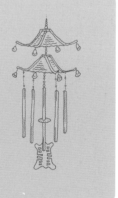

WEALTH VASES can be filled with semiprecious stones.

METALLIC WINDCHIMES activates the Northwest sector to enhance patronage luck.

7 THE SOUTHEAST: PROSPERITY LUCK

✳ THE SOUTHEAST IS THE PLACE OF THE SUN TRIGRAM, WHOSE ELEMENT IS WOOD. THE SOUTHEAST SIGNIFIES INCOME LEVELS. THE LUCK OF THE SOUTHEAST INDICATES ACTIVITY, WHICH GENERATES INCOME. IF YOU WISH TO ATTRACT INCREASED EARNINGS, ENERGIZE THIS CORNER.

A small waterfall, particularly if it has six levels, helps to generate auspicious chi and attracts prosperity.

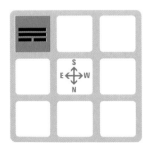

water pumps to simulate activity. You should landscape it with healthy plants and flowers. Waterfalls, especially if they have six levels of falls, are powerful in attracting prosperity. Water features need not be elaborate, nor be stocked with expensive fish. In feng shui, distinction is made only between yin water, which is still, and yang water, which is moving and filled with life chi.

Plants and an indoor garden in the Southeast will magnify growth chi for the home. Beautiful flowering plants amidst plenty of green grass suggest the blossoming of good fortune. When flowers stop blooming, you must get a fresh supply. In these days of instant gardens, you do not need a green thumb to harness the blossoming Sheng Chi of plants that will help all your plans come to fruition quickly.

The best way to activate money luck is to construct a small waterfall and keep its waters moving with fish, tortoises, and

CAUTION!

✳ **IT IS NOT GOOD** to have bright lights in the Southeast, as they will exhaust the chi of the corner.

8 THE NORTHEAST: EDUCATION LUCK

✳ THE NORTHEAST IS AN EARTH ELEMENT CORNER. THE RULING TRIGRAM IS THE MOUNTAIN TRIGRAM, KEN, WHICH SUGGESTS A TIME OF TRAINING AND PREPARATION FOR THE GOOD THINGS TO COME. ACTIVATE THIS CORNER FOR EDUCATION LUCK.

The powerful chi of the Northeast can be activated to bring excellent examination results, scholastic honors, and scholarships. In addition to using the Kua formula, select your student's most auspicious directions in which to face when studying or sitting examinations. Activate the Northeast of the student's room to attract scholastic luck. Energizing this corner with earth energy can be extremely potent. Crystals are the most powerful manifestation of earth energy and can be natural or synthetic, although natural crystals are better. The crystal sphere etched with a globe, however, is the most effective for harnessing education luck. Place a crystal globe on a table in the Northeast corner of your child's bedroom to activate education luck and you should see improvements right away.

It is also a good idea to invest in a single-ended natural crystal for your child. The crystal is a very efficient store of energy and knowledge. Let the crystal become a personal study companion amulet for your child. When you select one, first cleanse it of other people's energy by soaking it in a sea or rock salt solution for seven days and seven nights. Place it on a table in the Northeast when your child is studying and underneath the pillow when your child is sleeping. It can be taken into the classroom to bring the luck of examinations. Keep the crystal wrapped in silk or velvet when not in use.

A crystal globe or crystal placed in the Northeast corner of your child's bedroom brings education luck.

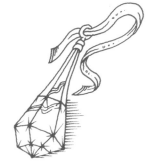

CAUTION!

✳ **IT IS NOT GOOD** to have bright lights in the Northeast, as they will exhaust the chi of the corner.

CHAPTER 14

KUA FORMULA OF EIGHT DIRECTIONS

✳ EIGHT MANSIONS OR DIRECTIONS FENG SHUI IS A PERSONALIZED FORMULA THAT CATEGORIZES PEOPLE AS BELONGING TO EITHER THE EAST OR WEST GROUP AND LIKEWISE DIVIDES HOUSES AS BEING EAST OR WEST BUILDINGS.

Investigate whether your house is good for you by checking whether you are a West- or an East-group person.

With very little effort, you can immediately investigate your compatibility with particular houses. When the house and the person belong to the same group, the house has an affinity with the individual and will bring good fortune. More significantly, the Eight Mansions Kua formula also reveals your lucky and unlucky directions based on your Kua number as derived from your gender and date of birth.

CALCULATING YOUR KUA NUMBER

1 Add the last two digits of your year of birth; if the result is a double-digit number, add the digits together so that you have a single-digit number.

2 If you are male, deduct this digit from 10 —the result is your Kua number

3 If you are female, add 5 to this digit— reduce to a single digit again, if necessary —the result is your Kua number

4 The formula is based on the Chinese lunar calendar, so if you are born in January or February, check to see if you need to deduct a year from your year of birth based on the exact date of the lunar New Year. Use the Chinese Calendar showing Chinese New Year dates (*see* pages 284–285) to determine this.

EXAMPLE: Male born on June 6, 1945
As the date of birth is after the start of the lunar New Year, there is no need to adjust it. Add the last two digits of year of birth: 4 + 5 = 9. Deduct this number from 10: 10 − 9 = 1, so the Kua number is 1.

Note: For males born after 2000, instead of deducting from 10, deduct from 9.

EXAMPLE: Female born January 2, 1958
As the date of birth is before the lunar New Year, the year of birth is adjusted to 1957. Add the last two digits of year of birth: 5 + 7 = 12. Reduce to one digit: 1 + 2 = 3. Add 5 to this number: 3 + 5 = 8, so the Kua number is 8.

Note: For females born after 2000, instead of adding 5, add 6.

KUA NUMBERS AND ASSOCIATIONS

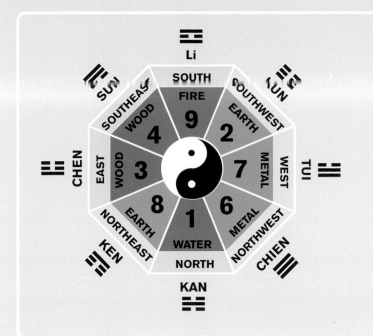

THE ILLUSTRATION SHOWS KUA NUMBERS AND THEIR CORRESPONDING DIRECTIONS PLACED AROUND THE PA KUA.

The East group numbers are 1, 3, 4, and 9; the West group numbers are 2, 5, 6, 7, and 8.

The directions have been categorized to reflect the yin and yang Tai Chi of chi energy.

Trigrams and related elements are also given here.

✳ DETERMINING EAST AND WEST GROUPS

Once you have your Kua number, you will know whether you are an East or a West group person.

• East group people have Kua numbers 1, 3, 4, and 9

• West group people have Kua numbers 2, 5, 6, 7, and 8

East group directions—East, Southeast, North, and South—are auspicious for East group people while West group directions are unlucky. East group people should ideally live in East group houses, which are defined as "sitting" on an East group direction. They also benefit from living in houses that "face" an East group direction. However, since the sitting direction is the exact opposite of the facing direction, East group people can maximize their luck by living in houses that have a sitting/facing axis direction of North/South, since both these directions belong to the East group.

West group directions—West, Southwest, Northwest, and Northeast—are auspicious for West group people while East directions are unlucky. West group people should ideally live in West group houses, which are defined as "sitting" on a West group direction. They also benefit from living in houses that "face" a West group direction. However, since the sitting direction is the exact opposite of the facing direction, West group people can maximize their luck by living in houses that have a sitting/facing axis direction of Northeast/Southwest, since both these directions belong to the West group.

Combine this information with that given in the diagram above and the table below to customize your personal space. For example, if your Kua number is 3, then you know that wood is your personal element and East is your direction, so having a wood floor and locating your space along the East sector of your room will benefit you. Likewise, if you sit facing East it will be beneficial for you. These suggestions are particularly suitable for people who live alone and for the feng shui of small office spaces.

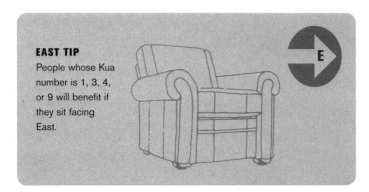

EAST TIP
People whose Kua number is 1, 3, 4, or 9 will benefit if they sit facing East.

✳ FINE-TUNING YOUR AUSPICIOUS DIRECTIONS

Your Kua number will also reveal your other auspicious and inauspicious directions. The Eight Mansions feng shui formula divides house space into eight sectors with each sector standing for one type of luck.

ATTRIBUTES OF YOUR KUA NUMBER

IN EIGHT MANSIONS FENG SHUI, YOUR KUA NUMBER IS CONSIDERED TO BE YOUR LUCKY NUMBER. IT ALSO TELLS YOU YOUR PERSONAL KUA ELEMENT AND YOUR PERSONAL TRIGRAM FOR FENG SHUI PURPOSES AS WELL AS YOUR MOST AUSPICIOUS COLOR(S) AND DIRECTION(S) FOR PERSONAL GROWTH.

KUA NUMBER	YOUR KUA ELEMENT	YOUR KUA TRIGRAM	BEST COLOR FOR YOUR HOME	BEST DIRECTION FOR PERSONAL GROWTH
1	Water	Kan	White	North
2	Earth	Kun	Red/Yellow	Southwest
3	Wood	Chen	Blue/Green	East
4	Wood	Sun	Blue/Green	Southeast
5	Earth	Kun/Ken	Red/Yellow	Southwest/Northeast
6	Metal	Chien	Yellow/White	Northwest
7	Metal	Tui	Yellow/White	West
8	Earth	Ken	Red/Yellow	Northeast
9	Fire	Li	Green/Red	South

EAST AND WEST GROUP HOUSES

THE EIGHT DIRECTIONS OF THE PA KUA SYMBOL REPRESENT EIGHT TYPES OF HOUSES, WHICH FALL INTO GROUPS OF EAST OR WEST HOUSES.

East houses sit in one of the East Group directions; West houses sit in one of the West Group directions. East houses are associated with the elements of Water, Wood, and Fire. This brings the harmony of the creative cycle: Water produces Wood, which produces Fire. To enhance feng shui use plants, flowers, bright lights, and water features near the front door or in the element sectors (see below). West houses are associated with Metal and Earth. Use windchimes and crystals in the relevant sectors to enhance the feng shui of these houses.

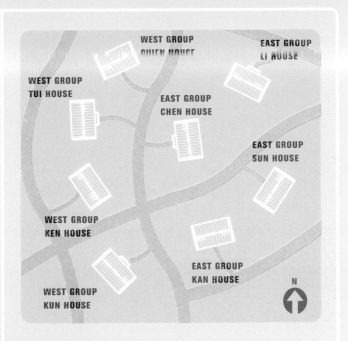

YOUR HOUSE GROUP AND ATTRIBUTES

TO DETERMINE IF YOURS IS AN EAST OR A WEST GROUP HOUSE, FIND THE DIRECTION OF YOUR FRONT AND BACK DOORS (FROM INSIDE LOOKING OUT). IF IN DOUBT, THE BACK DOOR IS THE DECIDING FACTOR. FOR EXAMPLE, IF YOUR BACK DOOR FACES NORTH AND YOUR FRONT DOOR FACES SOUTHEAST, YOURS IS A KAN HOUSE (NOT A CHIEN HOUSE).

	TRIGRAM	FRONT DOOR DIRECTION	BACK DOOR DIRECTION	ELEMENT
EAST GROUP HOUSES	Li	North	South	Fire
	Kan	South	North	Water
	Chen	West	East	Wood
	Sun	Northwest	Southeast	Wood
WEST GROUP HOUSES	Chien	Southeast	Northwest	Metal
	Kun	Northeast	Southwest	Earth
	Ken	Southwest	Northeast	Earth
	Tui	East	West	Metal

There are four sectors of good luck and four sectors of bad luck in any space, hence the name Eight Mansions. Where these types of luck appear in the sectors in your house depends on your Kua number. The type of luck are described in detail in the table opposite and their position is given in the tables overleaf.

The four types of good fortune luck are as follows:

✳ Sheng Chi: wealth and success

✳ Nien Yen: love and marriage

✳ Tien Yi: health and longevity

✳ Fu Wei: personal growth and development.

The four types of bad fortune luck are:

✳ Ho Hai: experiencing bad luck

✳ Wu Kwei (Five Ghosts): five kinds of bad people working against you

✳ Lui Shar (Six Killings): experiencing six types of misfortunes

✳ Chueh Ming: experiencing total loss.

You can use Eight Mansions feng shui to determine whether your bedroom has good or bad luck for you, and whether it has the type of good luck you want. Likewise, you can determine whether your main front door has the luck you desire, the ideal place for your kitchen and the best direction for you to sleep in.

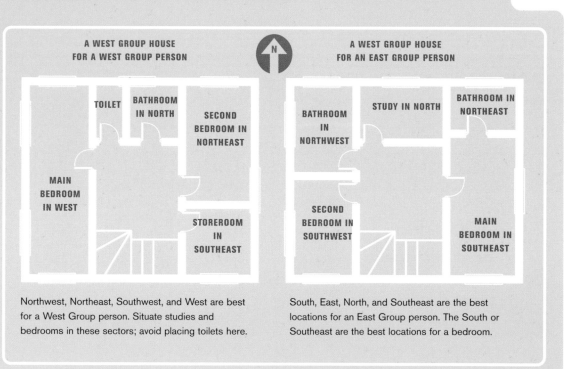

WEST GROUP HOUSE FOR WEST AND EAST GROUP PEOPLE

A WEST GROUP HOUSE FOR A WEST GROUP PERSON

N

A WEST GROUP HOUSE FOR AN EAST GROUP PERSON

TOILET

BATHROOM IN NORTH

SECOND BEDROOM IN NORTHEAST

MAIN BEDROOM IN WEST

STOREROOM IN SOUTHEAST

BATHROOM IN NORTHWEST

STUDY IN NORTH

BATHROOM IN NORTHEAST

SECOND BEDROOM IN SOUTHWEST

MAIN BEDROOM IN SOUTHEAST

Northwest, Northeast, Southwest, and West are best for a West Group person. Situate studies and bedrooms in these sectors; avoid placing toilets here.

South, East, North, and Southeast are the best locations for an East Group person. The South or Southeast are the best locations for a bedroom.

GOOD AND BAD LUCK LOCATIONS AND DIRECTIONS

GOOD LUCK

✳ **SHENG CHI (WEALTH)** signifies the place and direction that bring wealth and prosperity luck. In an ideal situation, this should always correspond to the entrance to your house or apartment building. When your sitting or facing direction corresponds to your Sheng Chi direction, make sure this part of the house is activated and you will enjoy prosperity luck.

✳ **NIEN YEN (LOVE)** signifies the place and direction that bring good luck in love and marriage. It also helps your descendants' luck. Sleep with your head toward this direction if you are keen to find a soulmate or if your life is lacking in romance and love.

✳ **TIEN YI (HEALTH)** pinpoints the room and direction that bring you the best health and longevity luck. Members of the family who are prone to illness should be given rooms that correspond to their Tien Yi direction.

✳ **FU WEI (PERSONAL GROWTH)** signifies the space and direction that bring the luck of outstanding personal growth. Schoolchildren and those pursuing educational programs benefit from this area of the house.

BAD LUCK

✳ **HO HAI (BAD LUCK)** signifies the place and direction of mild bad luck. If you stay in a Ho Hai room, you will find minor irritations annoying you. Projects will take longer to come to fruition and you will experience setbacks and disappointments.

✳ **WU KWEI (FIVE GHOSTS)** signifies the direction of relationship problems, bad luck associated with troublemakers, and gossip and scandal-mongering. Five Ghosts bad luck can sometimes be transformed into immense good luck by the auspicious feng shui charts using other systems and formulas such as Flying Star (*see* Chapter 15).

✳ **LUI SHAR (SIX KILLINGS)** signifies six types of misfortunes. The bad luck here can be described as quite severe and it comes in battalions. Illness, loss, death, loss of good name, loss of wealth, and loss of descendants are all misfortunes but in many different manifestations.

✳ **CHUEH MING (TOTAL LOSS)** signifies a state of total loss. This can mean bankruptcy or even destruction of the family. Never stay in a room afflicted by your personal Chueh Ming direction unless the Flying Star chart indicates a change of luck.

FINE-TUNING THE APPLICATION

✳ APPLY EIGHT MANSIONS BY MAKING SURE THAT YOU DO NOT
OCCUPY A ROOM CORRESPONDING TO ANY OF THE BAD LUCK
DIRECTION SECTORS.

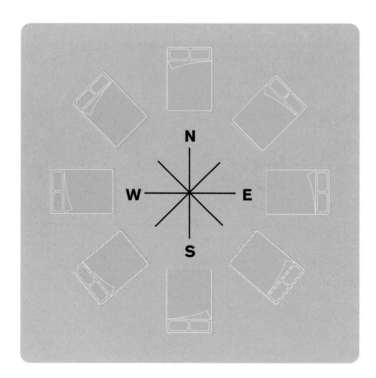

success, or sleeping with your head toward your Nien Yen direction if you want to find love. Likewise, you should face your Fu Wei direction while studying and your Tien Yi to recover from an illness. The feng shui possibilities are infinite and you can be as creative as you wish when you use your personalized directions. All you need is a reliable compass and the tables opposite to determine the eight directions for each of the nine Kua numbers.

Make sure you sleep with your head pointing in one of your good luck directions. Use the tables opposite to help.

When sitting, sleeping, or working you should try to avoid facing a bad luck direction. The key to good luck is to spend time in a room that brings you one of your four types of good luck, and to work facing one of your good luck directions.

You can fine-tune the application further by endeavoring to sit facing your Sheng Chi direction if you want wealth and

EAST GROUP: LUCK SECTORS

KUA NUMBER	1	3	4	9
SHENG CHI: WEALTH	Southeast	South	North	East
NIEN YEN: LOVE	South	Southeast	East	North
TIEN YI: HEALTH	East	North	South	Southeast
FU WEI: PERSONAL GROWTH	North	East	Southeast	South
HO HAI: BAD LUCK	West	Southwest	Northwest	Northeast
WU KWEI: FIVE GHOSTS	Northeast	Northwest	Southwest	West
LUI SHAR: SIX KILLINGS	Northwest	Northeast	West	Southwest
CHUEH MING: TOTAL LOSS	Southwest	West	Northeast	Northwest

WEST GROUP: LUCK SECTORS

KUA NUMBER	5 MALE	5 FEMALE	2 ALL	6 ALL	7 ALL	8 ALL
SHENG CHI: WEALTH	Northeast	Southwest	Northeast	West	Northwest	Southwest
NIEN YEN: LOVE	Northwest	West	Northwest	Southwest	Northeast	West
TIEN YI: HEALTH	West	Northwest	West	Northeast	Southwest	Northwest
FU WEI: PERSONAL GROWTH	Southwest	Northeast	Southwest	Northwest	West	Northeast
HO HAI: BAD LUCK	East	South	East	Southeast	North	South
WU KWEI: FIVE GHOSTS	Southeast	North	Southeast	East	South	North
LUI SHAR: SIX KILLINGS	South	East	South	North	Southeast	East
CHUEH MING: TOTAL LOSS	North	Southeast	North	South	East	Southeast

APPLYING EIGHT MANSIONS

✱ SINCE THIS IS A PERSONALIZED FORMULA, IT IS BEST PRACTICED BY INCORPORATING IT INTO YOUR LIFE USING YOUR MOST AUSPICIOUS DIRECTIONS FOR WORKING, SLEEPING, AND UNDERTAKING ANY KIND OF ACTIVITY.

It is worth investing in a good compass and learning to read directions accurately.

By learning your own set of good luck and bad luck directions and carrying a small compass, you will never be caught out. You will avoid, for example, being forced to face in a total loss direction.

It is important to establish whether you are an East or West Group person and whether you are living in an East or West Group house. West Group people living in East Group houses will find the distribution of luck in the house directly clashes with their personal good and bad luck directions. If you are either the father or mother of the house, the room you occupy should bring you good luck under both the house chart and your personal Kua number. If you are a child or relative, use your Kua number to select the rooms best for you and ignore the Eight Mansions chart for the house (a grid superimposed on the layout of the house showing the eight good and bad luck sectors).

USING EIGHT MANSIONS FORMULA

SE NIEN YEN	S SHENG CHI	SW HO HAI
E FU WEI		W CHUEH MING
NE SIX KILLINGS	N TIEN YI	NW FIVE GHOSTS

According to the Eight Mansions theory, every house can be divided into eight sectors, with each of the sectors corresponding to one of eight forms of good or bad luck.

EIGHT MANSIONS PRACTICE: GUIDELINES

✳ **ALWAYS SLEEP** with your head toward one of your best directions, selecting the direction that corresponds to what you most desire—wealth, health, love, or personal growth. Arrange your bed to tap your desired direction, but also take note of other bedroom taboos when doing this.

✳ **ALWAYS SIT** or stand facing one of your best directions when you work or when you are giving a presentation, asking for a raise, negotiating a contract, making a sale, interviewing for a job, making a speech, speaking over the phone, giving a performance… the list of applications is endless.

✳ **LOCATE THE MAIN ENTRANCE** of your home in a good direction sector and facing your good direction. This is a major feng shui feature, although note that Flying Star can supercede Eight Mansions regarding the best location and facing direction of the main door.

✳ **IF YOU ARE RELOCATING**, make sure that you will be moving from one of your good directions to get to your new location. This should ensure that you bring good fortune with you when you move.

✳ **LOCATE YOUR KITCHEN** in one of the bad luck direction sectors, as this will serve to suppress your personal bad

✳ **ARRANGE ALL KETTLES,** ovens, crockpots, and toasters so that electricity coming into the electrical appliance is from one of your good directions. This ensures that chi energy used to cook or boil water will be auspicious.

CHAPTER 15
FLYING STAR FORMULA OF PERIOD FENG SHUI

✳ FLYING STAR FENG SHUI IS ONE OF THE MOST POTENT AND FAST ACTING FORMULAS, WHICH IN RECENT YEARS HAS BECOME INCREASINGLY POPULAR AMONG FENG SHUI PRACTITIONERS. IT IS THE BRANCH OF COMPASS FORMULA FENG SHUI THAT DEALS WITH THE CHANGING CHI ENERGY OF TIME.

February 4, 1984

February 4, 2004

Flying Star Feng Shui introduces the concept of natal charts for houses and buildings. These charts are like a map of luck sectors and afflictions in any building, and they offer a basis for analyzing and diagnosing the feng shui of buildings and homes. The natal charts reveal the distribution of relationship and wealth luck in any building from one cycle of time to the next.

One cycle of time lasts twenty years. We are now in Period Eight, which began on February 4, 2004 and will end on February 4, 2024. The year 2004 is thus considered a benchmark year in the world of feng shui. The first year of a period is a time in which many significant changes will take place as the energy shifts and changes. Many countries will experience a change of leaders. Trends will change and the luck map of the world will also change. Flying Star Feng Shui introduces the predictive element into feng shui, as it is

February 4, 2004

February 4, 2024

concerned with fortunes of places and spaces over time.

Flying Star charts are drawn up based on the facing direction of buildings (including houses) as well as on the age of the building (the date of original construction or last renovation). The Flying Star natal charts can also incorporate month and year numbers to expand the feng shui investigation, thereby offering clues on how to improve your interiors from year to year and from month to month.

More to the point, Flying Star charts offer a map for capturing the wealth and relationship luck in any house or building. This is done by identifying and activating the auspicious Mountain Stars and Water Stars of the chart wherever they occur in the house. Typical examples of Flying Star charts are shown opposite, with the Mountain and Water Stars marked out (these are indicated by the small numbers to the top left and right of each square).

FLYING STAR PERIODS

Flying Star is one of the most exciting branches of compass formula feng shui. Its applications are powerful and work fast. Their potency comes from the combination of time and space to create an energy field inside any home so that luck comes pouring in.

Remember that while space and direction stay constant, time changes and each new cycle of time brings new energy influences that affect health, wealth, finances, romance, marriage, family, and personal growth. This is the exciting promise of Flying Star Feng Shui. If you know how to use it, your life will forever be brightened.

Period Eight will see a rise in the influence of countries and states that lie to the Northeast of any land mass.

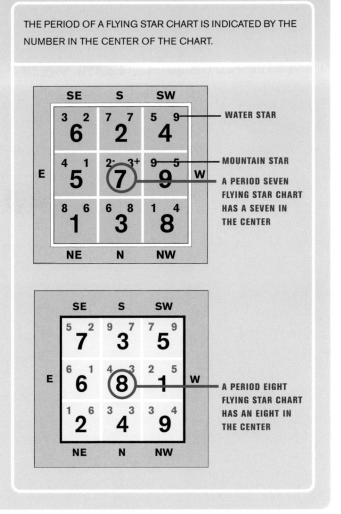

THE PERIOD OF A FLYING STAR CHART IS INDICATED BY THE NUMBER IN THE CENTER OF THE CHART.

WATER STAR

MOUNTAIN STAR

A PERIOD SEVEN FLYING STAR CHART HAS A SEVEN IN THE CENTER

A PERIOD EIGHT FLYING STAR CHART HAS AN EIGHT IN THE CENTER

THE AGE OF BUILDINGS

✳ FLYING STAR FENG SHUI IS BASED ON THE PREMISE THAT THE LUCK OF BUILDINGS IS NEVER STATIC BUT INSTEAD CHANGES WITH THE PASSAGE OF TIME. IT TAKES INTO ACCOUNT THE AGE OF BUILDINGS AND THE CHANGING ENERGY OVER TIME PERIODS.

When the Flying Star chart for a North-facing apartment in Period Seven is applied the auspicious double seven (Mountain and Water Star) is shown at the back of the house. This double becomes unlucky in Period Eight, when eight is the lucky number.

A full era of time is one hundred eighty years, comprised of three cycles lasting sixty years each—the Lower, Middle, and Upper cycles. Each cycle comprises three twenty-year periods and each period is ruled by a single-digit number, described as the reigning number of that period. We are presently living in Period Eight.

Natal charts are created according to the facing direction and age of the building under investigation. The age of a building refers to when it was built or last renovated. In any period there are sixteen different natal charts (*see* pages 138–145 for complete sets of charts for Period Seven and Period Eight), and in every chart there are nine grids, inside each of which are at least three numbers.

The chart demarcates space into nine sectors. The luck of the corresponding sector of the building, and the wealth and relationship luck indications of sectors of the house over twenty years, are read based on the numbers inside each sector.

LEARNING FLYING STAR FENG SHUI

LEARNING FLYING STAR REQUIRES BASIC KNOWLEDGE OF THE LO SHU SQUARE (SEE PAGE 48) AND ITS SEQUENCE OF NUMBERS, BUT THIS ▓▓▓ ▓▓ ▓▓▓▓▓▓▓▓ ▓▓ ▓▓▓▓▓ ▓▓▓ ▓▓ ▓▓▓▓▓. THERE ARE CONTROVERSIAL ISSUES IN FLYING STAR FENG SHUI THAT NOT ALL PROFESSIONAL PRACTITIONERS AGREE ON. UNLESS YOU HAVE COMPLETED A PROPER COURSE OF STUDY, YOU MAY FEEL SOME FRUSTRATION WHEN USING THESE CHARTS. PROFESSIONAL CONSULTANTS TEND TO BE SECRETIVE IN THEIR APPROACH TO FENG SHUI, SO IT IS USEFUL FOR YOU TO BE AWARE OF THE POSSIBLE DIFFERENCES IN APPROACH .

✳ **NOT ALL EXPERTS AGREE**
as to what constitutes the age of a building. Some say it is when a building is completely constructed. Others say it is when the building was last renovated, but they cannot agree on the precise definition of the word renovation. The house period is a vital issue, since this is the basis of the natal chart.

✳ **NOT ALL EXPERTS AGREE**
on how to determine the facing direction of any building. Some say it is where the house faces the road, others where it faces the most unencumbered view, and still others where the main door faces. This matter requires judgment and on-site investigation.

✳ **NOT ALL EXPERTS AGREE**
on the prescribed cures for Flying Star afflictions. A small minority stubbornly maintains that there are simply no cures other than to move out of afflicted rooms. Many others use the powerful practice of symbolic feng shui and five-element theory to prescribe successful cures for Flying Star afflictions.

While this book does not teach Flying Star Feng Shui in an academic format, there is more than enough information here to design excellent feng shui for your interiors, the kind of feng shui that will activate good fortune in the wealth and relationship sectors of your home.

With the Flying Star chart, anyone can identify the luckiest part of the home, and even extend this to identifying the luckiest part of each room. Once the lucky sector has been identified, the luck contained there can be activated using the feng shui methods outlined in this book.

SHORTCUT TO FLYING STAR FENG SHUI

✳ IN THIS CHAPTER IS THE COMPLETE SET OF FLYING STAR CHARTS THAT APPLY TO PERIOD SEVEN HOUSES, BUILDINGS, AND APARTMENTS (*SEE* PAGES 138–141; MOST OF US CURRENTLY LIVE IN PERIOD SEVEN HOUSES. THE CHARTS FOR PERIOD EIGHT ARE ALSO INCLUDED (*SEE* PAGES 142–145) AS MANY WILL BE RENOVATING OR MOVING INTO NEW PERIOD EIGHT HOUSES.

With these charts, it is likely that you'll be able to identify the one that applies to your home and analyze it by superimposing it onto your home layout plan. What you need to do is to learn how to select the chart that applies to your house.

HOW TO DETERMINE THE FACING DIRECTION OF A HOUSE

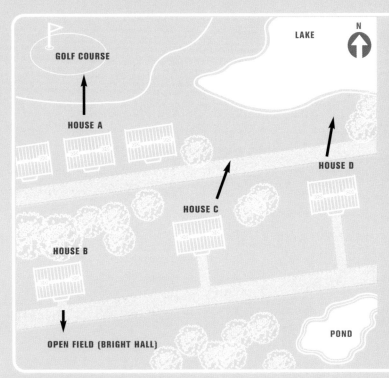

DETERMINING THE FACING DIRECTION OF A HOUSE CAN BE A CHALLENGE. ALTHOUGH ALL THESE HOUSES HAVE A MAIN ENTRANCE FACING A ROAD, SOME HAVE FINE VIEWS IN OTHER DIRECTIONS AND ON-SITE CONFIRMATION WOULD BE NEEDED.

HOUSE A has a view North from the back over a golf course.

HOUSE B looks South over a large open field. This is also the facing direction of the front door.

HOUSES C/D have a view Northeast/North toward a lake.

HOW TO USE FLYING STAR FENG SHUI

FIRST, you need to determine two things:

THE AGE OF YOUR HOUSE

✱ When was your house built? When was it last renovated? This determines the period of the building. Since Period Seven began in 1984, most readers' homes belong to this period, as many will have renovated their home in the last twenty years. If you renovate your home in the next twenty years, it will become a Period Eight house. This may be desirable, as the number seven is now very unlucky. If you can't renovate, you should use feng shui remedies to contain the impact of this number. The charts on pages 138–145 offer advice on which houses may need renovation or cure, but seek expert advice to confirm.

THE FACING DIRECTION OF YOUR HOUSE

✱ You will need a good compass that contains the three subdirections of each of the eight main directions (see page 130). Determine the facing direction of the house, not just the main door. Most often the door and the house face the same direction, but not always. Look at your house or apartment building from all directions. Consider the source of the most yang energy, usually the main road. Consider where the main door is facing and use this as the orientation unless the main door is facing a garage or a wall away from the main road.

✱ For apartment buildings and condominiums that have more than one entrance, determining the facing direction can be difficult. Look for the direction that faces the road or the best view (of distant hills, a city, a lake, over a pond or a stretch of grass) and use this as the facing direction of your house (see page 32). If in doubt, analyze a couple of charts to see which one best describes the present luck of your house.

HOW TO DETERMINE THE FACING DIRECTION OF A BUSINESS

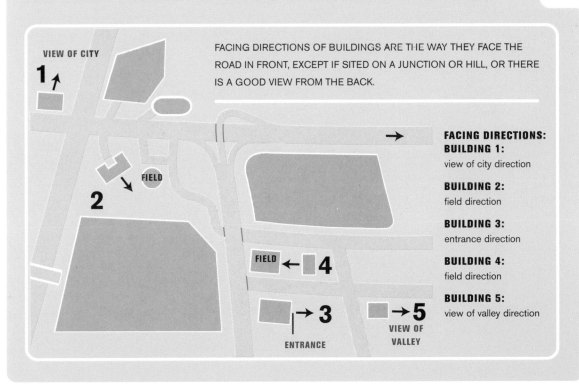

FACING DIRECTIONS OF BUILDINGS ARE THE WAY THEY FACE THE ROAD IN FRONT, EXCEPT IF SITED ON A JUNCTION OR HILL, OR THERE IS A GOOD VIEW FROM THE BACK.

FACING DIRECTIONS:
BUILDING 1:
view of city direction

BUILDING 2:
field direction

BUILDING 3:
entrance direction

BUILDING 4:
field direction

BUILDING 5:
view of valley direction

THE TWENTY-FOUR MOUNTAIN DIRECTIONS

✳ THIS IS THE NAME GIVEN TO THE TWENTY-FOUR DIRECTIONS USED IN FLYING STAR FENG SHUI. EACH OF THE EIGHT MAIN DIRECTIONS IS DIVIDED INTO THREE SUBDIRECTIONS, MAKING A TOTAL OF TWENTY SUBDIRECTIONS.

For good feng shui practice, you will need a compass that shows the three subdirections of each of the eight main directions.

This means that South becomes South 1, South 2, and South 3. West is West 1, West 2, and West 3, and so on. Each subdirection occupies fifteen degrees.

To help you determine your facing direction and find the chart that applies to your house, refer to the table given opposite and look for the direction that corresponds to the facing direction of your house.

If yours is a Period Seven or Eight building, you'll find the Flying Star chart that applies to your house on pages 138–145. More importantly, you will be able to identify your auspicious Water and Mountain Stars and activate them to increase your wealth and improve your relationship luck.

If you live in an apartment, consider the facing direction of the whole building and use it to identify the relevant natal chart. Remember to check the age of the building. Then, using the same natal chart,

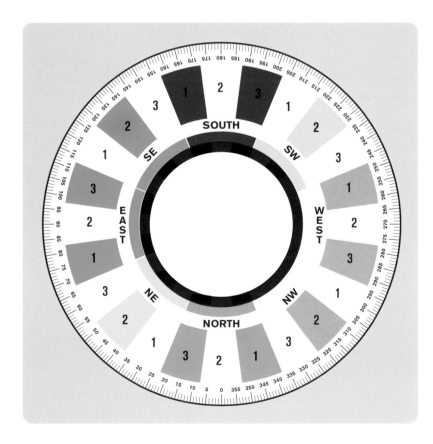

MOUNTAIN DIRECTIONS

SECTOR OF COMPASS (FOR FACING DIRECTION OF BUILDING/MAIN DOOR)	THE EXACT READING IN DEGREES USING A RELIABLE COMPASS
SOUTH 1	157.5 to 172.5
SOUTH 2	172.5 to 187.5
SOUTH 3	187.5 to 202.5
SOUTHWEST 1	202.5 to 217.5
SOUTHWEST 2	217.5 to 232.5
SOUTHWEST 3	232.5 to 247.5
WEST 1	247.5 to 262.5
WEST 2	262.5 to 277.5
WEST 3	277.5 to 292.5
NORTHWEST 1	292.5 to 307.5
NORTHWEST 2	307.5 to 322.5
NORTHWEST 3	322.5 to 337.5
NORTH 1	337.5 to 352.5
NORTH 2	352.5 to 007.5
NORTH 3	007.5 to 022.5
NORTHEAST 1	022.5 to 037.5
NORTHEAST 2	037.5 to 052.5
NORTHEAST 3	052.5 to 067.5
EAST 1	067.5 to 082.5
EAST 2	082.5 to 097.5
EAST 3	097.5 to 112.5
SOUTHEAST 1	112.5 to 127.5
SOUTHEAST 2	127.5 to 142.5
SOUTHEAST 3	142.5 to 157.5

superimpose it onto your apartment unit layout plan to undertake the analysis. You should also identify where your apartment is located in the building's natal chart. This gives you the general idea of the luck of your apartment, since you can see instantly whether the numbers in that grid are auspicious or not. This is one sure way of identifying the lucky apartments in any apartment building.

FAMILIARIZING YOURSELF WITH THE CHART

✳ TO GET THE MOST OUT OF YOUR FLYING STAR ANALYSIS, YOU MUST FIRST GET TO KNOW A FLYING STAR CHART SO THAT YOU WILL KNOW THAT THE STARS REFERRED TO ARE IN FACT NUMBERS. THEN YOU CAN DETERMINE WHICH STARS STAND FOR WEALTH AND WHICH ONES STAND FOR RELATIONSHIP LUCK. YOU WILL ALSO LEARN THE LUCKY AND UNLUCKY NUMBERS, AS WELL AS HOW THEY CAN BE ENHANCED OR REMEDIED.

When an auspicious Water Star flies into a sector in your home, you can activate it with a water feature.

1 LOOK AT THE COMBINATION of numbers inside each grid. The big numbers in the center are the period numbers. The little numbers on the left and right of the big central number are the Mountain Stars (on the left) and the Water Stars (on the right). These numbers indicate relationship and wealth luck, respectively.

2 NOTE THAT THE INTERPRETATION of the numbers takes into account how annual numbers impact the numbers of the Water Star, Mountain Star, and period star.

3 AUSPICIOUS WATER STAR NUMBERS are activated by the presence of water. If wealth is what you want, find the Water Star Eight and then build or buy a beautiful water feature to place there. Invest in an aquarium that allows you to have fish, moving water, and plants to create yang water.

4 AUSPICIOUS MOUNTAIN STAR NUMBERS
are activated with earth element objects. If
you want romance or a stronger marriage,
or if your husband is in politics and you
want to ensure continued support for him,
then look for the Mountain Star Eight in
your home and place a large natural crystal
in that corner. Or invest in a large
porcelain figurine, stone sculpture, or
painting of a mountain range. This will
vastly improve your relationship luck as
well as your health.

5 MONTH AND YEAR STAR NUMBERS will
also have an impact on your chart (*see*
Chapter 16). These exert influence on
every sector, and their impact changes
from year to year. When there is a
concentration of bad numbers in a
particular month, any negative effect is
considerably empowered.

**6 NOTE THAT WHEN BAD STARS OR GOOD
STARS** combine, they usually require a
catalyst—an external feature or structure—
to trigger an effect. Thus external symbols
and structures combine with Flying Star to
speed up good and bad effects. Symbolic
decorative pieces can have a vital
triggering effect on your luck. When a bad
annual star flies into a sector with unlucky
natal chart numbers, bad luck is triggered
much faster if a poison arrow is also
harming the sector.

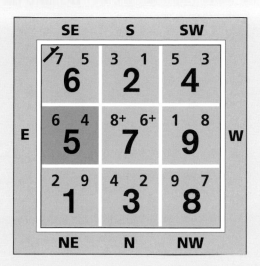

A Flying Star chart for a Period Seven house
facing Southeast. The auspicious Water Star Eight
is located in the West sector of the house.

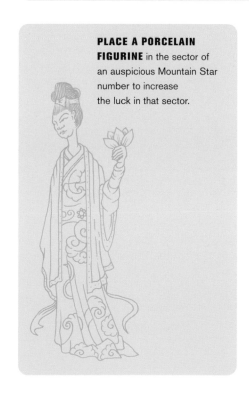

**PLACE A PORCELAIN
FIGURINE** in the sector of
an auspicious Mountain Star
number to increase
the luck in that sector.

UNDERSTANDING A FLYING STAR CHART

✳ ONCE YOU KNOW THE MEANINGS OF THE LUCKY AND UNLUCKY NUMBERS, YOU WILL FIND THE CHARTS EASY TO UNDERSTAND. STUDY THE NUMBERS OF THE WATER AND MOUNTAIN STARS IN THE CHART THAT APPLIES TO YOUR HOUSE OR APARTMENT. THEN YOU CAN DETERMINE WHICH ROOM IN YOUR HOUSE HAS WEALTH LUCK AND WHICH HAS AFFLICTIONS. YOU CAN ENERGIZE OR SUPPRESS ACCORDINGLY USING THE SYMBOLS AND CURES RECOMMENDED.

Study your charts to determine which sector in your house to activate for wealth.

✳ AUSPICIOUS NUMBERS

The auspicious numbers in any Flying Star chart are the numbers one, six, and eight.

The number eight will be the most auspicious number until 2024. It is also a number that is at the peak of its strength and vigor. Those with Kua Number Eight will experience extreme good fortune until 2024. Telephone and license plate numbers ending with the number eight will also bring good fortune.

The number six represents heaven and also the patriarch. When the Water or Mountain Star is six, activating it with suitable symbols or features will bring you luck from heaven.

The number one is also a particularly lucky number and it means that you are bound to be victorious.

Two other good numbers are the number four, which represents love and romance, as well as good fortune in research and scholarship, and the number nine. The number four is also excellent for those who work in the communication business, such a writers and teachers.

The number nine is symbolic of the fullness of heaven and earth. It is also a magnifying number, so when combined with eight it strengthens the good luck of the number eight and when combined with a bad number it makes the bad number's effect even worse.

✳ THE UNLUCKY NUMBERS

The bad luck numbers in Flying Star charts are two, three, five, and seven.

The number two brings illness and this must always be overcome with six-rod windchimes made of all metal. The rods should be hollow and have a coin with the Pa Kua symbol at the back. When the number two flies into your bedroom as the Mountain Star, it is the surest sign of illness. If it flies in as the Water Star, you are in for a worrisome time financially—enough worries to make you sick.

The number five is also known as the five yellow and this number is to be feared as it causes accidents, loss, and all kinds of severe mishaps. When the Mountain Star is five, it brings illness as well as loss. When the Water Star is five, it brings financial loss. The number five is at its most dangerous when the annual and monthly five are in the same grid, or when a nine has flown in to magnify its ill effects.

When you see the five in any sector you must immediately install the cure, which is the five-element pagoda. This is an all-metal hollow pagoda. Unscrew the pagoda and fill it with earth taken from your garden, then screw the pagoda back into place. This symbolically locks up the deadly Five Yellow.

The number three is known as the quarrelsome star that brings hostility and danger of misunderstandings and can lead to litigation. It causes obstacles to all your plans and at its most severe can be dangerous as well. It is the number that causes violence and anger to boil over. When you see the number three fly into your room as the Mountain Star, it will cause havoc in all your relationships. As the Water Star, it will cause you to fight with people over money matters. To control the number three star, you need something belonging to the fire element, hence

something red will be ideal, such as red curtains or red carpets.

The number seven is a violent star that causes burglary and creates the chi that leads to muggings or robbery. The number seven star can be overcome with water, but since you cannot place water inside the bedroom, another cure that is an image of the rhinoceros.

SUMMARY OF MEANINGS

✳ **THE NUMBERS TO FEAR ARE FIVE AND TWO** because these two numbers are the sickness numbers. Wherever they appear in any chart, if you stay or sleep in those sectors, you will suffer ill luck, get sick, or suffer misfortune.

✳ **THE NUMBER THREE** is a hostile number and it brings misunderstandings, quarrels, and fighting. If the three hits your room you could be faced with legal action.

✳ **THE NUMBER FOUR** is lucky for romance and brought literary luck in Period Seven, but it is unlucky in Period Eight. It must not be too near water as this can lead to sex scandals.

✳ **THE NUMBER NINE** has the power to magnify the ill effects of five and two. It is to be feared when it occurs with these two numbers. But on its own it is a good number encompassing the completeness of heaven and earth.

✳ **THE NUMBER SEVEN,** although lucky in Period Seven, in Period Eight turns dangerous and bloody, bringing burglary, robbery, and deadly accidents.

✳ **THE NUMBERS ONE, SIX, AND EIGHT** are the most auspicious numbers, but it is the number eight that is truly awesome. The energy of six is weak and needs to be activated.

THE FLYING STAR CHARTS

✳ FLYING STAR CHARTS ARE EXCELLENT FOR HIGHLIGHTING
AFFLICTED ENERGY OR AUSPICIOUS ENERGY IN THE SECTORS OF
A HOUSE. THE MOUNTAIN STAR AND THE WATER STAR ARE THE VITAL
LUCK INDICATORS OF THE CHARTS. THEIR NUMBERS ARE INDICATIVE
OF THE LUCK OF THE SECTORS THEY OCCUPY.

Depending whether it is a period, Water Star or Mountain Star number, the numbers in the Flying Star chart suggest overall luck or, more specifically, wealth luck or relationship luck, and highlight afflictions.

Afflictions manifest as illness, loss, failure, and the breakup of relationships. These show up as bad luck numbers (see pages 134–135) and cause ill health and material, physical, and financial problems.

Flying Star Feng Shui involves identifying these afflictions and protecting against their occurrence. Remedies require clever use of the Five Element Theory. Special symbols that signify Water, Fire, Wood, Earth, or Metal can be used with great potency to disarm the negative Flying Star numbers. These symbols include objects such as windchimes, longevity symbols, brass mirrors, crystals, candles, trees, plants, water, protector images, cranes, and tortoises.

Tortoises attract good fortune and protect you from bad luck.

✳ WATER STAR

The Water Star is placed on the right side of the Period number. This little number in each of the nine little grids of the chart will indicate whether the space in that grid has wealth chi. If the number is eight it indicates maximum wealth luck. If the number is five or two it indicates bad luck with money. The Water Star Eight is the key to wealth. When you find your Water Star Eight, activate it with a water feature—(*see* pages 160–165).

✳ MOUNTAIN STAR

The Mountain Star is usually placed on the left side of the period number. This little number here indicates relationship and health luck. If the number is eight it suggests excellent relationship luck, which is activated if there is a mountain nearby. Inside the house you can activate the area by placing a large natural crystal or special boulder in the relevant sector (*see* pages 166–167).

CHANGING HOUSE PERIOD

✳ IN FLYING STAR FENG SHUI, AS SOON AS THE TWENTY-YEAR PERIOD CHANGES, GENERALLY ALL HOUSES BUILT OR RENOVATED IN THE PRECEDING PERIOD SUFFER FROM A DECLINE IN ENERGY. IT BECOMES ADVISABLE TO CHANGE THE PERIOD OF YOUR HOUSE. UNLESS THE PRECEDING PERIOD'S CHART IS BETTER.

You can change the Period of your house through renovation.

All Period Seven houses are losing energy now that Period Eight has begun and residents of Period Seven houses will begin to feel a decline in their fortunes.

Generally, the advice of feng shui experts is to transform the declining energy through renovation so that the house is transformed into a Period Eight house.

There are circumstances when the decision to transform is not straightforward. For example, you might discover that the Period Seven chart for your house is far more favorable than the Period Eight chart would be. In this situation, rather than transforming your house and risk worsening your fortune, the advice is to wait a year or two to see how the new period affects your luck. If you then decide to change, use feng shui remedies to address any ill effects.

Traditionally, "renovation" is threefold:
✳ Changing heaven chi (renewing the roof of your house).

✳ Changing earth chi (replacing part of the floor with new flooring).
✳ Changing the main door.

If you are advised to change the period of your house, but it is impossible for you to undertake any kind of renovations, for example, you are renting a house or do not have available funds, the next best thing to do is to arrange for your house to receive a fresh infusion of yang energy. This can be achieved in the following ways:

✳ Have a big house party involving lots of positive people including children. Have music and plenty of food and open all the doors and windows to allow fresh energy to infuse your home.
✳ Paint your house using a slightly louder color than you have at the moment. The best color for Period Eight is yellow.

The Period Seven charts on the following pages include advice on whether transforming to Period Eight is advisable for your house.

FLYING STAR CHARTS PERIOD SEVEN SOUTH

SOUTH 1: THIS HOUSE MUST CONSIDER CHANGING TO PERIOD EIGHT.

SOUTH 2/3: THIS HOUSE MUST CONSIDER CHANGING TO PERIOD EIGHT BECAUSE OF THE DOUBLE 7.

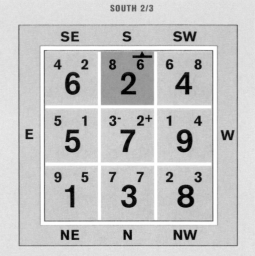

FLYING STAR CHARTS PERIOD SEVEN NORTH

NORTH 1: THIS HOUSE MUST CONSIDER CHANGING TO PERIOD EIGHT.

NORTH 2/3: THIS HOUSE SHOULD DEFINITELY CONSIDER CHANGING TO PERIOD EIGHT.

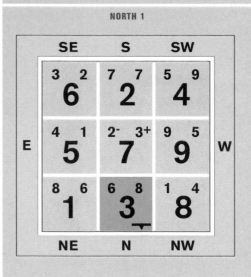
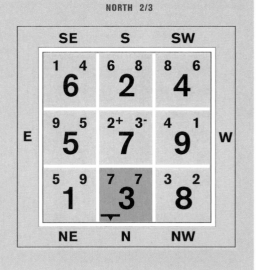

FLYING STAR CHARTS PERIOD SEVEN EAST

EAST 1: IF YOU HAVE NOT ALREADY DONE SO, CONSIDER CHANGING YOUR HOUSE TO PERIOD EIGHT.

EAST 2/3: YOU MUST SERIOUSLY CONSIDER CHANGING THIS HOUSE TO PERIOD EIGHT.

EAST 1

	SE	S	SW	
	8 4 — **6**	4 9 — **2**	6 2 — **4**	
E	7 3 — **5**	9+ 5+ — **7**	2 7 — **9**	**W**
	3 8 — **1**	5 1 — **3**	1 6 — **8**	
	NE	N	NW	

EAST 2/3

	SE	S	SW	
	1 6 — **6**	5 1 — **2**	3 8 — **4**	
E	2 7 — **5**	9- 5- — **7**	7 3 — **9**	**W**
	6 2 — **1**	4 9 — **3**	8 4 — **8**	
	NE	N	NW	

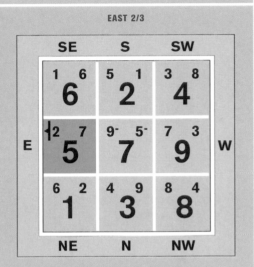

FLYING STAR CHARTS PERIOD SEVEN WEST

WEST 1: COMPARE THE CHART WITH THE PERIOD EIGHT ONE AND CHOOSE WHICH SUITS YOUR LAYOUT BEST.

WEST 2/3: AS FOR WEST 1, BUT IF YOU'RE PLANNING EXTENSIVE RENOVATIONS THEN PERIOD EIGHT IS BEST.

WEST 1

	SE	S	SW	
	4 8 — **6**	9 4 — **2**	2 6 — **4**	
E	3 7 — **5**	5+ 9+ — **7**	7 2 — **9**	**W**
	8 3 — **1**	1 5 — **3**	6 1 — **8**	
	NE	N	NW	

WEST 2/3

	SE	S	SW	
	6 1 — **6**	1 5 — **2**	8 3 — **4**	
E	7 2 — **5**	5- 9- — **7**	3 7 — **9**	**W**
	2 6 — **1**	9 4 — **3**	4 8 — **8**	
	NE	N	NW	

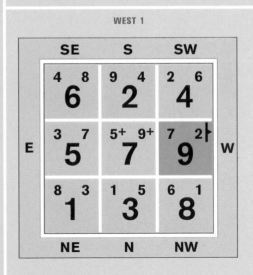
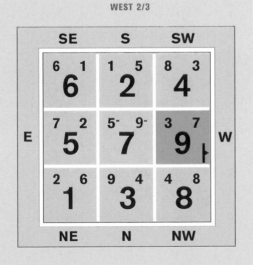

FLYING STAR CHARTS PERIOD SEVEN SOUTHWEST

SOUTHWEST 1 + 2/3: ALL SOUTHWEST FACING HOUSES SHOULD DEFINITELY CHANGE TO PERIOD EIGHT.

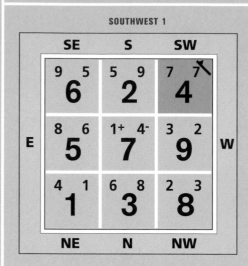

SOUTHWEST 1

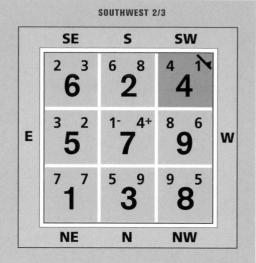

SOUTHWEST 2/3

FLYING STAR CHARTS PERIOD SEVEN NORTHWEST

NORTHWEST 1: I WOULD RECOMMEND CHANGING THIS TO A PERIOD EIGHT HOUSE.

NORTHWEST 2/3: YOU SHOULD CONSIDER CHANGING THIS TO A PERIOD EIGHT HOUSE.

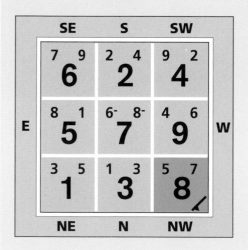

NORTHWEST 1

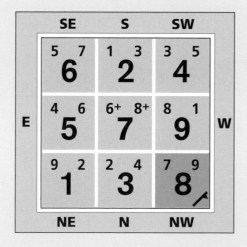

NORTHWEST 2/3

FLYING STAR CHARTS PERIOD SEVEN SOUTHEAST

SOUTHEAST 1 + 2/3: COMPARE THE PERIOD SEVEN AND EIGHT CHARTS TO DECIDE WHICH WORKS BEST WITH YOUR HOUSE LAYOUT

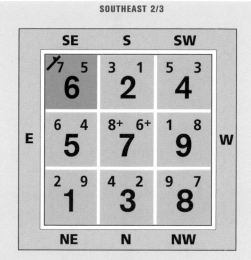

SOUTHEAST 1

	SE	S	SW	
	9 7 **6**	4 2 **2**	2 9 **4**	
E	1 8 **5**	8⁻ 6⁻ **7**	6 4 **9**	W
	5 3 **1**	3 1 **3**	7 5 **8**	
	NE	N	NW	

SOUTHEAST 2/3

	SE	S	SW	
	7 5 **6**	3 1 **2**	5 3 **4**	
E	6 4 **5**	8⁺ 6⁺ **7**	1 8 **9**	W
	2 9 **1**	4 2 **3**	9 7 **8**	
	NE	N	NW	

FLYING STAR CHARTS PERIOD SEVEN NORTHEAST

NORTHEAST 1 + 2/3: ALL NORTHEAST FACING HOUSES SHOULD DEFINITELY CHANGE TO PERIOD EIGHT TO ENJOY THE BENEFIT OF SUPERIOR CHI DISTRIBUTION IN THE HOUSE.

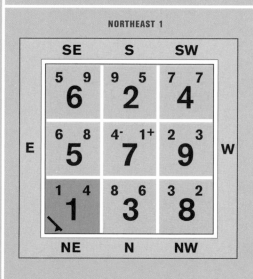
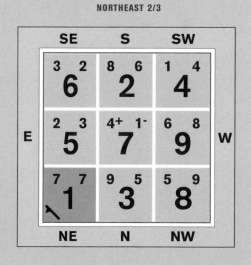

NORTHEAST 1

	SE	S	SW	
	5 9 **6**	9 5 **2**	7 7 **4**	
E	6 8 **5**	4⁻ 1⁺ **7**	2 3 **9**	W
	1 4 **1**	8 6 **3**	3 2 **8**	
	NE	N	NW	

NORTHEAST 2/3

	SE	S	SW	
	3 2 **6**	8 6 **2**	1 4 **4**	
E	2 3 **5**	4⁺ 1⁻ **7**	6 8 **9**	W
	7 7 **1**	9 5 **3**	5 9 **8**	
	NE	N	NW	

FLYING STAR CHARTS PERIOD EIGHT SOUTH

SOUTH 1: THIS HOUSE ENJOYS THE AUSPICIOUS DOUBLE EIGHT IN ITS SITTING PALACE.

SOUTH 2/3: THIS HOUSE ENJOYS THE AUSPICIOUS DOUBLE EIGHT IN ITS FACING PALACE.

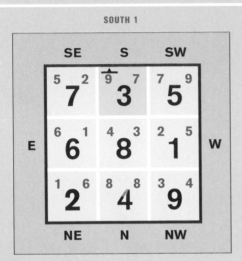

SOUTH 1

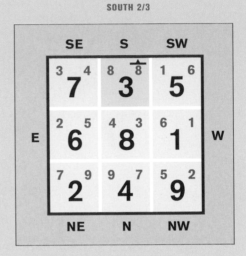

SOUTH 2/3

FLYING STAR CHARTS PERIOD EIGHT NORTH

NORTH 1: THIS HOUSE ENJOYS THE AUSPICIOUS DOUBLE EIGHT IN ITS FACING PALACE.

NORTH 2/3: THIS HOUSE ENJOYS THE AUSPICIOUS DOUBLE EIGHT IN ITS SITTING PALACE.

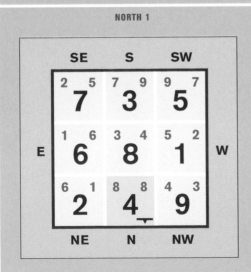

NORTH 1

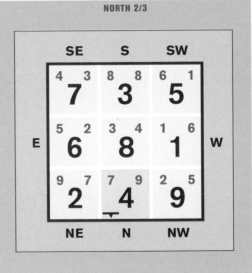

NORTH 2/3

FLYING STAR CHARTS PERIOD EIGHT EAST

EAST 1: THIS HOUSE ENJOYS THE AUSPICIOUS DOUBLE EIGHT IN ITS FACING PALACE.

EAST 2/3: THIS HOUSE ENJOYS THE AUSPICIOUS DOUBLE EIGHT IN ITS SITTING PALACE.

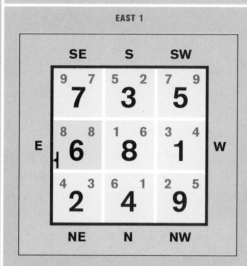

EAST 1

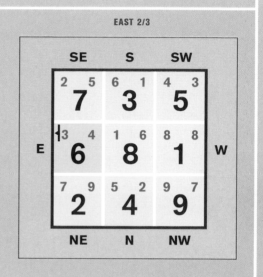

EAST 2/3

FLYING STAR CHARTS PERIOD EIGHT WEST

WEST 1: THIS HOUSE ENJOYS THE AUSPICIOUS DOUBLE EIGHT IN ITS SITTING PALACE.

WEST 2/3: THIS HOUSE ENJOYS THE AUSPICIOUS DOUBLE EIGHT IN ITS FACING PALACE.

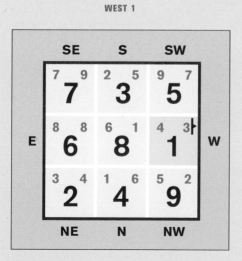

WEST 1

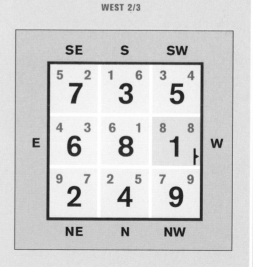

WEST 2/3

FLYING STAR CHARTS PERIOD EIGHT SOUTHWEST

SOUTHWEST 1 + 2/3: ALL SOUTHWEST FACING HOUSES ENJOY EXCEPTIONAL GOOD FORTUNE DURING THE PERIOD OF EIGHT.

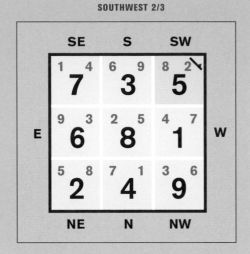

SOUTHWEST 1

	SE	S	SW	
	3 6 **7**	7 1 **3**	5 8 **5**	
E	4 7 **6**	2 5 **8**	9 3 **1**	W
	8 2 **2**	6 9 **4**	1 4 **9**	
	NE	N	NW	

SOUTHWEST 2/3

	SE	S	SW	
	1 4 **7**	6 9 **3**	8 2 **5**	
E	9 3 **6**	2 5 **8**	4 7 **1**	W
	5 8 **2**	7 1 **4**	3 6 **9**	
	NE	N	NW	

FLYING STAR CHARTS PERIOD EIGHT NORTHWEST

NORTHWEST 1: THIS HOUSE ENJOYS A VERY AUSPICIOUS MOUNTAIN STAR AT THE FRONT.
NORTHWEST 2/3: THIS HOUSE ENJOYS A VERY AUSPICIOUS WATER STAR AT THE FRONT.

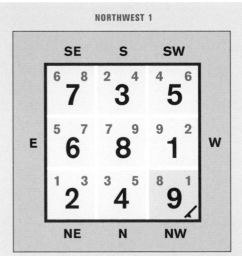

NORTHWEST 1

	SE	S	SW	
	6 8 **7**	2 4 **3**	4 6 **5**	
E	5 7 **6**	7 9 **8**	9 2 **1**	W
	1 3 **2**	3 5 **4**	8 1 **9**	
	NE	N	NW	

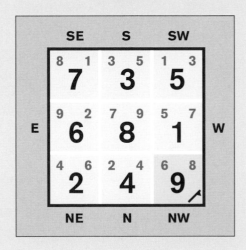

NORTHWEST 2/3

	SE	S	SW	
	8 1 **7**	3 5 **3**	1 3 **5**	
E	9 2 **6**	7 9 **8**	5 7 **1**	W
	4 6 **2**	2 4 **4**	6 8 **9**	
	NE	N	NW	

FLYING STAR CHARTS PERIOD EIGHT SOUTHEAST

SOUTHEAST 1: THIS HOUSE ENJOYS A VERY LUCKY FACING DIRECTION IN PERIOD EIGHT.

SOUTHEAST 2/3: THIS HOUSE HAS THE AUSPICIOUS WATER STAR EIGHT AT THE FRONT OF THE HOUSE.

SOUTHEAST 1

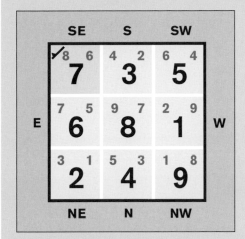

SOUTHEAST 2/3

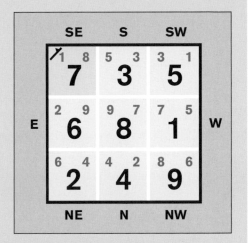

FLYING STAR CHARTS PERIOD EIGHT NORTHEAST

NORTHEAST 1 + 2/3: ALL NORTHEAST FACING HOUSES ENJOY EXCEPTIONAL GOOD FORTUNE IN THE PERIOD OF EIGHT.

NORTHEAST 1

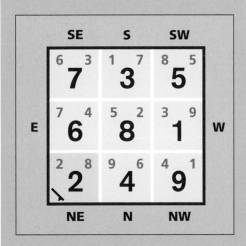

NORTHEAST 2/3

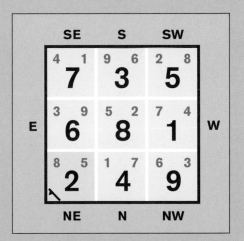

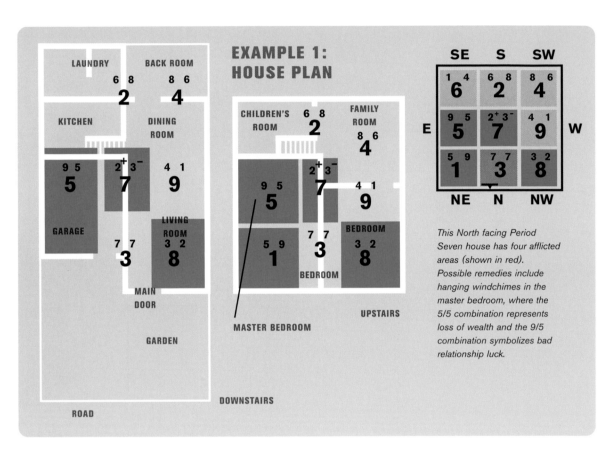

**EXAMPLE 1:
HOUSE PLAN**

LAUNDRY — 6 8 — **2**

BACK ROOM — 8 6 — **4**

KITCHEN

DINING ROOM

9 5 — **5**

2⁺ 3⁻ — **7**

4 1 — **9**

GARAGE

7 7 — **3**

LIVING ROOM — 3 2 — **8**

MAIN DOOR

GARDEN

ROAD

CHILDREN'S ROOM — 6 8 — **2**

FAMILY ROOM — 8 6 — **4**

9 5 — **5**

2⁺ 3⁻ — **7**

4 1 — **9**

5 9 — **1**

7 7 — **3**

BEDROOM — 3 2 — **8**

BEDROOM

MASTER BEDROOM

UPSTAIRS

DOWNSTAIRS

SE   S   SW

1 4 — **6**

6 8 — **2**

8 6 — **4**

E

9 5 — **5**

2⁺ 3⁻ — **7**

4 1 — **9**

W

5 9 — **1**

7 7 — **3**

3 2 — **8**

NE   N   NW

This North facing Period Seven house has four afflicted areas (shown in red). Possible remedies include hanging windchimes in the master bedroom, where the 5/5 combination represents loss of wealth and the 9/5 combination symbolizes bad relationship luck.

✳ EXAMPLE 1: A HOUSE

The example shows a Flying Star chart superimposed onto the layout plan of a two-level townhouse. This is a Period Seven house that is facing North 2/3. This chart reveals four afflicted sectors in this house (shown in red) and the chart is repeated on both levels.

In the East, the upstairs master bedroom has the 5/5 Water/Period Star combination that brings loss of wealth and the 9/5 as the Mountain/Period Star numbers bringing bad luck in relationships. Note that in Flying Star, these are unlucky combinations that spell problems, illness,

and bad luck. It is necessary to hang windchimes to control these negative numbers. Downstairs, these numbers are in the garage so the affliction is not serious.

The master bedroom must have metal energy to weaken the 9/5, otherwise the couple will suffer relationship problems and illness. In the second bedroom, we see the quarrelsome combination of 3/2 signifying the Mountain/Water Stars. Anyone staying in this bedroom will become quarrelsome and encounter hostility from others. Meanwhile, the bedroom in the North sector with the double 7, which was lucky until this period, has now turned unlucky.

✷ EXAMPLE 2: AN APARTMENT

For apartments, use the chart that coincides with the facing direction of the whole building and not the entrance to the apartment. Once you have determined the chart that applies to your building, superimpose it onto the apartment layout plan according to the compass directions.

Shown (in orange) in the example here are three auspicious rooms:

✷ THE FAMILY ROOM, which has the Water Star Eight

✷ THE MASTER BEDROOM, which has the Mountain Star Eight

✷ THE LIVING ROOM, which has the extremely lucky three-number combination of 1, 6, and 8

Residents of this apartment will definitely enjoy good fortune since the key rooms here are so auspicious. But the main door area has the Water Star 5 and this affliction must be overcome. It is vital to place a five-element pagoda or hang a metallic windchime in this part of the apartment to dissolve the evil influence of the Water Star 5 at the entrance. By doing this, residents are guarded against bad luck and can enjoy the good luck brought by the strategic occurrence of lucky water and Mountain Stars in the bedrooms and living room.

✷ UPDATING YOUR HOME FOR PERIOD EIGHT

Now that you have been introduced to Flying Star Feng Shui, be patient with yourself. The information in this book is sufficient for you to undertake simple yet accurate assessments of the luck distribution in your home. You will understand the time dimension in feng shui and by studying the monthly and annual charts, you will be able to update the feng shui of your home every year.

This apartment's chart is generally auspicious, with the particularly favorable Water Star Eight in the family room.

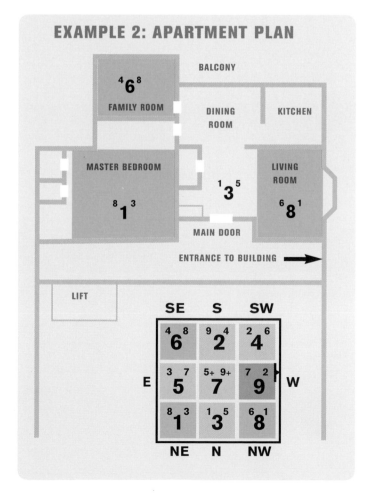

EXAMPLE 2: APARTMENT PLAN

ANNUAL UPDATES OF FENG SHUI AFFLICTIONS

✳ THERE IS A BRANCH OF FLYING STAR FENG SHUI, WHICH ADDS THE IMPORTANT DIMENSION OF ANNUAL UPDATES TO THE PRACTICE. THIS IS BASED ON THE PREMISE THAT THE CHI ENERGY OF HOMES AND BUILDINGS CHANGES EACH YEAR AND EVERY MONTH.

These cyclical movements of chi are represented in the annual feng shui chart, which applies to all houses. Each year's chart is based on the year's ruling number, also known as the Lo Shu number for the year. This number becomes the center number of the chart. The other numbers are inserted into the different sectors of the chart in the same sequence as the original Lo Shu Square (*see* page 48).

To update your feng shui effectively each year, you will need to understand about annual charts, such as the one shown here, as well as the different types of annual afflictions.

You can draw up this chart yourself once you know the Lo Shu number of the year. Note that the Lo Shu number for each New Year moves sequentially backward, so in 2005, the annual number is 4, in 2006 it is 3, in 2007 it is 2, in 2008 it is 1, in 2009 it is 9 and so forth.

The annual chart shows the different numbers that occupy each grid, and it also shows where the feng shui annual afflictions are located each year.

Updating the feng shui of your house or apartment means knowing what special measures you will need to take each year to counter the inauspicious luck caused by annual star afflictions when these enter into bedrooms or affect the main door of the building. Knowing about annual and monthly afflictions will help to give dynamic credence to your application of feng shui.

LO SHU NUMBER

YEAR	NUMBER
2004	5
2005	4
2006	3
2007	2
2008	1
2009	9
2010	8

ANNUAL CHART EXAMPLES

✱ THE LO SHU NUMBER OF 2004 IS FIVE; THIS NUMBER OCCUPIES THE CENTER OF THE CHART AND THE REST OF THE NUMBERS ARE PLACED INTO THE GRID FOLLOWING THE SEQUENCE OF THE LO SHU SQUARE. BECAUSE THE ORIGINAL LO SHU SQUARE ALSO HAS A FIVE IN THE CENTER, THE ANNUAL CHART FOR 2004 IS EXACTLY THE SAME AS THE LO SHU SQUARE.

✱ THE ANNUAL CHART FOR 2005 (THE YEAR OF THE ROOSTER) SHOWS THE POSITION OF THE THREE KILLINGS (SEE PAGES 154–155) IN THE EAST, ALONG WITH THE ILLNESS STAR, AND THE HOSTILE STAR IN THE SOUTHEAST, AND THE VIOLENT STAR IN THE NORTHEAST (SEE PAGES 156–157). THE GRAND DUKE JUPITER IS IN PART OF THE WEST (SEE PAGES 150–151).

GRAND DUKE JUPITER
AFFLICTS PART OF
THE SOUTHWEST

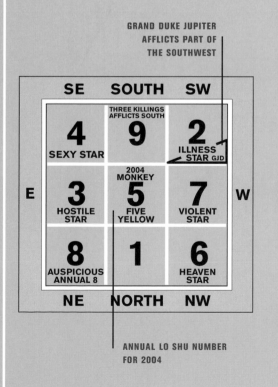

ANNUAL LO SHU NUMBER
FOR 2004

GRAND DUKE JUPITER
AFFLICTS PART OF
THE WEST

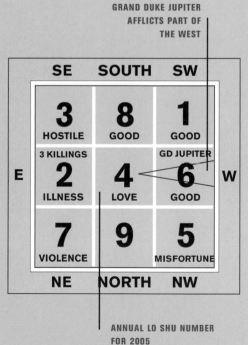

ANNUAL LO SHU NUMBER
FOR 2005

THE IMPORTANT AFFLICTIONS

✳ EVERY YEAR YOU MUST TAKE NOTE OF THE LOCATION OF THREE
IMPORTANT AFFLICTIONS. THESE ARE THE GRAND DUKE JUPITER, THE
DEADLY FIVE YELLOW, AND THE THREE KILLINGS.

The Grand Duke Jupiter is located in fifteen degrees of the compass corresponding to the Chinese astrological animal of each year.

The location of these three afflictions changes each year. The basis of the changes differ for each one of the three specified afflictions. Each of the three afflictions occupy different angles in terms of degrees—the Grand Duke occupies only fifteen degrees, the Five Yellow occupies forty-five degrees, and the Three Killings occupies ninety degrees, so the extent of their impact on the floor area of houses and buildings will differ.

Antidotes for controlling or overcoming these afflictions depend on where they are each year. There are safeguards that can be used according to which particular locations are afflicted.

To ensure protection from the ill effect of these annual afflictions, you should first note their location from year to year.

Next take note of the taboos—what you simply must not do so as not to incur the wrath of the afflictions.

The Five Yellow brings major financial loss and fatal illness; the Three Killings brings three kinds of bad luck associated with relationships, and the Grand Duke Jupiter brings defeat and failure. Knowing about these afflictions will help you to evade their various ill effects.

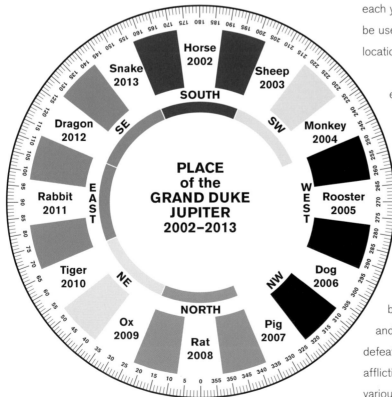

PLACE
of the
GRAND DUKE
JUPITER
2002–2013

Horse 2002
Snake 2013
Sheep 2003
SOUTH
Dragon 2012
SE
SW
Monkey 2004
Rabbit 2011
EAST
WEST
Rooster 2005
Tiger 2010
NE
NW
Dog 2006
Ox 2009
NORTH
Pig 2007
Rat 2008

THE GRAND DUKE JUPITER

✳ THE GRAND DUKE JUPITER IS THE NAME GIVEN TO AN ANNUAL AFFLICTION KNOWN AS THE TAI SUI IN CHINESE.

He is said to be the god of the year and is thus located in the fifteen degrees of the compass that correspond to the animal sign of the year. For instance, during the year of the Rooster, the Grand Duke is located in the West, which is the direction of the Rooster.

In the year of the Horse, he is in the South, and so forth. To ensure good feng shui throughout any year it is vital that you should never sit directly facing the Grand Duke's location for that year, even when that direction is your best direction according to other formulas of feng shui.

Never disturb the peace and quiet of the Grand Duke's palace. This means that you should not play loud music in the corresponding location. You also should not quarrel there, nor undertake renovations involving banging, digging, and demolition. If you do, the result will be loss, bad luck, and illness. This vital taboo applies even if you are planning to undertake spot renovations in the home.

In 2005 the Grand Duke occupies the direction of the Rooster, which is West, and in 2006 he occupies the direction of the Dog. Shown in the chart opposite are the directions of the Grand Duke indicated for the years 2002 to 2013. Once you know where to find the Grand Duke each year, it is easy enough to observe the taboos associated with him.

People born in the animal year directly opposite the ruling animal are in direct conflict with the Grand Duke. To cure this affliction, place the celestial protector Pi Yao in the Grand Duke's location. This heavenly creature with its horn and lion-dog face offers is a popular feng shui symbol (*see* page 266).

The Pi Yao is an excellent remedy against the Grand Duke Jupiter.

THE DEADLY FIVE YELLOW

✳ THE FIVE YELLOW IS THE MOST DEADLY OF THE THREE ANNUAL AFFLICTIONS, ESPECIALLY DURING YEARS WHEN IT FLIES INTO EARTH AND FIRE ELEMENT SECTORS.

The Five Yellow is at its most powerful when it afflicts the front door; counteract it by placing six metal coins above the doorway.

THE LOCATION OF THE FIVE YELLOW

YEAR	LOCATION
2004	Center
2005	Northwest
2006	West
2007	Northeast
2008	South
2009	North
2010	Southwest

This happened in 1999 when it flew to the South, a fire element sector. It also happened in 2001 when it flew into the Southwest, an earth element sector. In 2004, it occupies the center which is even more deadly. In these three sectors, the Five Yellow, being an earth element affliction, will have its evil essence considerably strengthened. The Five Yellow brings severe illness, financial loss, and obstacles to success. It is also known to cause hostility.

The Five Yellow is at its deadliest when it afflicts the main door or when it enters into your bedroom. When it afflicts your main door, use another door to enter the house throughout the year if you can, as the act of opening and closing the door activates the Five Yellow. If you cannot use another door, you will need to depend on the cures you put in place to exhaust the chi energy of the Five Yellow.

If it occupies your bedroom, it is activated by your presence and, if you can, it is a good idea to sleep in another bedroom. Otherwise, you will just have to strengthen the remedy for the Five Yellow.

✳ COUNTERACTING THE FIVE YELLOW

There are different ways to counter the Five Yellow, but perhaps the best method during Period Eight is to place a brass or golden metal five-element pagoda where the Five Yellow is located. Place two or three to strengthen the cure. The way to use the five-element pagoda is to unscrew its top, fill it with earth taken form your own home or apartment building, and then screw the top back on again. Symbolically locking up the earth keeps the Five Yellow under control.

You can also hang six-rod metal windchimes. The windchime should be made entirely of metal. The sound of metal caused by metal on metal in sectors occupied by the Five Yellow is an effective cure because the metal chi exhausts the earth chi of Five Yellow.

Feng shui masters always recommend using the exhausting cycle of the five elements rather than the destructive cycle to control the Five Yellow affliction.

Windchimes are an excellent antidote because they engage the power of the winds, but if you like you can also place six metal coins above the doorway, or six coins on either side of the door to exhaust the power of the Five Yellow.

Wherever the Five Yellow occurs in any home or building, it is important to keep the lights dimmed. This is because fire chi will strengthen the Five Yellow's earth energy. If you have spotlights in the sector of the house where there is the Five Yellow, for instance, these signify fire chi strengthening the Five Yellow, thereby making it more deadly.

Windchimes and pagodas are traditional feng shui remedies for the Five Yellow.

CAUTION!

✳ **YOU MUST NOT** undertake renovations in your home if the Five Yellow is at your front door. Certainly you must not cut, dig, or demolish any part of the home afflicted by the Five Yellow.

THE THREE KILLINGS

✳ THE THREE KILLINGS AFFLICTION IS KNOWN AS THE SARM SAAT IN CHINESE, AND IT IS ABLE TO BRING THREE TYPES OF MISFORTUNE ASSOCIATED WITH RELATIONSHIPS, IF YOU LET YOUR GUARD DOWN OR SIT WITH YOUR BACK TO IT. HOWEVER, REMEDIES EXIST TO COUNTER ITS BAD LUCK.

Unlike the Grand Duke Jupiter (*see* page 151), which must never be confronted, you must always confront the Three Killings, so face it head on. This means if it occupies the South, then you must face the South. Having the Three Killings behind you is asking to be stabbed in the back.

Rearrange your furniture each New Year so that you do not inadvertently have the Three Killings behind you. The best solution is to arrange living room and dining room furniture such that you never sit facing the Grand Duke and also never have the Three Killings behind you.

You should avoid doing any house renovations in sectors occupied by the Three Killings.

When planning home repairs and renovations, avoid such works in sectors occupied by the Three Killings. This is a troublesome taboo to observe since the Three Killings can occupy a large part of the house as they fly only to the cardinal directions, never into the secondary directions.

In the years of the Ox, Rooster, and Snake, Three Killings occupies the East. The cure is to shine a bright light in the corner or hang a metal windchime.

In the years of the Boar, Rabbit, and Sheep, Three Killings occupies the West. The cure is to place open water in this corner or shine a bright light.

In the years of the Monkey, Rat, and Dragon, Three Killings occupies the South. The cure is to use crystals or place open water here.

In the years of the Dog, Horse, and Tiger, Three Killings occupies the North. The cure is to place a strong plant here or use the strong earth energy of crystal.

REMEDIES FOR THE THREE KILLINGS

THE MAIN REMEDY FOR THE THREE KILLINGS
IS TO DISPLAY THREE CHI LINS—OR DRAGON
HORSES—IN THE PLACE OF THE THREE
KILLINGS. THESE CHI LINS ARE THE PERFECT
ANTIDOTE TO EXHAUST THE ENERGY.
HOWEVER, IF THE EAST IS AFFLICTED,
PLACING A BRIGHT LIGHT THERE WILL EASILY
OVERCOME THE THREE KILLINGS.

✳ When the Three Killings is in the West,
the remedy is a large bowl of water.

✳ When the Three Killings is in the South,
the remedy is three crystal spheres.

✳ When the Three Killings is in the North,
the remedy is live plants.

The idea is to exhaust the chi of the corner it
occupies. Do not use the destructive cycle of the
elements (*see* pages 40 and 221), as the
presence of the Three Killings is temporary.

THREE GREEN PLANTS

THREE CHI LINS

THREE CRYSTAL SPHERES

THREE ANNUAL STAR AFFLICTIONS

✱ THERE ARE THREE ANNUAL NUMBER AFFLICTIONS YOU SHOULD ALSO BE WARY OF, SINCE REMEDIES AND CURES MUST BE PUT INTO PLACE IN ORDER TO PUT THEM UNDER CONTROL; OTHERWISE, THEY ALSO HAVE THE POTENTIAL TO PLAY HAVOC WITH YOUR LIFE.

KEY

○ THREE STAR

○ TWO STAR

○ SEVEN STAR

A laughing Buddha wearing a red robe will help counter the Three Star in your bedroom.

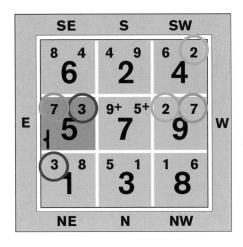

✱ THE HOSTILE NUMBER THREE STAR

Wherever the Number Three Star flies, there will be hostility, misunderstandings, and quarrels at best, and serious brushes with the law and at worst. The hostile Three Star is to be feared because it brings a great deal of inconvenience into your life and blocks your success path. People will find fault with you and blame you unjustly.

If your bedroom is occupied by the annual Three Star, you must immediately place something red and something metallic to counter the power of Three. Red carpets and curtains, tablecloths, and cushion covers are good, although you can also place the laughing Buddha wearing a red robe and carrying an ingot of gold.

When the main door into the house is occupied by the Number Three Star, the negativity affects everyone in the home. You must place a large object in red near to the doorway as well as a sword of coins tied together with red string. The Number Three Star is in the East in 2004 and in the Southeast in 2005—during these two years the number 3 star is extremely powerful and strong, so take care.

✳ THE ILLNESS NUMBER TWO STAR

There is also the Number Two Illness Star to contend with. In 2004, it occupies the Southwest. In 2005 it moves to the East. The Illness Star, as the name suggests, always brings illness and, depending on which direction it occupies, it causes illness in specific areas of the body. Thus, when it occupies the East and Southeast, it will tend to bring aches and pains relating to joints and limbs. If the affliction is more severe (that is, your bedroom has the Illness Star) then something could cause damage to your bones and limbs.

When the Illness Star occupies the South, it could bring diseases related to the heart, the blood stream, and the eyes. When it moves to the North, illness is usually associated with the kidney. When it occupies the Southwest or Northeast, illness has to do with the stomach and the womb. If it occupies the West or Northwest, then illness could be mental or have something to do with the head, lungs, or chest. The best cure for the Illness Star is all-metal windchimes because, like the Five Yellow, the Number Two Star belongs to the earth element.

✳ THE VIOLENT STAR NUMBER SEVEN

This was regarded as a very auspicious number in Period Seven. In Period Eight, however, the number seven reverts to its original nature, which is that it brings violence and bloodshed associated with metal energy such as knives and guns. It also stands for burglary and getting cheated. If the Number Seven Star flies into a your bedroom sector, be careful.

The best defense against it is to use yang water. Flowing water will dissolve all the violent energy brought by it. Water has the power to exhaust the metal energy of seven. Do not place crystals or windchimes in the West sector in 2004 as this is where this star resides in 2004. In 2005, the Number Seven Star is in the Northeast. In case it is not possible to move your water feature to the Northeast sector in 2005, you can place an image of a rhinoceros to press down hard on the potential of being robbed, mugged, or cheated.

All-metal windchimes act as a remedy against the Illness Star.

A picture of a large rhinoceros will help to counter the affliction of the Violent Star Number Seven.

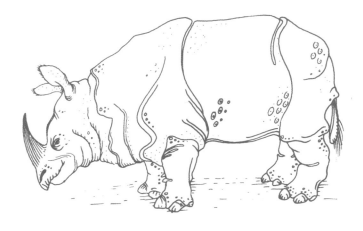

PART FIVE

EMPOWERMENT TECHNIQUES

THE KEY TO **FENG SHUI** PRACTICE IS TO UNDERSTAND THAT ALL CHI—GOOD OR BAD—NEEDS TO BE ACTIVATED FOR ITS EFFECTS TO MANIFEST. USUALLY GOOD AND BAD LUCK IS ACTIVATED WITHOUT OUR REALIZATION. FOR INSTANCE, OPENING A DOOR ACTIVATES THE CHI OF THE SPACE AROUND IT; TURNING ON BRIGHT LIGHTS ACTIVATES THE CHI IN THE LIT SPACE. SOUNDS AND ACTIVITY—SUCH AS CHILDREN LAUGHING OR FISH SWIMMING—CAUSE CHI TO MANIFEST GOOD OR BAD ENERGY. **FENG SHUI** TECHNIQUES CAN STRENGTHEN THE ACCUMULATION AND RELEASE OF SPECIFIC TYPES OF GOOD LUCK CHI, SUCH AS WEALTH LUCK OR RELATIONSHIP LUCK. THESE TECHNIQUES OFFER AMAZING RESULTS WHEN PRACTICED WITH THE COMPASS FORMULAS THAT TELL US WHEN A SECTOR IN THE HOUSE HAS GOOD OR BAD LUCK, OR WHEN A DIRECTION BRINGS US GOOD OR BAD LUCK.

CHAPTER 17
WATER EMPOWERING TECHNIQUES

✳ A LONG-STANDING TAOIST FENG SHUI MASTER ONCE TOLD ME, "IF YOU WANT TO USE FENG SHUI TO IMPROVE YOUR FINANCES, YOU MUST KNOW HOW TO FIND THE MONEY SPOT IN YOUR HOUSE OR PROPERTY, AND THEN YOU MUST BUILD A WATER FEATURE THERE. A BEAUTIFUL SWIMMING POOL IS GOOD."

When you have located the wealth spot in your property, you can activate money luck by incorporating a water feature or image there.

He was insistent that water feng shui based on Flying Star charts (*see* Chapter 15) is very potent for improving money luck. There are different feng shui theories about using water to activate wealth luck, but the

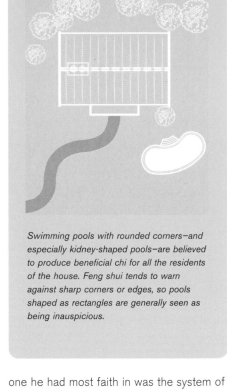

Swimming pools with rounded corners—and especially kidney-shaped pools—are believed to produce beneficial chi for all the residents of the house. Feng shui tends to warn against sharp corners or edges, so pools shaped as rectangles are generally seen as being inauspicious.

one he had most faith in was the system of feng shui that activates the Water Star or *siang sin* (the facing star), the wealth star of the Flying Star chart.

He said, "When you build a suitable yang water feature where a lucky Water Star is found, money will start to flow in." According to Flying Star feng shui, this wealth spot is where the "Water Star Eight" is located. Water always stands for wealth in feng shui, and the number eight is the most auspicious of the nine numbers when it refers to money and success in financial

FINDING THE WEALTH SPOT

matters. In every house, there are good and bad spots for placing water.

To empower your wealth spot, you need to activate it with an auspicious water feature—this may be outside in the garden or inside the house, especially in living areas frequented by residents. Identifying exactly where these wealth spots are takes into account certain time formulas, since all luck sectors, including money luck sectors, change over time.

Activating these sectors requires the building of small water features such as pools, ponds, or waterfalls. You can also use ready-made water features made of fiberglass or crystals.

If you have a garden, it is beneficial to activate the Water Star Eight in the garden with a significant water feature, preferably one that is deep and filled with clean, clear water. You can simultaneously activate the Water Star Eight inside the home itself, and if you like, you can also activate it in all the public rooms of your home.

In feng shui terms, water always represents wealth.

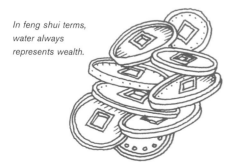

BASED ON FLYING STAR METHODS, THE WEALTH SPOT IN ANY HOME OR BUILDING IS WHERE THE WATER STAR 8 IS LOCATED. IF YOU HAVE A PERIOD SEVEN HOUSE, FIND YOUR WATER STAR 8 LOCATION BELOW (SEE PAGES 128–129 IF UNSURE ABOUT THE FACING DIRECTION):

IF YOUR HOUSE IS FACING...	WATER STAR EIGHT WILL BE IN THE...
SOUTH 1	Northeast
SOUTH 2 OR 3	Southwest
NORTH 1	North
NORTH 2 OR 3	South
EAST 1	Northeast
EAST 2 OR 3	Southwest
WEST 1	Southeast
WEST 2 OR 3	Northwest
NORTHEAST 1	East
NORTHEAST 2 OR 3	West
NORTHWEST 1	Center
NORTHWEST 2 OR 3	Center
SOUTHWEST 1	North
SOUTHWEST 2 OR 3	South
SOUTHEAST 1	East
SOUTHEAST 2 OR 3	West

Living, dining, and family rooms all benefit when the Water Star Eight corner is activated with small water features such as a rotating crystal sphere or a zen-like water feature. Apartment dwellers should also activate the Water Star Eight inside their homes. If the Water Star Eight is located on a patio or balcony that has a big picture window view, the Water Star takes on increased potency.

Similarly, if the Water Star Eight sector corresponds to the front of the house, it will be doubly auspicious. Ensure you place the water feature on the left-hand side of the main door (from the inside of the house looking out).

If you don't, the male partner may succumb to ideas of infidelity. Activating the Water Star Eight for the whole house activates the big Tai Chi of the house; activating individual rooms in the house activates the small Tai Chi. Both are equally potent in bringing wealth luck.

The fresh, flowing water of a fountain helps to energize wealth luck.

When the Water Star Eight is in the same sector as the main door, it is considered to be doubly auspicious. Activate the luck by putting a water feature in this sector.

CAUTION!

✳ **DON'T** place the water feature on the right-hand side of the main door (inside looking out). Water on the right of the main door can cause the husband to develop a roving eye!

ACTIVATING YOUR WATER FEATURE

AFTER YOU HAVE SUCCESSFULLY LOCATED YOUR WEALTH SPOT AND BUILT YOUR WATER FEATURE, IT IS IMPORTANT TO ACTIVATE THE FEATURE. HERE ARE SOME ACTIONS YOU ABSOLUTELY MUST TAKE TO ENSURE YOUR WATER FEATURE IS PROPERLY EMPOWERED:

1 Place the image of a dragon somewhere near the water feature. The dragon can be inside the water or at the side of the pond or waterfall. When there is a dragon nearby, the water will then be transformed into a powerful symbol of wealth luck.

2 Place a light somewhere near the water so that you can turn it on for at least three hours each day or night. This brings a burst of yang energy to the water feature. If it is located outside the house and receives copious amounts of sunshine, the light is not vital, but if it is inside the home you must have a light turned on.

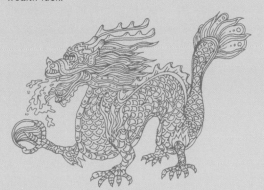

3 Place either fish or plants in the water to add life energy. When there is no life in the water, it can become yin water, which is unable to activate wealth luck. Fish—especially auspicious fish such as the goldfish, arrowana, or colorful guppies—bring the symbolism of abundance to your fishpond. Ensure your fish are happy and well-fed and that the water quality is correctly balanced for them. When fish appear lethargic and unhappy, they cannot create good luck for you. Ensure you have a good filtration system to continuously clean and oxygenate the water.

4 Finally, make sure that the water is kept "happy." You must not let it absorb your unhappiness or quarrelsome vibrations. The happier the residents of the home, the more auspicious the water will be. If you have a shouting match in the house, try not to have it in front of your water feature.

CREATING A FLOW OF WATER

✳ BUILDING A WATERFALL THAT BRINGS A FLOW OF AUSPICIOUS WATER TOWARD YOUR HOUSE IS AN AMAZINGLY POWERFUL WAY OF CREATING A FLOW OF GOOD FORTUNE AND RICHES TO YOUR HOME. IT BENEFITS THE ENTIRE FAMILY AND ALL OTHER RESIDENTS, INCLUDING HOUSEHOLD EMPLOYEES.

The waterfall suggests a flow of water, which is not the same as a water feature. A water feature symbolizes a body of wealth, while a flow is representative of an income stream.

The aim of having good feng shui is to ensure your family wealth is protected, and that it swells and expands with the years. This kind of feng shui usually benefits from having a body of water such as a swimming pool. A flow of water, however, suggests a continuous inflow of income.

When building a flow of water around your home, it is important that the flow is inward and that it passes your main door in an auspicious direction. If you build a waterfall in your garden, make sure the water passes your front door correctly and also that it does not visibly flow away from your house.

When there is a natural flow of water in, near, or around your property, consult the Yellow Emperor Classic of Internal Medicine on auspicious water flows rather than the Flying Star formula. The Yellow Emperor's ancient manuscript on feng shui is said to have been given to him by the Lady of Nine Heavens. He used it to inform the layout of his palaces and thus succeed in vanquishing his enemies and reuniting the people across the land. Since then, the work has been consulted with reference to landscape feng shui subjects.

Garden ponds can bring excellent wealth luck to residents provided they are kept clean.

AUSPICIOUS FLOW OF WATER PAST THE MAIN DOOR

WHEN YOU ARE LOOKING TO BUY OR BUILD A HOUSE AND YOU WISH IT TO BE EMPOWERED TO BRING YOU WEALTH FROM THE WATER TRY TO BUY OR BUILD ONE THAT IS ORIENTED SO THAT THE FLOW OF WATER IS AUSPICIOUS. THE INSTRUCTIONS FROM THE WATER DRAGON CLASSIC ARE AS FOLLOWS:

✳ When the water flows past the main door (from inside looking out) from left to right, make sure that the house and the main door are facing a cardinal direction, that is, North, South, East, or West.

✳ When the water flows past the main door from right to left (from inside looking out), make sure that the house and the main door are facing a secondary direction, that is, Northwest, Southwest, Southeast, or Northeast.

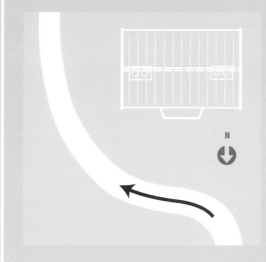

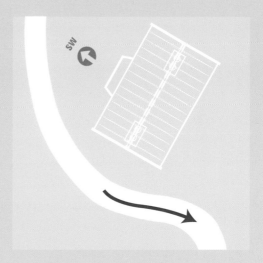

Water flows can bring great good fortune, but it can be difficult to direct the flow correctly. In many instances, building the water dragon (*see* page 280) in the garden has been fraught with difficulties when applying the water formulas of the Yellow Emperor Classic.

I would advise anyone wanting to build a waterfall to let it flow into a pond and not into a flow of water. The pond into which the waterfall flows should be located in the Water Star Eight location.

AUSPICIOUS WATER FLOWS: FURTHER EXAMPLES

SEVERAL FLOWS JOINING THE MAIN FLOW

WATER FLOWING INTO AN ENCLOSED POOL

CHAPTER 18

ACTIVATING MOUNTAIN STAR LUCK FOR RELATIONSHIPS

✳ THE MOUNTAIN STARS OF THE FLYING STAR SYSTEM OF FENG SHUI GOVERN ALL ASPECTS OF RELATIONSHIP AND HEALTH LUCK. WHEN YOUR ROOM IS VISITED BY AN AUSPICIOUS MOUNTAIN STAR, YOU WILL HAVE EXCELLENT RELATIONSHIP AND HEALTH LUCK.

Luck manifests in the way people react to you: with warmth, support, and goodwill. You will find it easy to make friends and will feel that the world is an agreeable place. When you activate an auspicious Mountain Star with the correct placement of mountain symbols, your relationships will become the source of extreme good fortune and you will enjoy good health as well.

Many of the feng shui masters from Hong Kong recommend mountain landscape paintings as part of their practice. A Taoist master explained to me that mountains are not only powerful symbols of support, but that they also signify the essence of the celestial dragon. It was then that I was introduced to the concept of Mountain Stars—the sitting stars or chor sin of feng shui terminology. When you activate the lucky Mountain Stars, your family luck and your descendants' luck will be superior, you will live to a ripe old age, and you will be able to enjoy your children and grandchildren.

Mountain peaks are yang energy and symbolize the essence of the celestial dragon.

✳ ACTIVATING THE MOUNTAIN STAR

There are several factors to consider when activating the Mountain Star Eight in any building. Those who own property will benefit from activating the Mountain Star Eight in their garden with a significant wall feature, preferably one that is high and clearly seen as a special feature of that part

FINDING THE AUSPICIOUS MOUNTAIN STAR EIGHT

✳ **BASED ON FLYING STAR FENG SHUI** (SEE CHAPTER 15), THE EXCELLENT HEALTH AND RELATIONSHIP SPOT IN ANY HOME OR BUILDING IS WHERE THE MOUNTAIN STAR EIGHT IS LOCATED. THOSE OF YOU WITH PERIOD SEVEN HOUSES CAN FIND THE MOUNTAIN STAR EIGHT LOCATION AS FOLLOWS:

IF YOUR HOUSE IS FACING...	MOUNTAIN STAR EIGHT WILL BE IN THE...
SOUTH 1	North
SOUTH 2 OR 3	South
NORTH 1	Northeast
NORTH 2 OR 3	Southwest
EAST 1	Southeast
EAST 2 OR 3	Northwest
WEST 1	Northeast
WEST 2 OR 3	Southwest
NORTHEAST 1	North
NORTHEAST 2 OR 3	South
NORTHWEST 1	East
NORTHWEST 2 OR 3	West
SOUTHWEST 1	East
SOUTHWEST 2 OR 3	West
SOUTHEAST 1	Center
SOUTHEAST 2 OR 3	Center

When Mountain Star Eight is activated in gardens with a high wall feature it is especially auspicious.

of the garden. They can simultaneously activate the Mountain Star Eight inside the home itself in all of the most important rooms where the family gathers, for example, the family room, the living room, and the dining room.

These rooms all benefit from activating the Mountain Star Eight corner with a mountain symbol. This can be a crystal geode that looks like a mountain or it can be a magnificent mountain photograph or painting. Those living in apartments have no choice but to activate the Mountain Star Eight inside their homes. If the Mountain Star Eight is located on a patio or balcony that has a big picture-window type view, and there is a view of mountains in the distance, the flying Mountain Star Eight takes on increased potency.

CHAPTER 19

USING SYMBOLS OF GOOD FORTUNE

✳ SYMBOLISM IS AN INTEGRAL PART OF FENG SHUI PRACTICE, ALTHOUGH IT IS SOMETIMES BRUSHED ASIDE AS INCONSEQUENTIAL. WITHOUT SYMBOLISM, FENG SHUI WOULD BE DIFFICULT TO UNDERSTAND AND PROBABLY IMPOSSIBLE TO PRACTICE.

Amulets are worn by many feng shui experts as protection against robbery and danger while traveling.

All of the remedies and cures needed to overcome feng shui afflictions are based on their symbolic overtones, usually associated with their element attributes and their protective or enhancing attributes.

Symbolic feng shui is one of the easiest aspects of feng shui practice. By merely placing decorative objects that symbolize vibrant good luck in a particular room, or wearing jewelry with a special feng shui symbol on the body, we can enhance the living chi around us, making our space and our auras a great deal more positive and auspicious.

Symbolism gives substance to the practice of feng shui in a contemporary context, as it complements all the formulas and techniques of feng shui practice. Symbols can be used as remedies or as decorative objects and there are symbols of prosperity, wealth, health, love, education, romance, and various types of success catalysts that enhance career luck and other aspirations. It is impossible to offer a complete list of good fortune symbols, since there are simply so many of them, but some popular symbols of good fortune have become standard to the practice of feng shui.

SYMBOLS OF WEALTH AND PROSPERITY

THE SAILING SHIP brings wealth from the winds and the waters. A golden sailing ship with its hold loaded with faux ingots and diamonds sailing into your house or office from your best Kua direction should bring increased income. The more ships you have the better, as each ship symbolizes a major source of income. Having more than one ship brings you many sources of income.

GOOD FORTUNE COINS bring wealth from heaven and earth. Grouped in threes, sixes, or nines, they are activated when tied with a red string or ribbon. When installing new carpet, get a few hundred of these coins, tie them in red, and place them under the carpet. Wealthy Chinese line their walls and floors with these good fortune coins when they build new homes. The coins can also be glued onto invoice books, stuck to cash registers, or taped to telephones and fax machines. They can even be the inspiration for feng shui jewelry.

WEALTH SPOUTING MONGOOSE brings wealth from the Gods. This is a lesser-known symbol of prosperity, but it is extremely powerful in bringing business luck. It resembles the wealth spouting rat that is carried by the Tibetan wealth Buddhas (known as Dzambhalas).

Images of this auspicious creature are best placed at table level, either on a bookcase or on the desk.

THREE-LEGGED TOAD attracts wealth and money into the home. The toad or frog as a symbol of money-making success is part of the many legends surrounding the Eight Immortals. The Chinese also believe that spawn of the frog falls from heaven, like dew, and that the spittle of the toad has powerful medicinal qualities. Indeed, one of the most popular cures for a sore throat caused by excessive smoking is the boiled spittle of the frog. The three-legged toad should be placed at floor level and the best places are under chairs and sofas. They can be facing in any direction, although many people prefer them not to look directly out of the house.

FISH SYMBOLS always signify abundance. The ultimate feng shui fish is the golden arrowana. The carp and the goldfish were the favorites long ago. All households can benefit from having a fishpond populated with these little symbols of abundance. Fish also come with happy water, which is one of the most potent energizers for wealth.

THE TRIBUTE HORSE brings wealth from the Eight Directions. This is the horse usually shown with the God of Wealth, Tsai Shen Yeh, and it is usually laden with ingots and other precious items. The tribute horse should be placed inside the house near the foyer and it should be heading in, not out. If possible, let the horse come in from your best Sheng Chi direction, as this signifies wealth luck.

FIVE-CLAWED DRAGONS are probably the most potent symbols of good fortune. Placing the five-clawed Imperial dragon image along the East wall of the living room will attract both wealth and success because the dragon epitomizes the pinnacle of success and prosperity luck. Remember to place a dragon beside your water feature, but do not make your dragon images too big. The nine-dragon screen should not be too large, since you may not be able to bear the power of nine large dragons. Usually, smaller images are best, especially when they are made in genuine gold and set as fine jewelry.

THE RED BAT brings abundance and great prosperity, especially when shown in a circular gathering of five red bats. This emblem is extremely popular as it signifies the five blessings from heaven, which are longevity, wealth, health, love of virtue, and natural death. A group of five red bats is the favorite Taoist symbol of prosperity and it can often be found on Chinese ceramics and furniture.

THE CHI LIN, or dragon horse, brings prosperity, success, longevity, illustrious offspring, and all-around good fortune in your finances. A single Chi Lin brings success at work, so it should be placed in the office. Placed as a pair, the Chi Lin protects the home and the family spirit; placed in threes, it overcomes the Three Killings, an annual feng shui affliction.

GOLDEN INGOTS always bring wealth and prosperity. They can be used in a variety of ways. You can be as creative as you wish, since there are no taboos to their placement in the home.

GOLDEN RICE BOWL AND CHOPSTICKS are excellent symbols of financial and work success. They signify that if you love your work, you will never lose your job and if you do not like your job, you will soon find something that you do like. The golden rice bowl suggests your livelihood is golden. Sets of golden bowls and chopsticks make auspicious wedding gifts.

FUK LUK SAU are the Three Star Gods that signify wealth, health, and prosperity. They are usually placed in the dining room and their presence in the house ensures continuity of good fortune. You should get the best you can afford, as these are the most basic good fortune symbols.

GEM TREES made from semiprecious stones signify the wealth tree and are extremely auspicious for bringing wealth luck into the home or office. The best are those encrusted with yellow gemstones, usually citrines, as these signify wealth luck. Place gem trees at table level and choose those with a solid trunk. This will ensure that your sources of wealth are strong and solid.

FUK   **LUK**   **SAU**

SYMBOLS OF LONGEVITY

THE CRANE signifies long life and good health. Flying cranes painted by the hundreds are much sought after as they symbolize immortality and are strongly identified with the attributes of long life, happiness, and smoothness in all endeavors. Place them as decorative images in your garden (in the South) or inside the house as part of furniture or ceramics decoration.

THE TORTOISE is the best symbol of longevity to have around the house. Have a real tortoise or turtle if you can. If not, then keep its image at the back of the house. The tortoise has multidimensional meanings and is one of the four celestial creatures, in fact, the only one still in existence. Many feng shui experts believe that the tortoise is the one symbol everyone should have in their home and office.

THE GOD OF LONGEVITY, also known as Sau, is probably the most popular of the Taoist deities. He is usually depicted in paintings or on ceramic and porcelain. Sau symbolizes a smooth and long life as well as a happy old age surrounded by children and grandchildren.

THE DRAGON TORTOISE not only brings a long and fruitful life but also a successful one filled with blessings. The dragon tortoise brings a good name, honor, and recognition to the family, and fabulous long life and good health to the patriarch. No home should be without the dragon tortoise. Worn on the left hand, it brings protection from premature death and courage in the face of unexpected trouble.

THE BAMBOO is durable and resilient, signifying longevity and fortitude in the face of adversity. The bamboo gives you the resilience to succeed in anything you undertake. Having a bamboo plant in the front part of your garden ensures that there will be longevity in any business you undertake. You will never lose your position or your wealth.

THE DEER brings speed, endurance, and long life. Phonetically the Chinese word for deer, lu, sounds like the word for good income and prosperity. The deer represents longevity of income and wealth. It is an excellent image to have in the office, especially when draped with a necklace of auspicious good fortune coins.

THE JADE CICADA is an emblem of immortality and also an amulet against office politics. It is best used as an amulet because carrying it inside your bag wards off premature death. It is also regarded as a symbol of long life, happiness, and eternal youth.

OTHER SYMBOLS OF GOOD FORTUNE

✱ **THE LONGEVITY SIGN** creates long-life chi and is an extremely powerful energizer of good health. Its presence around you is like an affirmation of good fortune attributes.

✱ **THE MYSTICAL KNOT** is a sign much favored by Chinese feng shui practitioners. It signifies endless love, endless opportunities, and success in all the professions. The mystical knot is also a special sign that is particularly auspicious during the current Period Eight and it is associated with many success-invoking rituals. Keep this symbol everywhere at home, at work, and even worn as a talisman of good fortune.

✱ **THE DOUBLE-HAPPINESS SYMBOL** is an affirmation of incredible happiness brought about by love, marriage, and excellent family life. It spells joyousness and cause for celebration so this symbol is excellent as a marriage-enhancing talisman. Placed in the Southwest or, better still, worn as a ring or a pendant, it attracts the happiness associated with marriage and family life.

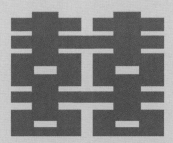

CHAPTER 20
WEALTH-ACTIVATING METHODS

 ✳ IN ADDITION TO DISPLAYING SYMBOLS OF GOOD FORTUNE IN YOUR HOME, YOU CAN ALSO TRY SOME OF THE WEALTH-ACTIVATING RITUALS AND ACTIVITIES THAT BRING PROSPERITY AND SAFEGUARD FAMILY FORTUNES. HERE ARE SOME IDEAS YOU MIGHT LIKE TO TRY.

Creating and consecrating a wealth vase ensures the preservation and growth of a family's fortunes. Chinese families keep their wealth vases forever and pass them down from one generation to the next.

A wealth vase may be made of earth or metal elements—porcelain, crystal, copper, brass, silver, or gold. The more precious the material, the more auspicious will the luck be that it brings.

The most important things to remember about the wealth vase are:

✳ its ingredients (*see* opposite)

✳ the method used to close it (*see* opposite)

✳ It must be kept inside a special, locked cupboard

✳ It should not face the front door, as this symbolizes wealth draining away.

You can make more than one wealth vase. When you become rich, you can make a wealth vase filled with better quality ingredients. This will increase your wealth even further.

HOW TO MAKE A WEALTH VASE

1 SELECT A VASE WITH A COVER.
Ideally, the wealth vase should have
a fairly wide mouth, a slender neck,
a fat body and a wide, solid base.

2 GATHER THESE ITEMS and place
them inside the vase:

✱ A God of Wealth in miniature.
This can be the laughing Buddha,
Tsai Sheng Yeh, or any of the wealth
gods that are part of the pantheon of
your culture. Ensure the Wealth God
inside the vase is facing inward.
✱ Three gold coins tied with red
string to signify wealth multiplied
tenfold.
✱ Nine Chinese coins in a red
packet to signify money donated
to charity.
✱ Ten clear crystals to ensure
a smooth life.
✱ Ten lapis lazuli globes to signify
the best of the world's treasures.
✱ Five types of dried foodstuffs
wrapped inside plastic bags.
Suggested foodstuffs are rice, dhal,
barley, sorghum, millet, or beans.
✱ Packets of semiprecious stones
or real diamonds and gold jewelry.

3 PLACE THE FOLLOWING secret
things inside the wealth vase to
increase its potency:

✱ Earth from a rich man's home.
You may not steal it; it must be given
to you willingly.
✱ Money from a rich man's pocket.
Again, it must not be stolen. It must
be given to you, perhaps as change
for your money.
✱ Pictures of six rich men
or women.
✱ A picture of a mansion.
✱ Money from nine rich countries.

4 WHEN YOU HAVE FILLED THE VASE
with all the ingredients you have
gathered you will need:

✱ Five pieces of cotton cloth
sewn into squares in the colors of
the five elements.
✱ Five cotton strings in the colors
of the five elements.

5 COVER THE VASE with its own
cover and place the fabric squares
over the cover, first white, then blue,
then green, then red, and finally
yellow on top. Braid the five-colored
string and tie the cloth firmly over
the vase. This effectively seals in the
wealth ingredients.

6 CONSECRATE THE VASE
with incense and aroma
sticks, then place
it inside a cupboard
in your bedroom
or deep inside
your house.

NB: The wealth
vase should
not be easily seen.
Never place anything
above it.

✳ USE SALT RITUALS TO CLEAR ALL YOUR DEBTS

If you are having financial difficulties and are indebted to many people, there are two potent rituals for clearing your debts.

RITUAL 1

1 Each Friday, buy a small packet of sea salt or rock salt and add a pinch of it to the cooking salt you are using in the kitchen. Done faithfully over time, it will bring you out of your financial difficulties.

2 When all your debts are reduced to a comfortable level, you can stop the ritual.

RITUAL 2

If your financial problems are severe and there is a danger of legal action, this ritual might help.

1 Take some salt from your cooking salt container on a Friday morning, and place it in a plastic container with some cinnabar powder and a small mirror that has been used to reflect the four corners of the house.

2 Roll two unripe limes in your palm for five minutes. Visualize all your financial problems flowing from your body and into the limes.

3 When you are done, place the limes inside the plastic container.

4 Take the container to a large drain or river and throw the biodegradable contents over your left shoulder into the river and, without looking back, return home.

This ritual is most potent when you do it three Fridays in succession.

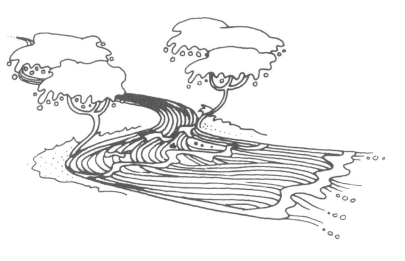

BUILD A SIX-TIER WATERFALL IN THE NORTH TO GET RICH

THERE ARE ONLY THREE SECTORS IN WHICH BUILDING A WATER FEATURE IS BENEFICIAL: THE EAST, THE SOUTHEAST, AND THE NORTH. OF THESE, NORTH IS BEST BECAUSE THIS SECTOR FEATURES THE WATER ELEMENT. BUILDING A SIX-TIER WATERFALL IN THE NORTH SECTOR OF YOUR GARDEN IS ONE OF THE MOST POTENT ACTIVATORS OF PROSPERITY LUCK. THE SIX TIERS REPRESENT CHI FROM HEAVEN.

Your waterfall need not be big, but the water should fall over six ledges. It is important to keep tortoises and fish in your waterfall, so design it carefully, complete with filter systems, and oxygenate the water to keep the fish and tortoises happy. Use auspicious plants to landscape the waterfall. You can place the Tibetan wealth Gods on the ledges. The ritual of having water flow down their bodies is the correct way of invoking the help of the Dzambhalas.

✱ TIBETAN WEALTH GOD
Dzambhala is the Buddhist god of wealth. He is magnificently decorated with jewelry, and has a big belly. His squeezes the neck of a mongoose with his left hand; the mongoose spits out coins or precious stones.

✱ AUSPICIOUS PLANTS
As a general guide, plants that have rounded leaves are auspicious, and the more succulent and green the leaves, the more auspicious the plant. Examples of auspicious plants include the jade plant, the lotus, and water lilies.

PART SIX

PROTECTIVE SYMBOLS AND RITUALS

IN **FENG SHUI**, PROTECTING YOUR HOME OR OFFICE AGAINST BAD CHI IS MORE IMPORTANT THAN THE CREATION OF AUSPICIOUS CHI. YOU WILL ALWAYS BENEFIT FROM USING A DEFENSIVE STRATEGY BEFORE USING **FENG SHUI** TO ENHANCE VARIOUS TYPES OF LUCK. SYMBOLISM PLAYS A BIG ROLE IN **FENG SHUI** AND MANY SYMBOLS ARE USED AS SOLUTIONS TO A RANGE OF FENG SHUI ILLS. THERE IS ALSO A PART OF FENG SHUI PRACTICE THAT IS PROTECTIVE IN NATURE. THIS CONSISTS OF SPACE-CLEARING RITUALS THAT ARE EXCELLENT FOR REFRESHING CHI, AT LEAST TEMPORARILY, UNTIL MORE PERMANENT FENG SHUI IMPROVEMENTS CAN BE MADE.

CHAPTER 21
USING SYMBOLS OF PROTECTION

✳ FENG SHUI PRESCRIBES DIFFERENT METHODS FOR PROTECTING THE HOME AND OFFICE AGAINST MISFORTUNES. THEY RANGE FROM THE SIMPLE PLACEMENT OF DOOR GODS, FU DOGS, AND OTHER PROTECTIVE DEITIES TO THE MORE COMPLEX APPLICATION OF SYMBOLIC CURES AND REMEDIES FOR SPECIFIC FENG SHUI ILLS.

Bad chi is often caused by hostile physical structures and by the passage of time. It can also be due to imbalances of yin and yang cosmic forces in the space around us. When yin is excessively dominant, it can cause fatal occurrences. Hence, we must be protective of our homes.

The Chinese pantheon of symbols and gods offers many items to incorporate into interior décor. You can also use symbols from your own culture. There are no religious connotations attached to the use of Chinese Taoist deities; practitioners can use alternatives from their own traditions.

KUAN KUNG: GOD OF WEALTH

✳ **KUAN KUNG** is the most popular of the Taoist protective deities. He is the God of War and also the God of Wealth. His countenance is fierce and his demeanor intimidating. There are many different versions of Kuan Kung. To protect your business it is best to have a wrathful Kuan Kung on horseback, wearing armor complete with banners and flags. This type of Kuan Kung is usually made of brass and on his body there will be nine dragons. This is the best Kuan Kung for those in competitive businesses or in a profession requiring protection.

Those who live a more sedentary lifestyle might find this Kuan Kung a little too fierce and intimidating. In that case, it is better to have a smaller, seated, less-combative version. Whichever posture of Kuan Kung you select, place it either looking at the front door (from any angle) or behind you if you work from home. Make sure the long sword is placed correctly (that is, pointed at or resting on the floor).

THE FOUR CELESTIAL GUARDIANS

THE GREEN DRAGON, THE CRIMSON PHOENIX, THE BLACK TORTOISE, AND THE WHITE TIGER ARE THE FOUR CELESTIAL GUARDIANS OF FENG SHUI LORE. IN THE OUTER ENVIRONMENT, THEY ARE THE PROTECTIVE HILLS AND MOUNTAINS THAT SURROUND A BUILDING. IN A CITY ENVIRONMENT, HILLS AND MOUNTAINS ARE REPLACED BY THE SURROUNDING BUILDINGS.

According to feng shui, these celestial creatures symbolically protect the home within their embrace. When a home enjoys the physical protection of dragon, tiger, and tortoise hills it is blessed with good fortune. In modern living environments it is usually impossible to enjoy the physical manifestation of the celestial guardians. One way to simulate their presence is to place symbols of them around the home—the dragon on the left of the house (facing out), the tiger on the right, the tortoise at the back, and the phoenix in front. The presence of these symbolic celestial creatures offers protection from bad feng shui.

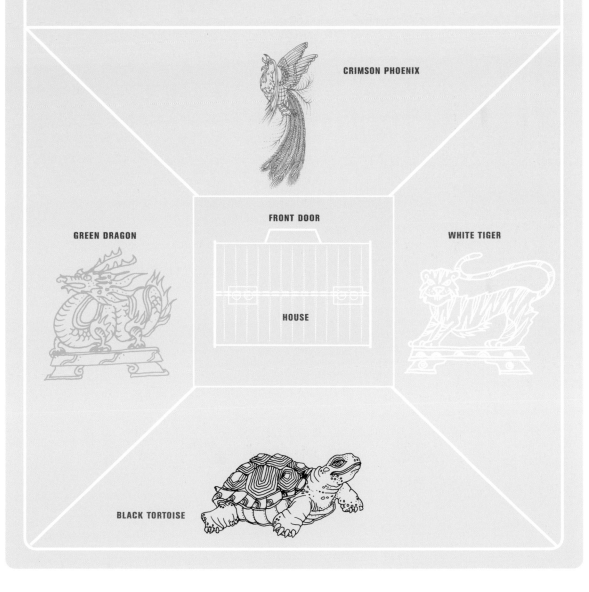

CRIMSON PHOENIX

GREEN DRAGON

FRONT DOOR

HOUSE

WHITE TIGER

BLACK TORTOISE

THE FOUR HEAVENLY KINGS

✳ THESE FOUR CELESTIAL BEINGS ARE KNOWN AS THE GUARDIANS OF THE FOUR DIRECTIONS. THEY ARE INCREDIBLY POWERFUL AND THEIR PRESENCE IN A HOME, ESPECIALLY IF THEY HAVE BEEN PROPERLY CONSECRATED, PROTECTS RESIDENTS FROM EVERY KIND OF MISFORTUNE, EVERY KIND OF EVIL FORCE, AND SPIRIT HARM COMING FROM THE FOUR DIRECTIONS.

MO LI CHING

MO LI HAI

There are stunning images of the four kings, each holding a personalized weapon with supernatural powers. They are always alert to negative influences and under their watchful presence, righteousness, honesty, and good moral character will always prevail in the home. They defend with tireless energy and their powers are said to be invincible. Put them in a place of honor at table level, preferably looking over the living area or at the main door.

MO LI CHING is the guardian of the East. His face is white and he carries both a spear and a sword. His weapon is made from metal, which controls the wood element of the East.

MO LI HAI is the guardian of the West. His face is blue and he carries a mandolin, which spews forth balls of fire. The fire element controls the metal element of the west.

MO LI HUNG is the guardian of the South. His face is red and he holds an umbrella, which, when opened, causes total darkness and when reversed causes earthquakes and tidal waves. Water controls the fire element of the South.

MO LI SHOU is the guardian of the North. He has a black face and he carries a pearl and a snake. Sometimes he is shown with a white rat and an elephant. He is also the guardian of wealth, and the king of the wealth gods.

MO LI HUNG   MO LI SHOU

ZHONG KUEI

The image of the red-robed Zhong Kuei (also spelled Chong Kwei) protects the home against spirit harm. He is usually depicted carrying a sword in his right hand and a flask of wine in the other. He also has a fierce countenance, but he is not as intimidating as Kuan Kung. His presence in any home is enough to "chase away all the ghosts and devils" from your life (that is, troublemakers and those who would seek to harm you).

FU DOGS AND PROTECTION

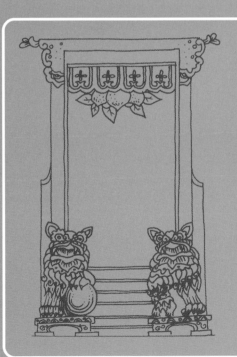

THERE IS A GREAT DEAL OF CONFUSION ABOUT FU DOGS, CHI LINS, AND LIONS. ALL THREE ARE EXCELLENT PROTECTIVE SYMBOLS, BUT LIONS ARE EXTREMELY POTENT AND MAY BE TOO STRONG FOR RESIDENTIAL ABODES. TRY INSTEAD EITHER THE WONDERFUL CHI LINS (WHICH ARE HORSES WITH DRAGON HEADS POPULARLY REGARDED AS THE CHINESE UNICORNS) OR BETTER YET, THE FU DOGS.

It is not difficult to recognize Fu Dogs. They are usually depicted as a pair, the male Fu Dog holding a globe to be placed on the right-hand side (inside looking out) of the door and the female Fu Dog holding a baby on the left side. If you live in an apartment, place them just outside the door. They can be placed at floor level or slightly higher. These wonderful dogs will protect you from being robbed or cheated, as well fending off burglars and harmful people.

CHAPTER 22
CLEARING PERSONAL SPACE RITUALS

CLEARING THE CLUTTER

✳ CHANGING ORIENTATIONS, DIRECTIONS, AND, WHERE POSSIBLE, DOORS IS NECESSARY TO CORRECT BAD FENG SHUI LONG TERM. PHYSICAL CLUTTER CAN ALSO CREATE MENTAL AND SPIRITUAL BLOCKS TO SUCCESS AND WELL-BEING. HOWEVER, SIMPLY DE-JUNKING YOUR HOME OR WORKPLACE WILL NOT NECESSARILY PROVIDE A SOLUTION. WHAT IS VITAL IS FIRST TO DISSOLVE BAD CHI USING SPACE-CLEARING RITUALS, WHICH ARE THE ESSENCE OF FENG SHUI DECLUTTERING.

There are four types of bad chi that space-clearing rituals can help to dispel at least temporarily. The most harmful chi is Chueh Ming Shar Chi, a killing chi that causes residents to suffer total loss—total loss of wealth, good name, descendants, prosperity, and happiness. This is not simply Shar Chi (which is translated as killing breath) but the most harmful chi and needs to be corrected or dispersed. Next is Six Killings Chi, known as Lui Shar Chi, and Five Devils Chi, also known as Wu Kuei Chi. These bring bad luck of a lesser degree. The fourth is hostile chi that brings mild bad luck and is known as Ho Hai Chi.

All four cause bad feng shui to manifest as loss of wealth, illness, loss of loved ones, loss of good name, and so forth. Feng shui offers methods to avoid or overcome these forms of bad chi.

After an argument, burn incense in the room to dispel lingering anger.

You can apply space-clearing practices to your room, your home, or your office. These practices can lighten the energies that surround you and that may have become heavy with imbalance.

It is a good idea to develop a routine to your space-clearing practices so that you will continually freshen up energies around you that may become stale.

You can use these simple methods to dissolve all sick and unhealthy energies, as well as temporarily dissolve inauspicious energies until you can introduce longer-term changes to improve either the orientation or the location of your furniture.

In particular, rooms that have been previously occupied by bedridden or sick persons, or a home that has just had a death in the family, will benefit from space-clearing rituals.

Improving the quality of energy around you can be done in different ways, and all cultures have the equivalent of the Chinese method of feng shui space clearing as well as land or building blessing rituals and ceremonies. How elaborate the rituals and ceremonies are depends on the individual. Some people are more comfortable with quick, simple methods, while others love elaborate ceremonies that involve the burning of fragrant incense accompanied by mantra chanting.

Burn incense around the room each time there is a particularly severe argument in the home, since it clears away any anger that may be lingering in the air and makes for better relationships. Over the years, it will help create greater harmony in the home. There will be fewer disagreements, less flaring of tempers, and less anger.

Do what makes you comfortable. Space clearing done once a month should be adequate. Complete space purification can be done twice a year and at least once just before the start of a new year.

Select from any of the methods that are outlined below as they are all effective in clearing space.

SPACE-CLEARING GUIDELINES

✳ Be clear that what you are doing is space clearing and not space enhancing.

✳ Think seriously and focus your mind on what you are doing.

✳ Relax and understand that you are clearing the energies around you and not praying to or invoking any spirits. This is vital.

✳ Undertake all space-clearing activities in the morning, after the sun has come up. Never undertake space clearing after the sun has set.

✳ Never do space clearing on an overcast or rainy day. You will always get better results when energized by a dose of precious natural yang energy supplied by the morning sun.

✳ Resist the temptation to perform space-clearing rituals for other people. There is an unwritten rule about disturbing the energy of space that does not belong to you unless you are possessed of a protective amulet. Observing this advice will protect you from being inadvertently hurt by hostile spirits that might be present in other people's space and who do not know you. In space clearing we are addressing only the invisible energy lines that affect our personal well-being.

RICE AND SALT RITUAL

THIS IS A POPULAR RITUAL USED BY OLD MASTERS. IT IS USED WHEN ENTERING A NEW HOUSE FOR THE FIRST TIME, OR WHEN TAKING OVER A NEW OFFICE. BEFORE YOU BEGIN THE RITUAL, MIX A PACKET OF RICE WITH A PACKET OF SALT. MAKE SURE YOU HAVE A SUFFICIENT AMOUNT OF THE MIXTURE FOR THE SIZE OF YOUR HOUSE OR OFFICE. SOME PRACTITIONERS RING BELLS AND BURN INCENSE STICKS WHEN THEY PERFORM THIS RITUAL.

1 Move around the perimeter of the house in a clockwise direction and sprinkle a mixture of raw rice grains and raw sea salt. Throw the mixture at the base of the wall and as you do so, think to yourself, "The rice is offered as charity to any wandering spirit so all co-exist in harmony, and the salt cleanses the space of all negative, sick, and hostile energies."

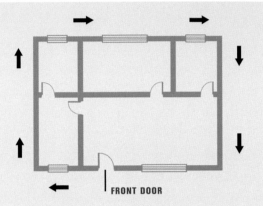

FRONT DOOR

2 After going around the outside of the house, do the inside of the house, going from room to room and moving in a clockwise direction around the room. Throw the rice and salt mixture on the floor and at the base of the walls.

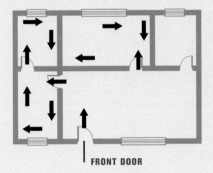

FRONT DOOR

3 At the front door, throw three handfuls from the inside outward and then throw three handfuls from the outside inward.

4 When you have finished, leave the rice and salt until the next day before cleaning them away. Do not use a broom to sweep—use a vacuum cleaner instead. The act of sweeping negates what you have done.

This symbolic power of the pagoda is invoked when it is incorporated into windchimes meant to reduce the bad luck of a particular corner or sector of the home. Some windchimes are made with several layers of roof levels above the rods to simulate the pagoda. The rods cause hostile chi to rise up through the hollow tube to be transformed into auspicious chi. In case any bad chi escapes, the pagoda will capture it.

✳ USING FANS

Historically, an effective way to shield yourself from bad energies was to carry a fan. Ladies usually carried these fans as symbolic protection against energies that might prove harmful. For example, suddenly meeting a funeral procession is considered bad luck and holding a fan can shield you from the excessive yin energy emanating from the funeral procession. Use a metal fan to symbolically wave away any bad energy that may have been left behind by someone else.

✳ USING A PAGODA

Pagodas are circular or octagonal buildings, usually seven or nine levels high. In feng shui, the pagoda symbolizes the best and safest place to capture and imprison negative chi. The pagoda is also an effective prison for wandering spirits that may do harm to the human race. If you hold a symbolic pagoda in your left hand while sprinkling rice and salt with your right hand, any wandering spirit with evil or bad intentions will take fright and run away.

Apartment residents can encourage good chi by opening two windows at a time once a week.

✳ USING AIR

If you live in a highrise apartment or condominium, or if you live in the mountains, you should incorporate the crisp and clear air into your space-clearing practice. Once a week, open your windows two at a time and invite the air from the outside to enter your home. Allow air to sail in slowly. If you open all the windows at the same time, air comes in too fast and can become hostile and damaging. Instead allow the air to flow in slowly and, if you can, let it meander by opening one window in one room and another in different room.

USING A FENG SHUI MIRROR

YOU CAN USE A CIRCULAR MIRROR TO ABSORB ALL THE BAD AND STALE ENERGY IN A HOME. SELECT A SMALL CIRCULAR MIRROR, ABOUT THREE INCHES (8 CM) IN DIAMETER. DESIGNATE IT AS YOUR FENG SHUI MIRROR AND ALWAYS USE THE SAME MIRROR. MIRRORS USED FOR SPACE CLEARING SHOULD NOT BE USED FOR OTHER PURPOSES.

1 Move around the rooms in the house, holding the mirror to reflect the walls and each corner. Concentrate on dark corners and places that are seldom used. Be especially thorough with toilets and kitchens.

2 When you have gone through the whole house, soak the mirror in salt water for a few minutes. This serves to cleanse and dissolve all the bad energy collected in the mirror.

3 Wrap the mirror in a cloth and keep it inside a cupboard.

NOTE
It is good practice to perform this sort of space clearing at least once a month.

This creates a flow that is not only gentle but also meandering.

The best time to do this is during sunrise, when the energies of the day are pure and crisp. During summer months when yang energy is strong, clearing the energies of your home at sunrise brings in yang energy that is not excessively strong. In the winter months you can do it during late morning or early afternoon when the sun gets stronger. While it might seem foolish to bring cold air into the home, the air actually brings in fresh yang energy that is good for the home.

The best time to open windows is at daybreak when the sun's yang energy is not too strong.

USING SUNSHINE

A VARIATION OF THE USE OF AIR IS THE USE OF SUNSHINE. NOTHING IS AS EFFECTIVE AS SUNLIGHT TO GET RID OF STALE ENERGIES CAUSED BY NEGLECT OF THE HOUSE.

✳ Open all the rooms and draw all the curtains to douse the whole house with sunshine. Sunshine is the greatest source of the precious life force—the yang energy that brings such wonderful good luck.

✳ If you have a garden, ensure that trees and plants do not become so dense as to block out the sun completely.

✳ Hang faceted crystals on all the windows that face the West to catch the strong afternoon sun, and on the East side of your home, open the windows to greet the morning sun.

✳ When you clean your furniture and floors, occasionally use clean water that has soaked up the sun for at least three hours to energize it.

✳ USING SOUNDS

The best application of sound is the use of special instruments like bells, cymbals, and bowls. Chanting mantras also works wonders. Indeed, almost all the religions of the world use a combination of sounds and prayers to bless any space. This is probably because sounds are so effective in purifying the vibrations of any space.

I have been told by Master practitioners that the simple act of clashing cymbals at the entrance to shops and at the four corners of rooms is sufficient to scare away negative energies. The sharp clanging sound of cymbals also scares away lingering naughty spirits who prefer to move to quieter areas. If you have a pair of cymbals, you can clash them three times in front of your main door before moving around your rooms in a clockwise direction and clashing the cymbals three times whenever you reach a corner.

WITH A BANG!

WHEN YOU SUSPECT THAT YOU HAVE A SEVERE PROBLEM WITH YOUR LIVING SPACE, AN EXCELLENT WAY TO REMOVE NEGATIVE ENERGY IS TO SET OFF A STRING OF FIRECRACKERS. THE USE OF A LOUD SOUND IS VERY EFFECTIVE IN CLEARING THE ENERGY INSIDE THE HOME.

A Chinese custom practiced during the lunar New Year involves hanging long strings of firecrackers from the highest level of the home down to the ground. The firecrackers are lighted from the ground up. These strings of firecrackers can be ten stories high, and they can take a full half hour to burn all the way to the top, in the process giving off loud noise and scattering bits of red paper all round the front entrance. Doing this is most auspicious since it ensures that the coming year will be cleansed of negative and inauspicious circumstances.

You can do the same with bells and bowls made of metal, especially those that have been designed to produce exquisite sounds. Some of the best bells and bowls give off sharp, clear notes when their sides are hit or rubbed with a leather or wooden mallet. They are often adorned with auspicious symbols or the wonderful omani mantras.

Bells are not rung like church bells. Bells used in space clearing are best when struck with a small wooden mallet. In the toilets and kitchens, storerooms and rooms that are not occupied, beat the bell a little louder than normal. These rooms will benefit immensely from the cleansing and any lingering stagnant energies will be dissipated.

Do the same thing with metallic bowls. Singing bowls are extremely powerful for completely purifying the immediate space around you (*see* pages 194–197 for a detailed description of using singing bowls for space clearing).

✳ USING LIGHTS

Another excellent method of cleansing the energy inside the home, especially when these energies have become excessively yin, is to use lights. Energy in the home turns yin when there has been a death in the family, especially if it occurs after a long period of illness.

After a funeral, you should wash the room, open all the windows, and turn on all

USING FRAGRANCES

✳ There has been a growing movement to popularize the use of fragrances to cleanse the space around us. Fragrances enhance the living space enormously. Lavender oil soothes the mind and brings out the creativity in people. Different types of fragrances are recommended to evoke different moods and to achieve different goals. Scented oils and waters lighten and enhance the energies around us.

the lights. You can also place Christmas lights in a broad-mouthed bowl and turn on the lights each night for three hours. Do this forty-nine nights in a row and the room will have been re-energized with a massive dose of yang energy. You can use this method in conjunction with the incense methods described below.

You can also use candles. Light six, eight, or nine candles. The numbers six and eight are very lucky; while nine represents the fullness of heaven and earth. Allowing the candles to burn continuously for three hours each night is sufficient. You can also use an oil lamp since it is clean, efficient, and economical. Remember that when using candles you should never leave an open flame unattended.

✳ USING INCENSE

Incense is believed to clean the energies in the air. This is not to be confused with space clearing which clears the air of negative chi. Purification involves dissolving bad energy and transforming it into good energy.

Clear your space first before attempting to purify it with incense and other enhancers. Space purification creates a good flow of auspicious Sheng Chi, and using incense is extremely effective because it represents the potent combination of fire with fragrance.

You can use any kind of fragrant incense for space purification, but use a special incense burner that has a handle. The incense holder should enable you to burn the incense while moving around the rooms of the home. This allows the smoke that rises from the burning herbs to mingle with the energies of each room, thereby purifying it.

The quality of space purification depends on the quality of the incense that you use:

✳ The Chinese and Indians prefer to use sandalwood incense for rituals and general purposes.

✳ Incense from India and Nepal tends to be stronger and more pungent and may be too intense for small homes.

The choice of incense is a personal matter. Try a few before settling on the one you like.

USING SPECIAL MOUNTAIN INCENSE

Incense purification works best when you burn mountain incense made from herbs or small plants that grow in the pure air of high mountains. A special blend of herbal incense collected from high up in the Himalayan mountain range contains extremely fragrant incense powder made from wild mountain plants from the Solu Khumbu region, near the base camp of Mt Everest. This holy region of the Himalayas is much revered by the Buddhists of Nepal, Tibet, and the surrounding area. They believe that the Lotus Buddha, the glorious Padmasambhava who brought Buddhism to Tibet, hid many of his secret teachings in caves found in this region.

The mountain plants that come from this region are considered to be so pure and special that it is extremely difficult to obtain them. You can look for your own blend of incense and when you find something you like, stick with it. To use this incense, burn a small piece of charcoal in an incense burner and sprinkle a tiny bit of the herbal incense mix on top. It is very fragrant. Let this fragrance permeate all the rooms of your home. Move in a clockwise direction and smell the incense as you move around the rooms.

CHANTING THE OMANI MANTRA

It is an excellent idea to chant a simple mantra as you move around the room with the incense burner. As the smoke rises and spreads around the room, chant the purifying omani mantra into the smoke so that as the smoke spreads, the mantra symbolically blesses the home.

The mantra is a six-syllable mantra that is chanted daily by every Buddhist of the Mahayana tradition, but it is also a mantra that is used by many non-Buddhists who recognize it as a powerful aid for their meditative practices. The mantra is Om Mani Padme Hum.

Buddhists recognize this as the mantra of their Buddha Chenrezig, the Compassionate Buddha, who is called Avalokiteswara in India and the Goddess of Mercy, Kuan Yin, by the Chinese, and Canon by the Japanese. By whatever name this Buddha is known, this mantra is regarded as a most powerful mantra. Those of you who wish to do so may chant this mantra 108 times while purifying the home with incense.

After you have finished all the rooms, silently think to yourself:

"I dedicate this purification practice and the chanting of this mantra to the harmony of my home, to the harmonious relationships between the members of my family, and to our harmonious relationships with outsiders so that we may all experience continued good health and happiness."

Non-Buddhists can also chant this mantra or can chant any other kind of purification prayer. The use of the mantra is optional. It is not really a part of feng shui. But I have discovered that incorporating any spiritual aspect in feng shui's Space purification adds much to the practice.

Kuan Yin, the Goddess of Mercy, offered the original mantra Om Mani Padme Hum.

✳ SINGING BOWL THERAPY– SPACE PURIFICATION

Let the singing bowl sit comfortably on a special cushion in your upturned left palm. Spend a few seconds tuning in to the heaviness of the bowl. Then take up the wooden mallet and gently strike the rim of the bowl.

Each person will hear a different kind of humming or singing sound. Some will hear deep undertones followed by a throbbing sound while others will focus in on undulating overtones. Strike the bowl again and again to get familiar with the sounds that envelope the room. Allow yourself to enter the sound waves created by closing your eyes lightly.

Over time you will become familiar with the bowl and be able to feel the vibrations of its sounds. Eventually, through the tones and undulating vibrations, you will be able to detect the initial disharmonies. After a short time, they improve and then harmonize. This is because the sound of the singing bowl will start to balance the energies around it. Once the energies become balanced, the singing bowl sings melodiously, converting the wonderful auspicious chi around the home into a delightful humming that soothes and calms you.

EXTERNAL CHARACTERISTICS

Singing bowls are found in different cultures where sounds feature prominently in spiritual rituals. The best singing bowls come from the Himalayan region in the Katmandu valley of Nepal. Originally brought to the West by spiritual tourists and New Age enthusiasts who sought to understand the sound phenomena in prayers and special ceremonials, the singing bowl is today enjoying ever increasing popularity.

Singing bowls come in different sizes. The ratio of the circumference and depth can vary but the bowl should ideally have a shining golden color, be fairly thick, and be perfectly round. Singing bowls can be polished or matte. They can be in any metallic shade. The most important characteristic is that when singing bowls are rubbed, hit, or tapped they produce a wonderful, pure sound. Even if you just tap the bowl with your fingernail it will emit a beautiful sound.

SEVEN TYPES OF METALS

The quality of the sound is determined by the thickness of the bowl's rim. Its humming resonance and singing vibrations

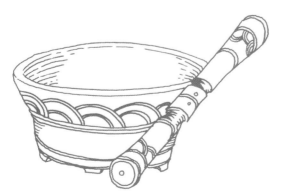

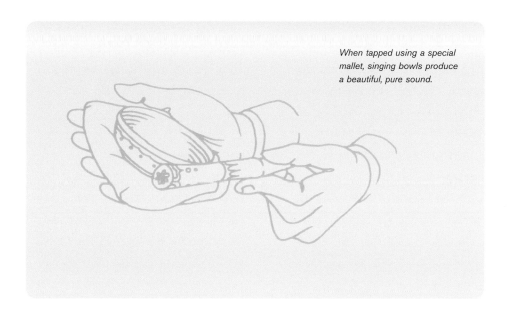

When tapped using a special mallet, singing bowls produce a beautiful, pure sound.

depend on its depth. To produce the special singing sound, the bowls should have a round crucible shape and be made from seven different metals: silver, gold, tin, copper, zinc, iron, and lead.

Adding real gold into the bowls not only improves the sound, but also symbolizes the auspiciousness of gold. The seven types of metals are a tradition. Gold represents the sun, the ultimate source of yang energy. Silver represents the moon the ultimate source of yin energy. Thus using silver and gold represents the union of yin and yang inside the bowl itself. The other metals each represent a planet. The proportion of each metal is a closely guarded secret, and the special bowls of some high lamas use metal alloys that are still a mystery to modern craftsmen.

Each of the seven metals produces an individual sound and together they produce an exceptional singing sound that pierces through the energy of space.

When you buy a singing bowl, spend some time getting to know it. All bowls have roughly the same sound but there are slight differences in the balance of the individual harmonics. The sound of each bowl is unique. Remember that every space and environment is a unique sounding board and will make the bowl resonate differently. In addition, every person possesses his or her own energies, which also change from moment to moment. The sound of the bowl can vary at different times.

As your living space gets purified with regular use, the singing sounds emitted each day will get purer and clearer and sharper to reflect the cleaner energies of the air around you. Develop an awareness of these improvements.

USING THE BOWL IN SPACE PURIFICATION

Hold the bowl in your left palm and walk slowly from room to room in your home. In each room strike the bowl three times, and move in a clockwise direction around the room.

Listen to the sounds coming from the bowl. Sounds produced in "dead" corners are often flat and dull while those that come from a lively part of the home tend to be sharp and clear. Learn to tell the difference. This first round through the home allows the bowl to resonate everywhere. It will balance the energies in your home almost instantly.

If you have a room you consider to be especially unlucky, place the bowl on a table with a cushion underneath. Let the bowl steady itself and then strike the rim of the bowl with the wooden mallet.

STRIKING THE BOWL WITH A MALLET

For space purification, create a continuous clear sound or a continuous humming sound as you move from room to room and from door to door. Striking the rim of the

bowl three times creates the first set of sounds. Let the sound ring out loud and follow its resonance. As the sound begins to fade, strike again, and keep doing this as you move around the room.

RUBBING THE BOWL WITH THE MALLET

You can also rub the mallet around the rim of the bowl in a clockwise direction. Keep a firm tension on the mallet and listen as a gentle humming sound grows in intensity.

If at first you cannot get the bowl to "sing" try striking the bowl first to wake it up before you start rubbing the rim. The trick is in the pressure of the mallet against the rim. Press the rim evenly and firmly.

When you get good at it, the sheer beauty of the sound will carry you away. This method brings out the harmonics of the bowl. When your bowl is singing nicely, begin to move slowly around the room. You should try to stay close to the walls so that any unbalanced energy that may be stuck to the walls gets cleansed and purified by the sound. Circle doors and windows three times.

FOCUS YOUR MIND

Singing bowl therapy can be done as often as you like; many people do it once every ten days. The special humming sound of the singing bowl not only attracts the good fortune, Sheng Chi, it also opens the chakras of the human body. Therefore, focus your mind and concentrate clearly on what you are doing.

Use singing bowl therapy only after purifying your space with incense. This fills the home with precious yang energy that is pure and balanced, especially when you use special mountain incense. The burning of these high mountain plants and herbs makes the air crisp and clear. When followed by the singing bowl, immense harmony is created.

Space purification of this kind is simple but immensely effective in creating a calming influence on all the residents in your home.

BENEFITS OF SINGING BOWL PURIFICATION

* Singing bowl therapy can enhance the energies of the living space.

* It can transform inauspicious energies into auspicious energies.

* It can activate the element energies of particular corners of your home.

* Many people feel uplifted after a space has been bathed with the harmonics and tones of a singing bowl.

* Sometimes the sounds even instill feelings of profound peace. The humming harmonics of the bowl massage the human psyche, thereby evoking a feeling of relaxed well-being.

* Singing bowls also massage the vibrations and wavelengths of the living space, thereby creating the harmony necessary for making homes hum with happiness. This is what feng shui is about, not just about creating auspicious space and wealth vibrations. More importantly, it is about putting us in touch with the soul and chi of the universe so that we live in harmony with each other and our environment.

FENG SHUI
A-Z

THIS SECTION PROVIDES YOU WITH A COMPREHENSIVE, ALPHABETICAL, AND

ILLUSTRATED DIRECTORY OF KEY WORDS IN **FENG SHUI** TERMINOLOGY.

USE IT AS AN EXTENDED GLOSSARY WHEN YOU ARE READING THE FIRST SECTION

OF THE BOOK OR AS A REFERENCE GUIDE WHENEVER YOU REQUIRE EXPLANATION

OR CLARIFICATION OF A SPECIFIC TERM OR TECHNIQUE. YOU WILL FIND THE TERMS

LISTED IN THIS SECTION ARE CLEARLY CROSS-REFERENCED BACK TO THE MAIN

SECTION OF THE BOOK FOR WHEN YOU NEED ADDITIONAL INFORMATION.

FENG SHUI A-Z

A

ABACUS

The abacus was developed in ancient China use as a calculator by literate businessmen. An abacus is a favorable indication that business will be good. Displaying a bronze abacus in the Northwest area of your home or office will bring financial support from influential people. Place an abacus in the Sheng Chi sector of your work desk to boost business and increase income. Retailers can energize each cash register with an abacus to multiply sales and profits. (*See* p. 83 for more details.)

ABUNDANCE

You can use feng shui to manifest abundance in your life. The Eight Manifestations of abundance are wealth, health and longevity, children (descendants' luck), a good name (fame and recognition), influence and authority, a solid career, loving family and marriage life, and wisdom.

Actively energize for these eight manifestations of luck by placing specific symbols for each type of luck in the respective corners of your home or living room. (*See* pp. 102–113. *See also* Eight Aspirations, p. 227.)

AERIALS

Aerials are antennas, cell towers, and satellite dishes, all of which can cut through chi. Preferably one should avoid living in a building that faces these magnets of energy. If you have no choice, use a mirror to reflect the chi, but make sure the aerials are fully reflected, so the entire force of negative energy is sent back. (*See also* Poison Arrows, p. 266.)

AFFLICTIONS

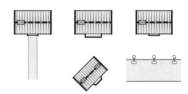

Straight paths   *Corners of buildings*   *Lampposts*

High ground   *Land sloping down behind house*

Feng shui afflictions manifest in physical afflictions and intangible afflictions, both equally troublesome.

Intangible afflictions are usually invisible, caused by Flying Star numbers (see Chapter 15) that reflect the changing fortunes of time.

Physical afflictions are caused by structures that assume the energy of harmful arrows bringing killing energy (Shar Chi). They include straight roads, edges of buildings, and obstacles in front of the entrance door, such as lampposts and signboards.

Physical problems can also be caused by exposure to the elements such as wind and water, for instance being situated on top of a hill, or when there is sloping ground or a lower level behind the house, signifying a lack of support. (*See* pp. 12 and 22–25.)

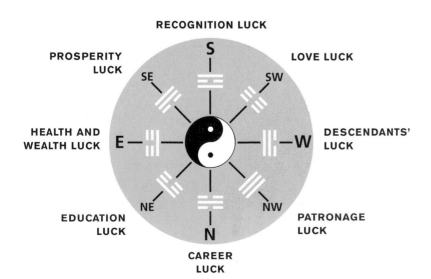

RECOGNITION LUCK
S

PROSPERITY LUCK
SE

LOVE LUCK
SW

HEALTH AND WEALTH LUCK
E

DESCENDANTS' LUCK
W

EDUCATION LUCK
NE

PATRONAGE LUCK
NW

CAREER LUCK
N

AIR CONDITIONERS

Air conditioners should never be placed directly above the bed or even on a wall beside it, since the blasts of cold air create yin wind eddies which can cause illness and sleepless nights. Position your air conditioner further away from the bed. (*See* p. 41 for more details of yin and yang.)

ALMANAC

The T'ung Shu, or Chinese Almanac, originated more than 4,000 years ago and contains the largest number of divination systems ever bound in a single book. The heart of the book is the calendar, based on the Chinese lunar and solar systems for calculating days and seasons of the year. The T'ung Shu contains auspicious dates for undertaking various activities from starting a new business to cutting your hair to performing planting and harvesting rituals.

Historically, senior officials within the Imperial Court compiled this calendar. Today, astrologers in Hong Kong and Taiwan compile the Almanac. (*See* Chinese Calendar, pp. 284–285.)

ALTAR

An altar in the home is best placed directly facing the door, so that it is immediately visible upon entering the home. The altar may also be placed in the Northwest section of the house or living room, since this sector represents the trigram Chien, in turn symbolizing the state of heaven and heavenly deities.

GUIDELINES TO DEITY PLACEMENT

1 Deities should always be placed indoors or have a roof over their heads. If you have an outdoor shrine, ensure that the altar is properly covered.

2 The deity should not be placed under an exposed overhead beam.

3 Never place your deity on the same wall as a toilet, directly below an upstairs toilet, or facing a toilet.

4 The deity should not be placed either directly facing or directly beneath a staircase.

5 The deity should not be placed in a bedroom in which the inhabitants make love.

Wherever you place your altar, always ensure that your Buddha, Kwan Yin statue, or any other deity, is placed on an elevated table. The most suitable dimension for altars is at least 60 inches (250 cm) high.

Keep the altar clean at all times. Leaving two small dim lamps on continuously offers light to the deity and attracts good chi. The lights are not too yang, but activate the chi of the Northeast corner to create benefits for the children of the home. (*See* p. 113)

AMETHYST

This purple semiprecious stone transforms negative energy into positive energy. It can be used to increase psychic abilities, quiet the mind, and focus your ability to make right decisions.

If you desire smooth working conditions, a thriving business, and harmony in the household, harness the power of the amethyst. Place an amethyst tree in any of the earth corners in your office (Northeast, Center, or Southwest).

Amethyst trees are made of wire branches and hold hundreds of amethyst stones as leaves. Your relationships with family, friends, and business associates will improve; even your sex life can benefit from displaying an amethyst tree.

Another popular method for tapping the energy of the amethyst is to wear amethyst beads around your wrist or neck. Amethyst chi will keep you in harmony with the world.

The amethyst geode is a powerful feng shui device for keeping husbands faithful. For this magical Taoist ritual to work well, the husband should sleep on the left side of the bed and the wife on the right. Place an amethyst geode tied with a piece of red string under the mattress at the foot of the wife's side of the bed. (*See* p. 74 for more details.)

AMULETS

Amulets are powerful protective symbols worn on the body for protection. They often overlap with the spiritual beliefs of different cultures. In feng shui, the tortoise and dragon are seen as powerful symbols of protection (*see* pp. 13–15). Fashioned into fine jewelry, these symbols are decorative and protective.

Taoist amulets can be made of special characters written on colored rice paper, then folded and worn inside gold or silver containers. In the past, mothers ensured their children's safety by adorning them with amulets blessed by the local temple.

Amulets are also worn to attract good fortune since wearing abundance attracts abundance. Jewelry made of gold, diamonds, jade, and pearls is purported to bring the luck of prosperity, good health, and power. Gold symbolizes the wealth of the earth, so wearing it is always propitious. (*See* p. 169 for more details.)

ANGLES

Sharp edges can be harmful if they face places where you sit or sleep. Sharp angles are created by square pillars or protruding table corners, or formed where two walls meet. The best way to deal with offensive angles is to place plants directly in front of the sharp angle. (*See* pp. 30–31.)

ANIMAL SIGNS

(*See* Zodiac, p. 283 and Chinese Calendar, pp. 284–285.)

ANNUAL STAR NUMBERS

The numbers 1 to 9 placed in a nine-sector Lo Shu grid indicate the distribution of chi luck for a given year.

	SE	S	SW	
	LUCKY **6**	GRAND DUKE **2**	LUCKY **4**	
E	5 YELLOW **5**	HORSE 2002 **7**	LUCKY **9**	W
	LUCKY **1**	3 KILLINGS **3**	MOST AUSPICIOUS **8**	
	NE	N	NW	

The chart illustrated here is the annual chart for the most recent year of the Horse–2002. In this chart, the center number is 7 and all other numbers are placed in the different compass grids. The year's luck can be determined according to the attributes assigned to these numbers. (*See* pp. 134–135 for more details. *See also* Lo Shu Square, p. 255.)

ANTIDOTES

Generally speaking, there are cures and antidotes for all feng shui ills. Some are better than others and choosing the correct antidote marks the skill of the feng shui master. Some common antidotes are noted here.

✱ Bright lights dissolve negative energy. Keep lights on at night for at least three hours.

✱ Yang energy–lights, sound, and bright colors–overcomes excessive yin energy.

✱ Windchimes diffuse bad energy and overcome illness.

✱ Pa Kua mirrors deflect Shar Chi caused by physical poison arrows. Use only as a last resort. Hang the mirror high above your front door, facing outward.

✱ Bells and singing bowls purify stagnant or afflicted space. This is a temporary cure and must be done regularly for greatest effectiveness.

✱ Crystals soften excessive yang energy. These symbols of the earth element are excellent antidotes.

✱ Colors improve element imbalance. Colors are also fabulous for balancing yin and yang chi.

✱ Flowers, plants, and trees block out Shar Chi and strengthen wood element energy.

✱ Curtains and blinds deflect negative energy and effectively shut out harmful sights and structures.

✱ A reliable compass is necessary for arranging your seating and living areas auspiciously.

✱ Element therapy corrects disharmony. Learn the productive and destructive cycles of the elements to practice this effectively. (*See* pp. 40–41 for more details.)

ANTIQUES

Old furniture or decorative items can be harmful to the home due to leftover energy. You may not know who last owned the piece, nor the quality of the chi that still clings to the antique. It may contain negative energy.

If you like collecting antiques, reduce the effect of negative energy by rubbing raw sea salt all over the piece with a damp cloth. Leave the salt on the furniture for seven days, letting it drop off on its own. This will neutralize any yin energy that may be bound to the antique. Be sure to open any drawers and place some salt into them. Another method is to place a piece of bright red paper under the antique. Set antiques

outside in bright sunshine for a
while as well.

It is extremely risky to keep antique
cannons or firearms in the house, since
they may have "tasted" blood before
and are therefore particularly potent.
(*See also* Cannons, p. 212.)

APARTMENTS

For apartments as for condominiums or
townhouses, some basic rules apply
with respect to shapes. Square or
rectangular shapes are preferable to
irregular ones.

Tools such as mirrors and lights are
useful aids in "regularizing" an uneven
layout. Mirrors can make L-shaped
apartments appear rectangular. Lights
can extend missing corners by shining
outward to correct the situation. (*See*
pp. 24–25 for more details. *See also*
Corners, p. 218.)

*Below: Plan the layout of the rooms
according to the Flying Star natal chart
so that all lucky sectors are "tapped"
for good fortune.*

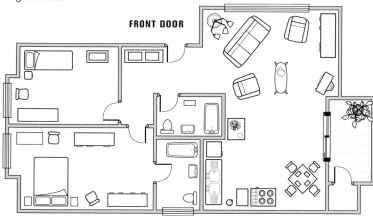

FRONT DOOR

*Below: Although it can be impossible
to achieve a regular shaped apartment,
an irregular shape and layout create
awkward corners that need attention.*

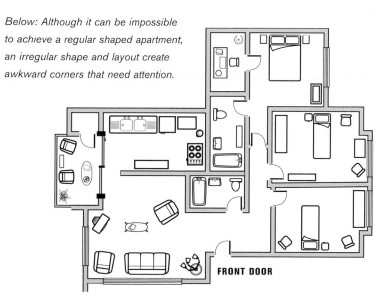

FRONT DOOR

AQUARIUMS

Aquariums provide good feng shui
when placed in the correct corners of
your home, office, or shop. Activating
the Southeast corner of your office with
a bubbling water feature will attract
wealth. An aquarium with lively fish is an
excellent water feature and, since it also
symbolizes growth and activity, it is an
excellent energizer.

Aquariums come in many designs.
Favor those that are easy to maintain and
conducive to healthy fish. (*See* pp. 54
and 104 for more details.)

ARCHWAYS

Archways can be auspicious if not
overdone. Round, curved archways
symbolize luck from heaven. An archway
is more conducive to harmony than is a
square walkway in the home. Archways
suggest the circular shape representing
the element of gold. They are especially
lucky placed in the Northwest and West
areas of the home, but best not seen in
the East and Southeast. (*See* pp.
22–23 for basic shapes for houses.)

ARMCHAIR FORMATION

The armchair formation in landscape
feng shui represents the classical
Green Dragon/White Tiger formation
that ensures excellent feng shui.

The armchair formation
recommends that the home has higher
land at the back (known as the Black
Turtle) to provide support akin to the
back of an armchair. The left-hand side
of the home should be higher, as this is
deemed to be the place of the Green
Dragon. The land to the right of your
home is the place of the White Tiger,
which should be lower than the dragon.

If land on your right is higher than land on your left, the Tiger can become overbearing and dangerous. In front of the home should be a small hump representing the Red Phoenix, which acts as the "footstool." The Armchair formation may be difficult to find naturally, but it is acceptable to artificially create this formation.

Historically, Green Dragons, White Tigers, Black Turtles, and Red Phoenixes were metaphoric references to hills and mountains. In modern cities, buildings are now regarded as hills and mountains. (*See* pp. 13–16 for more details. *See also* Landscape Feng Shui, p. 252.)

ARROWS
(*See* Poison Arrows, p. 266.)

ARROWANA

The arrowana, or dragon fish, with its silver scales and sleek sword-like body, has been used for years to bring good fortune.

The arrowana is best kept singly or in threes or fives. Arrowanas should never be kept in pairs. When the arrowana is well fed and healthy, it emits a pink or golden glow; which is said to bring good fortune. Only strong, brant arrowanas have the capacity to bring you great wealth.

The aquarium that houses this fish should not be cluttered—a large aquarium with nothing but water will serve to accentuate the beauty and graceful movement of the fish. The aquarium is best kept in the North corner, the water corner, or in the East or Southeast, which are wood corners, since water is harmonious with wood. Never keep an arrowana aquarium in your bedroom. (*See also* Aquariums, p. 203.)

ART
Works of art in the home or office can cause good or bad feng shui without your awareness. The subject, colors, and orientation of paintings all have feng shui implications; therefore, it is important to consider your paintings seriously before decorating.

When selecting paintings for the home, observe the following useful tips:

Avoid abstract art in colors that clash with the element of the wall on which you are hanging the painting. Thus do not hang artwork that depicts metal objects or that is painted substantially in white or metallic colors in the wood corners (East or Southeast). The element of metal destroys wood and the disharmony of the painting will create problems in the wood corner and anyone occupying it.

The Northwest wall is the best place to hang a portrait of the founder of your company, as this area activates the luck of the trigram Chien, which will create exceptional mentor luck.

Landscape art is the best choice for the office to create harmonious feng shui. A mountain painting behind where you sit symbolizes support. This is a good feature to add to your office.

A painting of a river or stream in front of your work desk simulates water bringing you great good fortune. Never hang paintings of rivers, lakes, or waterfalls behind you.

A picture of a large open field in front of you symbolizes the bright hall. This symbolism is enormously lucky, since it represents a complete and total absence of obstacles. An open field lends ease to your business and your career. Fruit and flowers also symbolize abundance and good fortunes.

Avoid depictions of wild animals such as lions, tigers, or eagles inside the home or office. They serve best

Traditionally regarded as a white horse, the Tribute Horse is an excellent symbol to have in the house as it signifies that everyone respects and honors you. Its symbolism started during the Sung Dynasty and the horse was often depicted with symbols of prosperity.

outside, to protect you and your family, but inside the home they can bring ill fortune and illness.

Artwork depicting symbols such as the tribute horse are excellent choices. A popular painting is of the famous tribute horse of the Sung Dynasty being led into the presence of the emperor. The horse represents loads of wealth and gold being carried to your home. (*See also* p. 255 for more details.)

ASPIRATIONS, EIGHT

(*See* Eight Aspirations, p. 227.)

ASTROLOGY

Many people confuse feng shui with Chinese astrology because the Chinese systems of divination also use the basic concepts of feng shui. The two most popular systems of Chinese astrology are:

✳ Purple Star astrology (*see* p. 267), which divides a person's luck into twelve houses and then places the "stars" within the houses according to your day and year of birth.

✳ Four Pillars astrology (*see* p. 236), which uses the day, month, hour, and year of your birth to chart the eight characters of your destiny as well as the Luck periods of your life.

ATRIUMS

Atriums are inauspicious when they are small and deep, as this form causes chi to be trapped and become destructive. When atriums resemble spacious courtyards, they become benevolent, bringing chi from above to mingle auspiciously with earth chi from below. (*See also* Courtyards, p. 219.)

ATTICS

Small rooms at the top of houses can be auspicious or harmful depending on how spacious or cramped they are. When the attic is small with no windows, chi tends to stagnate at the apex of the home. Yin energy collects and this is not auspicious. If you have an attic, make sure there are windows and that the ceiling is a reasonable height. (*See* pp. 38–39 for more details.)

AUSPICIOUS FENG SHUI

Good fortune in feng shui usually refers to eight categories of luck and these include:

✳ wealth and prosperity
✳ a loving family and relationships
✳ health and long life
✳ a happy marriage (or love life)
✳ good children
✳ the patronage of mentors
✳ a solid education
✳ a fine reputation

(*See* pp. 82–83 and 102–103 for more details. *See* also Eight Aspirations, p. 227.)

B
BAD FENG SHUI

This means the opposite of good luck. A series or cluster of misfortunes can be due to inauspicious feng shui. If your family continually experiences illness, loss, accidents, or problems, perhaps some structure or alignment is hurting your home. Fortunately, almost every bad feng shui feature can be diffused.

Afflictions may be caused by annual energy changes. Thus, when the front door, bedroom, or center of your home is affected by negative energy based on the time of year, then sickness, loss, and other manifestations of bad luck may occur. (*See* p. 41 for causes of Shar Chi in the home.)

BALANCE

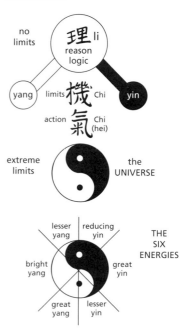

Ensuring the proper balance of yin and yang in your living space is a central feng shui concept. This balance is struck between the cosmic forces of yin and yang, two opposing yet complementary energies.

Yin is darkness; yang is Light. Yin is cold; yang is warmth. Yin is female; yang is male. Yin is passive; yang is active. Yin is rain; yang is sunshine. Everything that exists consists of both these energies. Without one there cannot be the other. Without darkness, what is light? Without cold, what is heat? (*See* p. 41 for more details of balancing yin and yang. *See also* Yin Yang Symbol, p. 283.)

BALCONIES

A balcony facing the front door is bad feng shui, as it causes chi and thus good fortune to fly in and just as quickly out again. To correct this affliction, set up a screen forcing the chi to meander.

A large balcony facing a fantastic open space or a beautiful view may be considered the "facing direction" of the home, even if the main door is not there. This is an important point when you undertake Flying Star chart analysis. (*See* Chapter 15 for more details.)

MAIN DOOR FACES BALCONY

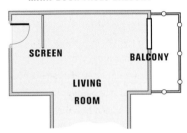

BAMBOO

Bamboo is an excellent feng shui plant signifies a life of good health and longevity.

Bamboo stems can be used in the same way as windchimes with hollow rods or wooden flutes. They should be hung in a pair, slanted toward each other at the top in such a way as to allow auspicious chi to rise up and counter the negative chi emitted from the overhead beam. Unlike windchimes, there is no sound to transform the chi into friendly energy, so tie the stems together with a piece of red string to bring out the necessary yang energy.

Bamboo stems are also an excellent tool for slowing down chi. Rooms at the end of long corridors often suffer from Shar Chi rushing toward them. To slow down this fast-moving chi, hang bamboo stems in the same way as above, with a red string tied between them. (*See* p. 172 for more details.)

BANKING

Banking is categorized under the water element; therefore, placing an auspicious water feature in the North or Southeast is highly recommended. You can also build a water feature in front of the bank building (be sure the water flows toward the building and not away from it). (*See* pp. 162–163 for more details.)

BARBECUE PITS

These are best placed on the South side of the yard in the fire sector. Never place barbecue pits or grills in the Northwest, since this represents the unlucky "fire at heaven's gate" situation. Also ensure that the pit or grill is not placed in the East or Southeast wood sectors, as the fire will symbolically burn the wood, thus burning away both health and wealth.

Because barbecues represent fire, they will activate this element, bringing recognition and fame to the family. This is also the sector of the middle daughter, so holding barbecues in the South sector will assist her in her schoolwork and personal development. (*See also* Fire, p. 233.)

BASEMENT

Feng shui does not advocate living or sleeping below street level; therefore, neither basement bedrooms nor apartments are auspicious. If you have no choice, however, you can enhance the chi by installing bright lights at the entrance to raise the energy and encourage chi to flow into the home. If the apartment opens into a garden at the back, the feng shui is improved. (*See* p. 15 for lifting energy details.)

BATHROOMS

Minimize the size and décor of your bathrooms and keep the doors to your bathrooms closed at all times when not in use. There is no need to decorate large bathrooms. They do not bring good luck. (*See* pp. 61, 206 for more details. *See also* Toilets, p. 278.)

BATS

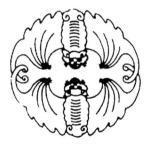

Although often associated with witches in the West, bats—especially red bats—have signified abundance in prosperity, happiness, and longevity to the Chinese for many years. The origin of this association comes from the sound of the creature's Chinese name, Pian Fu; the word Fu sounds like the word for happiness and good fortune.

Bats are usually painted cinnabar red, the color for joy, and depicted in fives to represent the five blessings from heaven: wealth, health, longevity, love of virtue, and a natural death. A group of five red bats is the yang symbol of prosperity, and takes on greater significance when placed in a circle around the longevity symbol to indicate abundance for your whole life.

A family of bats taking up residence in your home is an exceptionally good omen that heralds immense good fortune and success for the household. (*See* p. 170 for more details.)

BAY WINDOWS

Bay windows are not usually recommended in feng shui. Although the circular shape represents heaven, in a bay window the circle is incomplete. Despite this, a bay window located in your auspicious direction signifies a protrusion, which brings good luck. (*See* p. 53 for more details.)

BEADED CURTAINS

Beaded curtains can cure afflicted doorways. Two doors facing each other across a corridor will cause quarrels and misunderstandings, particularly between the people who occupy these two rooms. To soften the negative effect of this layout, hang a beaded curtain across the doorway to give the illusion of the door being closed.

A door facing half of another door (i.e., only part of each door is cutting into the other) has a worse effect. A plant can act as a divider between the doors, but beaded curtains are not suitable in this case. (*See also* Doors, p. 222.)

BEAMS

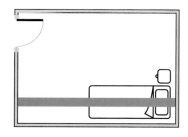

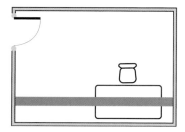

Protruding overhead beams cause problems inside the home and office. Sleeping or working directly under an exposed overhead beam is a serious affliction. Move your bed or desk or hang a five-rod windchime or two hollow bamboo stems tied with red string to overcome the negative chi. (*See* p. 30 for more details of beams. *See also* Ceilings, p. 213.)

BED POSITION

The position of your bed is important, as you are most vulnerable while asleep and this time is also used for growth (physical for children, and mental and spiritual for adults).

To properly position your bed, tap one of your auspicious directions using the Kua Formula (*see* pp. 114–121).

Observe these rules in positioning your bed:

✳ Never sleep with your feet directly facing the door.

✳ Make sure your bed does not face a mirror, television, or any other reflective surface as it brings a third party into the picture.

✳ Make sure your headboard is solid, and placed against a wall, or at least a board or cabinet. A bed "floating" in the middle of the room signifies a lack of support and will cause many sleepless nights.

✳ Avoid waterbeds, which symbolize a lack of support. They can cause serious problems in your relationships—both at work and in your love life.

✳ Do not place your headboard directly under a window. If you cannot avoid this position, cover your window with heavy drapes when you are sleeping.

✳ If you wish to sleep diagonal to the walls in your bedroom, make sure you build a solid board against which to place the headboard. (*See* p. 65 for more details.)

BEDROOMS

Remember that the bedroom is a place of rest. The energies that prevail should be more yin than yang, so avoid overactivating the bedroom with an excess of good fortune symbols. A bedroom that is too yang will create sleeping difficulties and insomnia.

Water features are generally auspicious, but in the bedroom they do more harm than good. Sleeping with water behind you—in the form of a fountain, a fishbowl, or even a painting of water—can result in financial loss. It is, however, acceptable to decorate your bedroom in shades of light blue to enhance relaxation and calm. Black (or dark blue), representing water, should not be prominent in the bedroom.

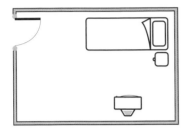

Avoid the TV facing the bed.

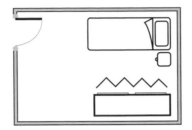

Avoid the wardrobe facing the bed.

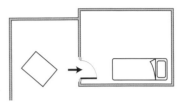

Keep furniture away from the door.

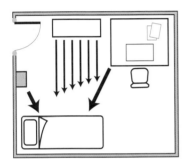

Avoid bookshelves and sharp corners facing the bed.

Mirrors: The use of mirrors to create a spacious feel in the bedroom is a common mistake in modern interior decorating. Whether attached to furnishings or affixed to the ceiling, the reflective edge of mirrors in the bedroom sends Shar Chi onto the sleeping person or couple.

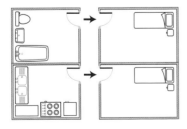

Kitchens or bathrooms afflict bedrooms.

This negative chi will cause quarrels, misunderstandings, ill health, and even unfaithfulness. Anything with a reflective surface, even a television set, should be kept out of the bedroom or covered with a cloth each night.

Flowers and plants: Growing plants are potent symbols of yang energy and therefore unsuitable for the bedroom. Plants in a girl's bedroom will work against her chance of happy romance. Plants featured in a couple's bedroom will cause frequent quarrels. The only time flowers or plants are justified in the bedroom is when someone is recuperating from an illness and needs the yang energy to recover.

Open shelves: Shelves should always be covered, particularly in the bedroom, where they do the most harm. If such shelves face your bed, each one will send little poison arrows toward you throughout the night. If you cannot cover open shelves with doors, ensure the shelves are filled with books aligned flush with the edge of the shelves (to take away the negative chi of the edge).

Sleeping direction: The time you spend sleeping will benefit from the application of good feng shui. Your head should point toward one of your four good directions while you are sleeping. Determine your "good and bad" directions using the Kua Formula. (*See* pp. 64–65 for more details.)

BEDS

Avoid the door touching the bed.

Beds should be placed in the best corner based on the Flying Star natal chart of the home.

A good feng shui bed has auspicious dimensions and is decorated with colors that harmonize either with the element of the corner in which the bed is placed, or with the sleeping person's Kua self-element. Use the element of the corner to determine colors, as this will make the bed auspicious for more than one person.

If you wish to use red, dark red or maroon is better than bright red. Bedspreads are best in solid colors. Avoid abstract designs with arrows or triangles, which represent the fire element and symbolize poison arrows. (*See* p. 62 for more details.)

BEGONIAS

Blue begonias are excellent plants for the North part of the garden. They simulate and energize the water element of the North. (*See also* Flower Gardens, p. 234.)

BELLS

Bells are excellent cures for afflicted earth element corners as well as for space clearing and for attracting the yang energy that brings customers into any retail store.

When hung above doors or on door handles, the tinkling sound of these little metal bells creates good chi each time someone enters. Bells are particularly effective in selling items such as jewelry, clothing, and accessories.

Bells are most effective when tied with a red ribbon. Red activates the intrinsic yang energy of the bells. The ideal number of bells should be six or seven, tied to the handle of the shop or hung above the door.

Tiny tinkling bells can also be placed inside along the West or Northwest wall or on the ceiling facing the entrance of the door to entice the precious Sheng Chi to enter. (*See* p. 83 for more details.)

BIG TAI CHI

This important and vital dimension of feng shui refers to different types of living spaces. Big Tai Chi refers to the environmental space that makes up a house or building property. Small Tai Chi means individual rooms. Everything you apply to the big space can also be applied to the small space. The ramifications of understanding this small point are big indeed! (*See* pp. 34–35 for more details.)

BIG WATER

This phrase refers to any natural water that surrounds a home or building that can be tapped to improve overall feng shui. (*See also* Water, p. 280.)

BIRDBATHS

Birdbaths are excellent water features suitable for the North, East, and Southeast sectors of your garden. Ensure that the water is clean at all times. The more birds that visit your birdbath, the better the energy created by this water feature. (*See also* Water, p. 280.)

BIRDS

Birds represent the celestial phoenix, and a sculpture of birds, especially in the South sector of your living room or garden, brings the luck of new opportunity. However, keeping birds in cages is extremely bad feng shui as it symbolizes imprisonment, curbing your ambitions, an inability to fly, and a block to attaining dreams. (*See* pp. 68–69, 82, and 103 for more details.)

BIRTHDATES

Used in Eight Directions or Mansions and Four Pillars Feng Shui, birthdates are required for calculating personalized lucky and unlucky directions.

The Eight Mansions Formula provides your Kua number. Using this number, refer to the table that details your four auspicious and four inauspicious directions.

The Four Pillars method is the same as the Eight Characters (Paht Chee) method of fortune telling. It requires your date of birth according to the lunar calendar and the hour of your birth. (*See* Chinese Calendar, pp. 284–285.)

BLACK HAT SECT

The Black Hat Sect (BHS) is a popular school of feng shui, which uses the fixed Pa Kua method to activate. This lineage incorporates input from different schools and was widely popularized in the US by Professor Lin Yun of Berkeley, California. It is a synthesis of Tibetan and Chinese Buddhist, Taoist, and folk wisdom. It also incorporates a system of transcendental cures. (*See also* Pa Kua, p. 263.)

BLACK TORTOISE

One of the four celestial creatures of feng shui mythology, the Black Tortoise, brings support, longevity, and protection.

Terrapins, smaller cousins of the turtle, also bring good fortune. If you wish to keep a terrapin or turtle, keep only one in the North sector of your house. Do not worry that your pet will feel lonely—terrapins are natural loners. If you are unable to keep a real turtle, a figurine of a tortoise in the North corner will effectively symbolize the tortoise energy.

In the Tibetan system, the turtle is regarded as the ultimate protective symbol. Antique religious paintings from Tibet, showing all the protective amulets, are usually painted on the belly of a turtle.

The Black Tortoise is also one of the animals that make up the "armchair" formation in Landscape Feng Shui. (*See* pp. 13–15 and 181 for more details. *See also* Lo Shu Square, p. 255.)

BLUE FLOWERS

Blue flowers symbolize the element of water, thus they are good for the North (career), East (health), and Southeast (wealth) sectors of the garden or yard. Colors are powerful enhancers and offer a creative way to perfect the feng shui of your garden. (*See also* Flower Gardens, p. 234.)

BLUE ROOF TILES

Water on top of the house signifies danger associated with overflow. Try to avoid having blue roof tiles on your home. The best colors for tiles are standard shades of red and maroon. (*See* p. 137 for details of roof renewal.)

BOARDROOMS

The best location for the boardroom of a corporation is diagonal to the entrance, deep inside the office. It is not advisable to have the boardroom on the top floor nor to have too many doors, which lead to disharmony. (*See* pp. 76–83 for details about businesses.)

BOATS

Boats as symbols of good fortune can bring good luck from the winds and waters. If you live on a boat, activate it with decorative symbols. *See also* Sailing Ship, p. 271.)

BODY FENG SHUI

The practice of improving your living space can be extended to enhance your personal space and the aura that surrounds your body. Wear clothes in colors that complement your natural chi and, if possible, genuine gold and diamond jewelry fashioned into auspicious symbols.

Creating an aura of abundance and good health works best for those with a positive outlook on life. The principles of the five elements and their cycles of production and destruction hold the secrets of aura enhancement. (*See* p. 22 for the Five Elements theory. *See also* Wu Xing, p. 282.)

BODY PARTS AND ORGANS

Experienced feng shui masters are able to diagnose and warn of impending illness as well as offer clues as to its nature by investigating the feng shui of rooms in an individual's home. When the element directions are afflicted, illness associated with those body parts may result.

Analysis identifies rooms afflicted by bad Flying Stars as well as annual sickness stars, which change every year. Once afflicted rooms are identified, element analysis is used to identify body parts or organs associated with the afflicted locations. (*See* pp. 88–90 for more details.)

BONSAI TREES

Genuine Bonsai plants can last for many years as part of a miniature garden that soothes the spirit. However, Bonsai trees—varieties of large trees that were stunted artificially over many years—also signify the antithesis of growth. Thus, they can be harmful for businesses and commercial enterprises. If you have them in your home, avoid placing them in the wood corners (East and Southeast) or garden. Placed in the North, they cause the least harm.

If you are retired, and growth and material success are no longer the central focus of your life, the Bonsai

tree's "old soul" spirit might suit your aspirations. (*See* p. 95 for trees.)

BOOK OF CHANGES

(*See* I Ching, p. 246.)

BOOKSHELVES

Exposed bookshelves represent knives and therefore bad feng shui. Cover exposed bookshelves in your office or study with doors. You may also fill the shelves with books aligned to the edges of the shelves to eliminate the poison arrows (*See* pp. 31 and 86 for more details. *See also* Poison Arrows, p. 266.)

BOULDERS

These symbols of earth energy can be used as powerful remedies. Tied with red string, boulders can be an antidote to poisonous chi. They can strengthen the auspicious mountain stars found in Flying Star natal charts. (*See also* Flying Star Feng Shui, p. 235.)

BOUNDARIES

Mark out the boundaries of your personal space on your floor plan before superimposing the Pa Kua or the Lo Shu chart or compass.

When using compass formulas, it is vital to get accurate measurements and compass readings to establish the parameters of your space according to directions, locations, and elements. (*See also* Compass, p. 218.)

BOWLS

Bowls of still water are effective in overcoming the "fire at heaven's gate" affliction of the stove or fireplace in the Northwest sector of the home or kitchen.

Bowls can also serve as wealth bowls when filled with symbols such as coins, semi-precious stones, and ingots to symbolize that your wealth has arrived. Place in the corner of the living room diagonal to the entrance door.

Enhance the bowl further by placing auspicious symbols such as the three-legged toad inside the bowl. (See p. 169 for more details. See also Singing Bowl, p. 273.)

BREATH

Auspicious house layout (below): chi meanders from front door to back door.

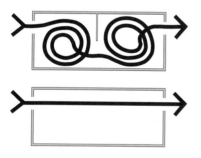

Inauspicious house layout (above): chi moves in a disastrous straight line from front door to back door.

The breath of the dragon is the cosmic chi—the force that circulates in the environment, floating across water and land, indoors and outdoors, permeating every inch of the earth's surface. Chi is the invisible energy that vibrates across the world and attracts extreme good luck wherever it settles.

Locations that enjoy the best Landscape Feng Shui are those where the Green Dragon exhales its magical cosmic breath. (See pp. 13–15 for more details.)

BRICK WALL

This feng shui remedy blocks out unwanted and inauspicious sights such as structures that send negative chi to the home. It is also an effective block against oncoming straight roads should your home be located at a T-junction. (See also T-intersections, p. 276.)

BRIDGES

Bridges near your home will be auspicious if they have three, five, or nine bends. They may be straight or curved, beamed, arched, suspended, or floating. They can be made of stone, lumber, or cane. In China, bridges that are built to enhance the feng shui of gardens are usually built of stone, and the space beneath is usually a semi-circle. (See also Garden, p. 238.)

BRIGHT HALL

A grassy park, football field, or meadow creates an auspicious "bright hall" (known as the ming tang in Chinese), which enables good chi to enter.

Sheng Chi first accumulates and settles in the bright hall before entering the home. A bright hall in front of your main door will bring great fortune and your plans will proceed smoothly and successfully. Schools and colleges with a playing field located directly in front of the main entrance usually produce excellent graduates.

Do not try to achieve the bright hall effect at all costs. If there is a statue or structure facing the front door, it is better to give up the bright hall effect than to suffer the poison arrow. (See pp. 15 and 17 for more details.)

BROOMS

Brooms, mops, and cleaning materials should never be exposed in the home, but always kept hidden when not in use. They can sweep away good luck as well as bad. Exposed brooms are particularly bad fortune if left in the dining room, which symbolizes your rice bowl, or your livelihood, being swept away. (See also Good Luck, p. 241.)

BUDDHA STATUES

Holy objects such as Buddha statues must occupy a place of respect in the home. Paintings and statues of Buddha should never be treated as decorations or furniture. The best place for displaying your Buddha statue is the Northwest sector of your foyer or living room. (See also Altar, p. 201, and Fat Buddha, p. 232.)

BUILDINGS

Buildings simulate mountains in feng shui analysis. In ancient times, surrounding hills and mountains determined the quality of the feng shui terrain. Because feng shui is symbolic, in today's cities, buildings make up the landscape and surroundings and are now analyzed in the same way hills were in the past. Roads often take the place of rivers in the analysis. (*See* pp. 26–27 for more details.)

BUSINESS

Business feng shui focuses on creating wealth and prosperity luck. Career professionals as well as budding entrepreneurs recognize the potency of feng shui in increasing turnover and improving the bottom line. In business feng shui should be seen in the same light as a legitimate business expense. When opening a retail store or a business branch, take into account the feng shui dimension in the overall planning. (*See* pp. 76–83 for more details.)

BUSINESS CARDS

Cards that contain feng shui features will attract good business luck for you. Color combinations also have feng shui implications. Black and blue text on white cards is auspicious, but red text is not.

Do not place anything pointed directly at your name or your company name. Your name above the company name puts you in control. When your name is below the company name, you may become a workaholic, working only for the company. (*See* pp. 78–79 for good fortune in business.)

C
CACTUS

Cactus and other prickly plants create tiny slivers of poisonous energy that can cause illness and misfortune. Cactus plants are best placed outside the home or office where their thorns serve to protect you from incoming Shar Chi. (*See also* Shar Chi, p. 273.)

CALENDAR

There are two calendars in the Chinese system, lunar and solar.

The lunar calendar is observed for calculating astrological charts and the official Chinese New Year. The start of each lunar year varies from year to year.

The solar calendar (also called the Hsia) was used to calculate growing and harvesting seasons and was measured according to the official arrival of spring and autumn. Each year, the solar calendar starts on the 4th or 5th of February, known as Lap Chun. Flying Star Feng Shui observes the months and New Year of the solar calendar. (*See also* Chinese Calendar, pp. 284–285.)

CALLIGRAPHY

Artistic calligraphy demonstrates the power of chi in the brushstrokes. Good calligraphy contains auspicious chi and if the word itself is also auspicious, it is even more highly prized. When you hang calligraphy in the home, use red as the background color to make the calligraphy "come alive."

Words with abundant meanings are revered and include words such as Fuk, which means "good luck," and Sau, which means "longevity." (*See also* Chi, p. 215, and Fuk Luk Sau, p. 237.)

CANNONS

Cannons can effectively deflect Shar Chi caused by sharp or hostile objects facing the home entrance. Use this remedy as a last resort, since the negative force sent out by cannons is potent.

Cannons are tools of defense, but it is best not to hurt your neighbor with objects placed in front of your home. Remember that objects facing outward influences the chi all around. Antique cannons that have been to war carry serious killing chi and can be dangerous. (*See* p. 27 for more details.)

CANOPY

A canopy, like an umbrella, is a symbol of protection. A canopy shading a balcony or terrace is excellent feng shui as it tempers excessive yang energy from the sun. (*See also* Yang Energy, p. 282.)

CARDINAL DIRECTIONS

Each of the cardinal directions—North, South, East and West—occupies an angle of 90 degrees. In feng shui, the cardinal directions are considered yang and their corresponding numbers are thus all odd numbers: 1 for North, 9 for South, 3 for East, and 7 for West.

Cardinal directions are extremely significant in Compass Formula Feng Shui. (*See* pp. 42–43 for more details.)

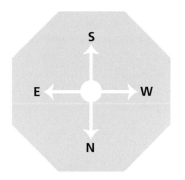

CAREER LUCK

Career luck is represented by the direction of North. Activate the Northern corners of your home or office with suitable good fortune symbols or the element of this sector. Since North is the water element, an aquarium full of energetic fish will energize this corner.

Colorful guppies, especially those with long tails (symbolizing a good ending) and neon-type yang colors on their bodies are a good choice. Their vigorous swimming creates the precious yang energy needed to give your career a boost.

Career luck is manifested in success. When activating luck at work, be prepared for an increasing workload and responsibilities along with more opportunities for advancement. (*See* pp. 104–105 for more details. *See also* Desks, p. 222.)

CARPET

Never put your company name on your carpet. Allowing people to walk over your name means you will never have good luck. (*See* pp. 78–79 for good fortune in business.)

CASH REGISTER

Energize retail business with coins and bamboo. Attach three old Chinese coins tied with red string, yang side up, to the side of the cash register. The yang side has four Chinese words, the yin side only two. Hang hollow bamboo stems tied with red string above the cash register. Let the stems hang perpendicular, tilted toward one other to ensure business longevity. (*See* pp. 78–79 for good fortune in business.)

CEILINGS

Ceilings should not be less than eight feet high or you will be weighed down with problems. At least four feet (1.2 m) of space above the tallest person in the home is ideal.

Ceiling designs should not have corner angles or ornate designs that can appear threatening. Beams are not recommended, although if they are part of an overall design that covers the entire ceiling, they do less harm than if they stand alone as heavy overhead structures. Paint your ceiling white or at least a bright color. Do not paint your ceilings blue or black. (*See* p. 33 for home decoration.)

CELESTIAL CREATURES

The four celestial creatures of feng shui are the Green Dragon and the White Tiger of the East and West as well as the Black Tortoise and the Crimson Phoenix of the North and South. Each brings a specific aspect of luck to the house that they collectively embrace. The dragon brings wealth and prosperity; the turtle brings patronage and support; the phoenix brings opportunity and recognition, and the

tiger brings protection against dark forces. Together, and when oriented correctly vis-à-vis each other, the celestial creatures symbolize perfect feng shui.

Historically, natural landforms in the environment provided the presence of these creatures but, as cities grow, these creatures are taking on an increasingly symbolic manifestation. Their "presence" in your surroundings protects your home and attracts good fortune.

The dragon was especially popular and many buildings and public places carried the image or form of the dragon. Today, we can do the same with all the creatures, although the Tiger is the most ferocious of the four and you may wish to activate it only out-of-doors. Those who are born in Tiger years should also be wary, as they may be able to take the energy of the tiger, but other members of the family may not. (*See* pp. 13–15 for more details. *See also* Chinese Calendar, pp. 284–285.)

CENTER OF THE HOME

The heart of the home is extremely important. All systems of feng shui emphasize the need for a golden and abundant heart place. Keep yours pulsating with precious yang chi.

The Flying Star system of feng shui recommends a big, spacious center that reflects the importance of this part of the house. The best center room is the dining room. Eating within the heart of the home attracts abundance.

What not to have in the center of the home are staircases, kitchens, toilets, or bedrooms, as they place undue importance on the activities

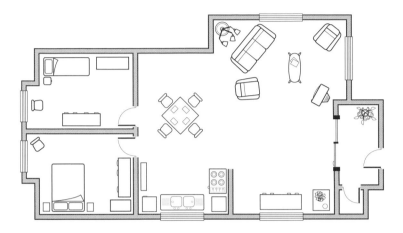

The center of the apartment should be spacious and preferably be the dining area.

within them. If either a bathroom or storeroom is in the center of the house, paint the outside of the door bright red and place a plant inside. (*See* Flying Star Feng Shui, p. 235.)

CHAIR

Shapes and dimensions of furniture can pose feng shui concerns. Most important is the chair you sit in to do work: make sure it has a solid back for support. A flimsy chair at work can cause problems with your boss and colleagues. Sit in a full-backed chair with arm rests for best results. Used together with your Kua directions, this will lead to promotions, better prospects, a salary raise, and the strong support of your boss. (*See also* Furniture, p. 237.)

CHAKRAS

Strictly speaking, the chakras of the human body are not part of feng shui practice; however, because chakras are the seven energy centers of the body, it is a good idea to be aware of them.

Many Taoist masters recognize the importance of meditation to their practice since opening the chakras enhances their focus and concentration. (*See also* Body Feng Shui, p. 210.)

CHANDELIERS

Chandeliers create excellent feng shui either inside or outside the home, and are especially effective in the Southwest. The combination of fire (lights) and earth (crystal) brings romance and love luck to members of the household. If possible, activate the Southwest of the whole house with a chandelier, rather than the Southwest of a single room. This powerful effect will benefit the entire family. If you do not have a chandelier, you can place crystals next to a bright stand lamp—the effect is the same. (*See* pp. 57–59 for more details of South corner activation.)

CHANG KUO LAO (ZHANG GUO LAO)

One of the Eight Immortals, Chang Kuo Lao is said to have lived in the seventh or early eighth century and is the patron

of the elderly. He is depicted riding a mule and carrying a bamboo tube-drum with iron sticks. If elderly parents or grandparents live with you, hanging Lao's image in your home will ensure that they live to a ripe old age and have a natural death. (*See also* Eight Immortals, p. 227.)

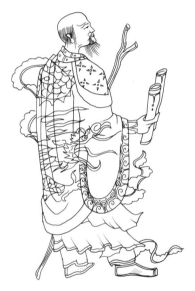

CHARTS

In feng shui, charts usually refer to Flying Star natal charts, which are drawn up in accordance with compass formulas, which can then be interpreted. The natal chart shows the distribution of the different types of chi inside any building or abode.

Flying Star charts are not to be confused with Eight Mansions charts, which also outline the chi distribution inside the home. These are also not to be confused with Four Pillars charts, which are destiny analysis charts. Many people confuse the practice of Four Pillars astrology with feng shui, but the sciences and charts are different. (*See* Flying Star Feng Shui, p. 235.)

CHEN TRIGRAM

Chen, the trigram of thunder in the East, signifies the eldest son and belongs to the wood element. Thunder, a life-giving force that rises from earth to power the new growth of spring, represents a rousing shock, potentially petrifying, but also exciting and productive. (*See* p. 106 for more details.)

CHI

Chi is the dragon's cosmic breath and the key to good feng shui. Chi is an intrinsic force, invisible to the eye, but nevertheless potent. The closest translation to the word chi is "energy."

The practice of feng shui implies the presence and accumulation of auspicious Sheng Chi, or "growth breath" along with protection from negative Shar Chi, which is translated as "killing breath." (*See* pp. 7–9 and 38–39 for more details. *See also* Shar Chi and Sheng Chi, p. 273.)

CHI KUNG

This style of physical training allows you to effectively move your chi, or intrinsic energy, through a series of slow exercises. Chi Kung can help overcome serious illnesses and in recent years has become extremely popular in the West where it is also called Qigong. (*See also* Illness, p. 246.)

CHI LIN

The mythical Chi Lin (also called Qi Lin and Kei Loon) is depicted with the head of a dragon, the body of a horse, and the scales of a fish. This fabulous symbol of good omens, prosperity, success, longevity, illustrious offspring, and enchantment is especially lucky for those in the military.

Endowed with magical qualities, Chi Lin emerged from the Yellow River bearing on its back the mythical map from which the legendary Fu Hsi (founder of the I Ching) derived the written characters of the Chinese language.

Chi Lin attracts the powerful cosmic breath of the dragon. Display this symbol in your workplace to bring promotion opportunities and prosperity. (*See also* I Ching, p. 246.)

CHIANG KAI-SHEK

Chiang Kai-shek, a Chinese leader, fled to Taiwan after unsuccessfully leading the Kuomintang against the communists under Mao Tse Tung. Many feng shui masters are believed to have fled with him and it has been speculated that

Chiang and a whole generation of generals and business leaders in Taiwan benefited from the excellent feng shui knowledge as a result. Much of this expertise in Taiwan is still secret, but recently many trade secrets have leaked out to the rest of the world. (*See also* Mao Tse Tung, p. 257.)

CHIEN TRIGRAM

This is the ultimate yang trigram. This first trigram in the I Ching is made up of three unbroken lines and placed in the Northwest quadrant of the Yang Pa Kua. This trigram symbolizes the patriarch and thus the Northwest corner of any home governs the luck of the male paternal. (*See* p. 111 for more details. *See also* Pa Kua p. 263.)

CHIEN LUNG (QIAN LONG)

Emperor from the Ching Dynasty credited with advancing feng shui. During Chien Lung's reign, arts and culture flourished in China. He implemented proper feng shui features into the Forbidden City, which had been plagued by fires and other problems since its construction. Chien Lung reportedly decreed that the young princes of the realm were to be housed in the eastern palaces, which were covered with green roofing tiles to energize the wood element. (*See also* China, p. 216.)

CHILDLESSNESS

This may be the result of a feng shui affliction if both spouses are in good reproductive health. It may also be cured using feng shui after exploring all other avenues.

If attempts to conceive a baby meet with no success, change the sleeping location and direction of the husband. Use the husband's Nien Yen direction according to the Kua formula in the Eight Mansions system, which is a very powerful system.

Also, place a precious elephant near the bed. The elephant symbolizes good descendants' luck. Placing special paintings that depict children in the bedroom will also aid in conception. (*See* pp. 70–71 for more details.)

CHILDREN

Children are the next generation, one of the Eight Aspirations. Energize the West side of the house for achieving descendants' luck, but the children themselves—especially the sons—should sleep in the East wing, or in their personal auspicious locations based on compass school formula. (*See* pp. 86–87 for more details.)

CHILDREN LUCK

(*See* Descendants' Luck, p. 221.)

CHINA

Feng shui originated in China, but for centuries the common people were not allowed to practice it. Emperors guarded the feng shui master's knowledge jealously and until the first half of this century, feng shui was forbidden in China. It is only with the opening of China that feng shui, which had thrived outside, was brought back into its homeland by business investors from Hong Kong. (*See also* Chien Lung, p. 215.)

CHINESE NEW YEAR

Chinese people throughout the world celebrate the start of the lunar year with many cultural rituals to ensure continued prosperity for the family. Include the following in your Chinese New Year celebration:

✳ Hang lanterns to attract wonderful New Year Chi. Keep the home brightly lit.

✳ Display fresh flowers around the home, preferably four different types to signify good luck throughout each of the four seasons.

✳ Grow green plants to advance your career luck. The higher the plants grow, the better your luck.

✳ Complete all housekeeping chores by the last day of the old year, so sweeping on New Year's Day won't result in wealth being swept away.

✳ Make sure your home is well stocked with food to symbolize abundance. Have plenty of oranges, plums, and kumquats on hand to signify wealth.

✳ Wear new clothes, preferably red in color to signify yang chi. Never wear white or black on New Year's Day.

✳ Give red packets filled with money to children, employees, and workers who have been of service to you in the past year.

✳ Add a new red packet filled with coins and currency to the old ones at the bottom of your rice urn to symbolically add to the family's wealth. Fill the urn to the brim with rice. If your luck in the past year has been bad, get a new rice urn decorated with auspicious symbols. (*See also* Rice Urn, p. 269.)

✳ Plant a new tree in the garden to symbolize new Sheng Chi, or growth energy.

✳ Display all the symbols of good fortune: mandarin oranges to signify gold; narcissus and other bulb plants to signify career luck; pussy willows to signify longevity. Most importantly, create a wealth tree by hanging real currency and coins on a tree.

✳ Serve plenty of sweet treats—cakes, tarts, chocolates and so forth—to ensure that the coming year will be "sweet."

✳ Be sure your altar is clean and filled with offerings. A mountain of flowers, sweets, and incense symbolizes generosity and will bring good luck by starting the flow of giving and receiving into your household. (*See also* Altar, p. 261.)

✳ Having a Lion dance is an excellent idea, since it will bring sound and happiness vibrations into the home. Let the lions roll a few baskets of gold into your house—the gold can be faux ingots or mandarin oranges. (*See also* Dragon Dance, p. 224.)

CHOPSTICKS

Using chopsticks and a rice bowl instead of fork and spoon lends significance to dining. Never place chopsticks upright into the rice bowl as this signifies death or heavy loss. Instead, use golden chopsticks and a golden rice bowl to attract the significance of abundance. Always place chopsticks together on the table, either flat or on a chopstick holder decorated with a longevity symbol. (*See also* Abundance, p. 200, and Longevity, p. 256.)

CHRYSANTHEMUMS

This flower is greatly favored during the New Year. Vibrant chrysanthemums convey so much strong yang energy that they instantly pull good luck into the home.

Chrysanthemums signify a life of ease and durability and are particularly appropriate offerings on the altar. Anything that you want to last - be it love, success, or luck—can be augmented by displaying these beautiful yellow flowers. When combined with other symbols of longevity, such as pine or bamboo, the crane or the deer, the indication of longevity is strengthened. (*See also* Longevity, p. 256.)

CHU YUAN CHUAN

The infamous Emperor Chu Yuan Chuan, founder of the Ming Dynasty, was reputed to be the second cruelest emperor of China. He started life as a peasant but later gained credence as a leader of a people's rebellion that crushed the Khans, thereby forming a new dynasty. Upon becoming emperor, he was told that his great success was due to good feng shui, so he rounded up all the feng shui masters in the land and had them executed. He then reportedly flooded the land with fake feng shui texts. (*See also* China, p. 216.)

CHUEH MING

This is the total loss direction in Eight Mansions Feng Shui Kua formula. It is imperative that you neither sit facing nor sleep with your head toward your personal Chueh Ming direction. (*See* pp. 118–119 and 184 for more details. *See also* Total Loss, p. 278.)

CLOTHES

When your clothes balance and harmonize with your chi, they attract good luck. Be sure that the elements of your clothes do not harm your self element.

Torn clothes (even intentionally ripped jeans to look hip) attract poverty energy, which often translates into ill fortune. Unflattering clothes have the same effect; in addition, they make you feel bad about yourself, depleting your yang chi and causing you to feel lethargic. Take time to change out of your pajamas in the morning and throw away baggy, shapeless "home clothes." (*See also* Good Luck, p. 240.)

COINS

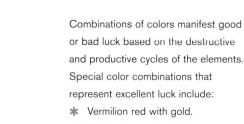

Old Chinese coins or replicas of such coins are potent tools for activating wealth. The circle and square shapes of authentic Chinese coins together represent heaven and earth. Tie three coins together with a red string and hang them on the inside of your front door to indicate that the money is already inside your house. (*See* p. 169 for more details. *See also* Cash Register, p. 213.)

COLOR

Color amplifies the elements and good color combinations bring good luck. Color therapy in feng shui is directly related to the concept of the five elements, which are represented by certain colors as summarized here:

Wood element	**brown and green**
Fire element	**red, yellow, and orange**
Metal element	**white, gold, silver, bronze, and chrome**
Earth element	**ochre and light yellow**
Water element	**blue, purple, and black**

Combinations of colors manifest good or bad luck based on the destructive and productive cycles of the elements. Special color combinations that represent excellent luck include:

* Vermilion red with gold.
* Dark rich purple with chrome or silver.
* Black with white.

Other good color combinations are:

* Two blues and one green.
* Two browns and one red.
* Two reds and one yellow.
* Two yellows and one white.
* Two whites and one blue.

Unlucky color combinations include:

* Two blues and one red.
* Two reds and one white.
* Two whites and one green.
* Two greens and one yellow.
* Two yellows and one blue.

(*See* pp. 28–29 for more details.)

COLUMNS

Columns, especially square stand-alone columns, can cause severe feng shui problems. Square columns have four sharp edges that send out poisonous Shar Chi. Deflect and dissolve this chi by placing plants against the edges or wrapping mirrors around the columns. Columns should never face the main entrance, either inside or outside, so in this case, the door or the column should be moved. (*See also* Sharp Edges, p. 273.)

COMPASS

The compass is the most important feng shui tool for determining accurate orientations (i.e., direction and location of any space). Always use a solid reliable compass to take precise directions. Stand square with the compass at waist level. (*See* pp. 42–43 for more details. *See also* Facing Direction, p. 231 and Sitting Direction, p. 273.)

COMPUTERS

Contrary to what you may have heard, computers do not necessarily cause bad feng shui; indeed, placed in the West or Northeast, computers energize these corners. Display screen saver images according to where your computer is used. Here are some suggestions:

* In the North, East, and Southeast, display swimming fish.
* In the South, Southwest, and Northeast, display mountain scenery.
* In the West and Northwest, display inventions and heroes.

(*See* pp. 52–59 for more details.)

CONCEPTION

Childless couples trying to start a family should first activate descendants' luck by sleeping in the Nien Yen direction of the husband. (*See* Eight Mansions, p. 121, for directions.)

Second, hang a painting of children near the marital bed. Third, have a young child born in the year of the Dragon roll across the bed three times or place a small representation of a dragon beside the bed to stimulate the precious yang energy needed. (*See* p. 109 for more details. *See also* Childlessness, p. 215.)

CROCKPOTS OR RICE COOKERS

Feng shui warns against placing the stove or even a crockpot in the Northwest of the kitchen, because this corner represents the primary breadwinner of the family, and the fire element will burn away the luck.

The Northwest corner also represents heaven; so cooking in the Northwest indicates "fire at heaven's gate." The Northwest is of the metal element and a stove represents fire, the only element capable of destroying metal. This serious feng shui defect should be corrected immediately by placing an urn of yin water nearby (yin water is still water with no life in it). (*See also* Yin Energy, p. 283.)

CORNERS

The protruding corner of the bathroom may be supporting or destroying the chi of the door.

Protruding corners create vertical sharp edges that send out negative energy, thereby creating havoc in the household. The corner can be nullified by placing a tall bushy plant against it.

Another type of protruding corner is the presence of a room that juts out of a regular-shaped house. Use element analysis to assess protruding corners. If the corner is located in the South and the main door is located in the West, the corner "destroys" the door because fire destroys metal.

Apply the Eight Mansions Kua formula to missing corners. If the missing corner would have been unlucky, then so much the better. But if the missing corner is lucky for you personally or represents a corner you wish to activate for the attributes it symbolizes (e.g., Southwest for love) then visually extend the corner using a wall mirror or install a bright light to shine into the missing corner. (*See* pp. 114–1223 for more details of Eight Mansions. *See also* Mirrors, p. 258.)

CORPORATE LOGOS

(*See* Logos, p. 255.)

CORRIDORS

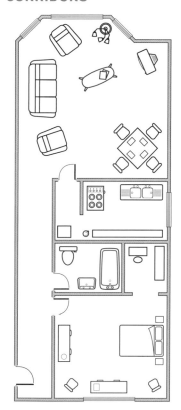

Long, narrow, straight corridors can become poison arrows that cause disharmony in relationships. The symbol of the arrow sends Shar Chi through the office or home, causing gossip, quarrels, and misunderstandings.

If your room is at the end of a long corridor, you will bear the brunt of most of the quarrelling. If your room opens off the corridor, you will have problems with the person occupying the room opposite you. Slow down the flight of the fast-moving chi by placing plants, art, and windchimes along the corridor.

If your apartment feels like a corridor, hang art on the walls and use a wall mirror to broaden the space. (*See* p. 38 for more details.)

COSMIC BREATH

The Sheng Chi that brings good fortune is lyrically described as the cosmic breath of the Green Dragon. Feng shui is about tapping into this breath, attracting it into the home, and encouraging it to settle and accumulate. (*See also* Feng Shui, p. 233.)

COURTYARD

An inner courtyard represents good feng shui for the heart of the home by enabling heaven and earth chi to meet, thus bringing auspicious chi into the very core of the home. If you have a courtyard, ensure that it is kept clean and filled with auspicious symbols. It is best to create an inner garden decorated with stones resembling dragons, Chi Lin and tortoises. (*See also* Atriums, p. 205.)

CRANES

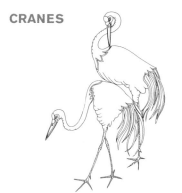

These beautiful long-necked birds with a red tuft of feathers at the forehead are popular symbols of longevity. They are often seen in Chinese art pieces or are depicted with the God of Longevity. Place statues of these cranes in either the West or the South of your garden. They will attract good health and happiness to your family. (*See* p. 172 for more details.)

CRIMSON PHOENIX

The phoenix signifies wonderful opportunities for bringing a good name, wealth, and prosperity to the family.

This magical celestial creature of the South (Feng Huang) is the "king of all feathered creatures of the Universe." The phoenix appears once every thousand years when times are auspicious and a good leader sits on the throne. The image of a phoenix placed in the South brings fresh opportunities into your life. The phoenix is also represented by low-lying foothills. When these appear in the South of your environment, the Crimson Phoenix is present. (*See* pp. 13 and 181 for more details.)

CROSS

A cross opposite your house or office brings severe bad luck. The sign of the cross (whether an X or a +) is an inauspicious sign. Crosses can be found in church spires or structural features of neighboring buildings. The best way to escape the effects of a cross is to use a different entrance. If you cannot, try to hang a large Pa Kua mirror to counter the cross. (*See also* Pa Kua Mirrors, p. 264.)

CRYSTAL BALLS

Crystal balls are even better than crystal points, because the shape represents the smoothness of plans and of life itself. Six crystal balls in the home will attract sheer abundance and happy, peaceful chi.

Crystal balls can be made of any kind of crystal although natural quartz crystals are more powerful than synthetic lead crystals. (*See also* Crystal Globe, p. 87.)

CRYSTALS

Crystals are effective energizers, especially if placed in the Southwest corner (the corner of "big earth"). Natural quartz crystal clusters are excellent symbols of mother earth.

Before displaying crystals, soak them for seven days and nights in sea salt water to dispel any negative energy they may be carrying. (*See* p. 67 for placement of crystals.)

CUL-DE-SACS

The feng shui interpretation of a dead-end street is "no way out," and therefore, not usually recommended. However, a cul-de-sac is sometimes a place where cosmic growth accumulates. Observing this feature will permit you to tap into great good fortune.

A gently curving road to a cul-de-sac is one indication of benevolent chi. Gather this chi by opening your gate, door, and windows to the empty road that represents the cul-de-sac. (*See also* p. 25 for more details.)

CURES FOR FENG SHUI ILLS

When feng shui misfortunes occur, it is usually possible to implement cures or remedies. Even if not completely successful, they do make a difference in the severity of the affliction.

Cures range from physical structures built to block, dissolve, or deflect bad chi, to carefully placed symbols to absorb or dissipate negative chi. Nine basic cures are summarized below.

1 Use the cycle of the five elements when a particular corner or direction is afflicted.

2 Use lights to generate the powerful yang energy that dissolves unwanted Shar Chi. A bright light in a dark corner immediately dispels stagnant or harmful yin chi.

3 Sounds make excellent feng shui cures because sound signifies life. Radios, stereos, and television sets are excellent remedies for opening cramped corners and narrow corridors.

4 Pets are powerful cures for stale or unhappy chi. Noisy pets—especially dogs—will never allow the home to become silent, therefore Yin energy will not become dominant.

5 Trees, walls, and other features can block off unsightly views or poison arrows. Sand pits, angled mirrors, and even a variety of Pa Kuas deflect unfriendly or hostile chi.

6 Mirrors and other reflective objects serve to reflect back any hostile chi being sent your way by secret poison arrows.

7 Water, especially yin water, is a powerful cure. An urn of still water in the kitchen will dissolve the dangers of an inappropriately placed stove. Yin water also absorbs quarrelsome energy. Change the water at least once a week.

8 Objects that move can also be powerful feng shui tools. The wind generated by a fan placed in front of a sharp corner will dissolve the Shar Chi of the edge.

9 The Yin Pa Kua and other hostile objects can push back negative chi, but use these only as a last resort.

(*See also* Good Fortune, p. 240.)

CURVED KNIFE

A curved knife can protect against bad feng shui when traveling to the East or Southeast. Swipe the air three times in that direction before setting out. (*See also* Knives, p. 251.)

CUTTING CHI

Unlucky cutting chi occurs when nearby structures or features resemble the cutting edge of knives or other sharp instruments. Multilevel roads, open shelves, and sharp circular roads can form this feature. Block the offending structure from view with trees, a wall, curtains, or screens. (*See* pp. 16–18 for more details.)

CYCLES OF CHI

The enhancing, weakening, and controlling cycles of the five elements according to the theory of Wu Xing. There are productive and destructive cycles to the universal elements of wood, fire, earth, water, and metal.

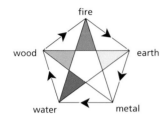

THE PRODUCTIVE CYCLE

…explains the productive nature of the elements: wood produces fire, which produces earth, which produces metal, which produces water, which produces wood, and so on.

THE EXHAUSTIVE CYCLE

…is the direct opposite of the Productive Cycle: fire exhausts wood, which exhausts water, which exhausts metal, which exhausts earth, which exhausts fire and so on.

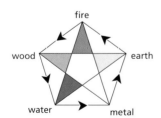

THE DESTRUCTIVE CYCLE

…expresses the controlling nature of the five elements: fire destroys metal, which destroys wood, which destroys earth, which destroys water, which destroys fire, and so on.
(*See also* Wu Xing, p. 282.)

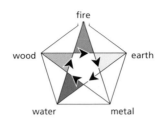

D

DEER

Deer are symbols of longevity often depicted with the God of Longevity. (*See* p. 173 for more details.)

DEITIES

In feng shui, all deities are Taoist unless otherwise noted. They symbolize specific aspirations such as wealth and longevity. Images of these deities in the home attract vibrant chi. (*See also* Gods and Goddesses, pp. 239–240.)

DEMARCATING FLOOR PLANS

It is necessary to demarcate the sectors of the home to assess chi distribution. Three ways to demarcate the floorplan are summarized here.

1 Superimpose the nine-sector Lo Shu grid onto your house plan and study the sectors one by one.

2 Superimpose the compass of directions onto the floor plan so it resembles a pie chart with slices indicating the different directions.

3 Examine the floor plan on a room-by-room basis.
(*See also* Floor Plans, p. 234.)

DENG XIAO PING

Deng is the Chinese leader who transformed China into a free market economy. His rise to the most powerful man in China during the 1980s was supposedly the result of good feng shui. Legend has it that this latter day "emperor" of China benefited from the excellent feng shui of his ancestral home. Three peaks visible from his home were a sign indicating that a descendant of the family would become the supreme leader. (*See also* China, p. 216.)

DESCENDANTS' LUCK

To activate children's luck in the home, it is necessary to activate the West, but the children, especially the eldest son, should sleep in the East. Use wood energy to bring this part of the living room alive with yang chi. The best representations of wood are lush plants. (*See* pp. 70–71 for more details. *See also* Children, p. 216.)

DESIGN

Motifs, shapes, and colors all have feng shui connotations. Develop different motifs for each of the five elements and then use them according to the directions symbolized by each element. For example, using the water motif for rooms in the North enhances the water element there. Use this table to determine the element motifs or symbols most suitable:

Direction	Motif
North, East, Southeast	*Water*
South, Southwest, Northeast	*Fire*
West, Northwest	*Metal*
Southwest, Northeast	*Earth*
East, Southeast	*Wood*

(*See also* Wu Xing, p. 282.)

DESKS

Properly energized, your desk can attract excellent work luck. To check for dimensions, refer to the feng shui ruler, found on p. 49. Energize your desktop with objects symbolizing the five elements. Use a Lo shu grid and a compass to mark the corresponding direction of each of the grids, then energize your desk according to the meanings of the different directions.

On the East corner of your desk, place a bowl of fresh flowers. On the Southeast corner, place a small green plant. On the West, your telephone, and on the Northwest, your computer. On the North place your cup of coffee or your daily glass of water. On the South side, place a red lamp and on the Northeast a crystal paperweight. And on the Southwest corner place a globe, preferably made of lapis or crystal.

Determine your Kua number to find out your best sitting direction. With the aid of a compass, mark the direction you should face to welcome luck. Sit in that position as often as possible.

Keep your office desk tidy and clean. Clutter can cause many unnecessary problems. Energize your office desk with the presence of a Ru Yi, the symbol of authority, if you wish to rise to the upper echelons of the company. Place metal coins if you desire wealth, and symbols of growth such as crystal and gem citrine trees if you desire success.

Finally, make sure that you never have your view blocked with a stack of files or paperwork. Let your view be unencumbered by keeping the space in front of you empty. (*See* pp. 52–53 for more details.)

DESTRUCTIVE CYCLE

(*See also* Cycles of Chi, p. 221.)

DINING ROOM

This important room benefits from good feng shui. When located in the middle of the home, the dining room signifies the family at the heart of the home.

The dining room should always be on an equal or higher level than the living room and should not be next to a bedroom or bathroom. Do not have the dining room at the end of a long hallway, as this is an unlucky room.

Food on the family table can be symbolically doubled with a wall mirror to indicate prosperity. To energize the "stomach" of the home, hang paintings of luscious flowers and ripe, juicy fruits. (*See* pp. 34–35 for more details.)

DINING TABLE

Tables are auspicious when they come in lucky shapes. Of the four auspicious shapes for dining tables—round, square, rectangular, and octagonal—the round shape is best as it symbolizes everything proceeding smoothly. Round is also the shape that signifies gold. Thus, round tables symbolize the creation of wealth and prosperity. (*See also* Furniture, p. 237.)

DIRECTIONS

(*See also* Compass, p. 218.)

DOOR GODS

Military Door Gods originated in the Tang Dynasty. They are based on two loyal generals, Chin and Yu, who stood guard over the emperor's quarters through the night to ensure the son of heaven would sleep peacefully,

undisturbed by spirits or ghosts. The guards themselves succumbed to their nocturnal duties, so the emperor commissioned court painters to draw two pictures of fully armed generals onto the entrance doors into his private quarters. The generals came to be known as military Door Gods and were eventually drawn one with a white face and one with a black face.

The civilian Door Gods appear less threatening. These Gods are also displayed in a pair, but are drawn in court robes, giving them the appearance of courtiers rather than fighters. Their protective powers are symbolic rather than actual and they guard against bad luck rather than ghosts and spirits. If you paint these Gods on your front doors, be sure the doors are painted red. (*See also* Gods and Goddesses, pp. 239–240.)

Use the symbolic protective powers of the civilian Door Gods to guard against bad luck.

DOORS

The size, number, and positions of doors have important feng shui implications. The main door is especially important. Ensure that no hostile structures in the outside environment harm this door.

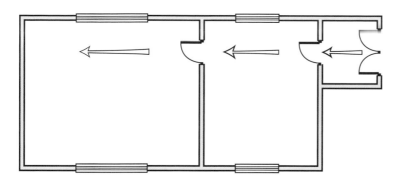

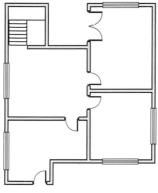

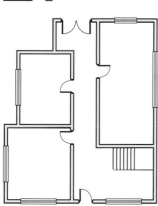

Top: Chi rushes into the house too quickly. Put up a screen to avoid this.

Middle: The main door is bigger than the inner doors and chi will meander auspiciously through the layout.

Above: Front and back doors form a straight line, which is inauspicious.

Be conscious of these taboos:

* Doors should not be placed one behind the other in a straight line.
* Doors should not open awkwardly against each other.
* Doors should not directly confront one another.
* The main door should not be smaller than other doors.

(*See* pp. 30 and 38 for more details.)

DOUBLE HAPPINESS

An excellent and popular feng shui symbol is "double happiness," which is the Chinese word for happiness, written twice. This symbol activates wedding luck. If you hope to find romance or a mate, place this symbol in the Southwest corner of your house or wear it in the form of a ring. (*See* pp. 75 and 173 for more details.)

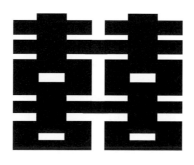

DOUBLING

The concept of doubling wealth is part of feng shui amplification. Doubling anything auspicious makes the outcome even better. The daily income of a restaurant or retail shop should also be doubled with a wall mirror reflecting the cash register. Mirrors all around the shop will double the number of customers. (*See also* Wealth Luck, p. 281.)

DRAGON

The dragon is the most important symbol in feng shui and Chinese folklore. According to legend, there are nine dragons, each a celestial creature that has largesse over an aspiration of humanity. All nine dragons are portrayed on a beautiful wall in the Forbidden City in Beijing. In addition to the earth dragon, are the wind dragon, sea dragon, water dragon, sky dragon, fire dragon, golden dragon, mountain dragon, and heavenly dragon.

Also known as "the art of harnessing wind and water," feng shui is about capturing and creating Sheng Chi, the dragon's precious cosmic breath. The dragon is traditionally associated with East; thus, the image of a dragon on the East side of the office or home will bring good fortune. Gardens can be activated using the dragon symbol, by setting plants in a winding flowerbed on the East side of the house.

When using the dragon symbol, there are several taboos that should be noted.

1 Never place a dragon in the bedroom; it is much too yang for a place of rest.

2 Dragons made of wood, ceramic, or crystal are fine for the East, but avoid dragons made of gold, cloisonné, or other metals in the East, as metal destroys wood. Use gold dragons in the West and Northwest to activate and complement water features.

3 A desk carved with dragon imagery can bring good luck, but not everyone has sufficient yang energy to sit at such a desk. Everyone can benefit from the dragon image, however. Remember that the dragon should not be too large or too fierce.

4 Displaying nine dragons in the house will make you extremely ambitious, although it may also cloud your judgment. When dragon energy becomes excessive it can cause a premature fall from power. Always treat dragon images with great respect.

5 Placing dragons beside water features makes the water feature more potent. This is one of the secrets of Taoist feng shui and the effect is simply magical. (*See* p. 170 for more details.)

DRAGON AND PHOENIX

Dragon and phoenix are the ultimate yang and yin symbols of Chinese cosmology and mythology. The dragon is the symbol of male vigor and fertility. The phoenix symbolizes yin splendor and female beauty when placed with

the dragon. (Alone, the phoenix takes on yang characteristics and male essence.) Together the dragon and phoenix symbolize the emperor and empress in a fruitful marriage blessed with success and prosperity. As a

popular image in marriage celebrations, especially during the tea drinking ceremony, the union of these two symbolic creatures attracts wealth and descendants' luck. (*See* p. 68 for more details. *See also* Crimson Phoenix, p. 219, and Green Dragon, p. 241.)

DRAGON CARP/ DRAGON GATE

The dragon carp swims upstream against the current and then leaps across the dragon gate to become the dragon. Displaying a dragon carp or dragon gate in the home brings scholastic and career success for the younger generation. (It is interesting to note that carps that fail to make the leap into genuine Dragonhood are forever stamped with the mark of having tried and failed, and this explains the red patch on the carp's forehead. (*See* p. 87 for more details.)

DRAGON DANCE

The dragon dance is usually held to celebrate such occasions as important openings, Chinese New Year, and so forth. Usually a hundred martial arts experts are involved in performing a good dragon dance to create auspicious chi. (*See also* Chinese New Year, p. 216.)

DRAGON FISH
(See Arowana, p. 204.)

DRAGON HORSE
(See Chi Lin, p. 215.)

DRAGON TORTOISE

This legendary symbol combines the awesome powers and attributes of the dragon and the tortoise, two of the four spiritually endowed creatures of Chinese symbolism. The creature has the body of a tortoise, the head of a dragon, and is depicted sitting on a bed of coins and gold ingots. In its mouth is the symbolic coin of prosperity and on its back is a baby tortoise. Like the Chi Lin, this creature of the imagination demonstrates the use of symbolism to enhance the physical environment. This image is multifaceted.

* The tortoise, reportedly able to live 3,000 years without food or air, symbolizes longevity.
* The dragon symbolizes success, courage, and determination. The tortoise's transformation into a dragon indicates impending good fortune in career and business.
* The base of gold ingots signifies tremendous wealth and prosperity.
* The coin in its mouth signifies increased income.

* The baby tortoise on its back symbolizes wonderful descendants' luck.

Place this symbol on your desk in the North or East sector, but not directly in front of you. Confronting a powerful symbol is asking for trouble. Alternatively, place this symbol behind your desk to signify support of both the dragon and the tortoise. (See p. 172 for more details.)

DRAINS
By applying the water dragon formula, the humble drain can be harnessed to bring extreme good fortune. Drains should always be free flowing, since blocked drains are obstacles to your ventures. Clean drains regularly and ensure that they flow past the main door in the correct direction. Determine the direction from inside the house, looking out.

* For homes where the main door faces North, South, East, or West (one of the cardinal directions), drains should flow from left to right.
* For homes where the main door faces a secondary direction (Southeast, Southwest, Northeast or Northwest) the drain should flow from right to left.

(See pp. 94–95 for more details. See also Jade Water Belt, p. 249.)

DRIED FLOWERS
Dried preserved, or pressed flowers are purveyors of yin energy and are not recommended for homes. While silk flowers can generate the good chi of fresh flowers, dry flowers cannot. Potpourris, however, are excepted as

they are seldom displayed and used only for their fragrance. (See also Flower Gardens, p. 234.)

DRIVEWAYS

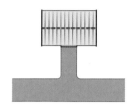

A curved driveway brings better luck than a long, straight one.

A long straight driveway that ends directly at the main entrance like an arrow brings severe bad luck. It is better to let the driveway curve or meander. A circular driveway is most auspicious since the round shape signifies gold. (See pp. 12–18 for more details.)

DZAMBHALA (ALSO JHAMBALA)
This God of Wealth is believed to answer the prayers of the poor. There is also the tradition of making wealth vases that invoke the Dzambhala's help. Part of the Mahayana Buddhist tradition, this deity is not mentioned in Chinese feng shui texts. The Taoist ritual of making wealth vases ritual had been relatively secret for hundreds of years. This is also a Tibetan tradition, and the knowledge of such vases is secret and powerful. (See pp. 174–175 for more details. See also Wealth Vases, p. 281.)

E

EARLY HEAVEN ARRANGEMENT

This refers to the arrangement of trigrams around the Yin Pa Kua, which are used as defensive Pa Kuas. Such symbols usually come with a mirror in the center and hung above doors to deflect harmful chi coming from sharp structures in the environment. (*See* pp. 98–99 for more details.)

EARTH LUCK

Earth is one of the five elements that are part of the Wu Xing theory. Earth luck comes from the practice of spatial arrangement. Earth luck complements heaven luck (tien chai) as well as humanity luck (ren chai). The compass sectors that signify earth are the Southwest (big earth) and Northeast (small earth).

The center of the home also represents earth energy. It is important for earth chi to be present in healthy doses for a home to be lucky.

The most effective symbol of the earth is the globe. When placed in Northeast, it harnesses luck for the children. In the Southwest and center of the home it magnifies and improves the luck of the family while in the West and

Northwest it leads to prosperity by harnessing the productive cycle in which the element earth produces gold in the metal sectors. (*See also* Wu Xing, p. 282.)

EAST

The traditional home of the dragon and, in the Later Heaven arrangement, the place of the big wood element.

In this part of the home, the chi signifies the essence of growth, reflected in the wood element. In Imperial China, this place was reserved for the heirs to the Dynasties. At all costs, keep a healthy store of yang energy here. Do not allow stagnant energy to accumulate in the East. (*See* pp. 106–107 for more details.)

EAST GROUP

Everyone benefits from either the West or the East group of directions, depending on individual Kua numbers. Kua numbers 1, 3, 4, or 9 belong to the East group. The East group's auspicious directions are Southeast, North, East, and South.

East group people will benefit from using their directions. They should avoid using the West group directions, as those are inauspicious for them. (*See* pp. 115–116 for more details. *See also* Kua Numbers, p. 251.)

EAST HOUSE

According to the direction of the main door, this is a house that faces an East group direction. The sitting direction is directly opposite the facing direction of the house. Thus all houses that face West, Northwest, North, or South are deemed to be East houses.

Under Eight Directions or Mansions theory, the chi of all East group people is compatible with these houses. This guideline can create problems for those following the Kua formula. People trying to tap their Sheng Chi direction for the main door, whose Sheng Chi is either East or Southeast, will discover that by facing either of these directions they will NOT be living in an East house. Under the formula of Eight Mansions not everyone is able to tap their best Sheng Chi direction as the main door direction. (*See* p. 117 for more details.)

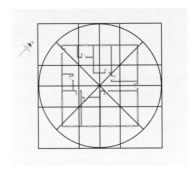

Eight Mansions theory involves superimposing a grid of directions onto a layout of your house.

EDUCATION LUCK

This is one of the eight aspirations that can be activated to benefit your development. Education luck can be activated to benefit college students and schoolchildren. The technique is simple: activate the earth element by placing meaningful symbols in the Northeast corner of the bedroom or living room.

Place a crystal globe to strengthen the earth element of the Northeast corner. Placing three fish on a crystal globe is also an effective energizer. (*See* pp. 84–87 for more details.)

EIGHT ASPIRATIONS

The Eight Aspirations can be activated in their particular sectors by the items highlighted in this diagram.

The eight aspirations are the types of luck associated with the eight sides of the Pa Kua. North represents career aspirations; South symbolizes aspirations related to recognition and fame; East stands for health; West for children; Southwest for love, marriage and family; Northeast for wisdom and literary luck; Southeast for wealth; and Northwest for mentoring. To attract the luck associated with these aspirations, just "activate" the compass corner that signifies each type of luck.

Career luck is activated by water features in the North. Recognition comes with the shining of a bright light in the South. Wealth is attracted to homes where the Southeast corner is filled with lush growing plants. Fresh flowers in the East signify good health. Children and mentor luck arrives when gold is placed in the West and Northwest respectively, and excellent academic luck comes when the Northeast is properly activated with crystal globes. (*See* p. 113 for more details.)

EIGHT DIRECTIONS

Reference is frequently made to the eight directions: North, South, East, West, Northwest, Northeast, Southwest, and Southeast. The study of feng shui involves the investigation of luck in these directions of the house.

Familiarize yourself with the compass where North is measured as magnetic North. All formulas use the directions of the compass to describe the distribution of different types of chi. (*See* p. 130 for more details.)

EIGHT IMMORTALS (OR PA HSIEN)

These are the Taoist Immortals whose presence in the home brings good fortune and protection from people with bad intentions. They are a class of human beings who have been deified and possess magical powers. Legend has it that everything they touch turns to gold. Displaying their presence in the home creates the chi of immortality as well as great success luck. Each of them represents a different condition in life—poverty, wealth, aristocracy, commoner, old age, youth, masculinity, and femininity. (*See* p. 93 for details.)

CHANG KUO LAO

Seventh-century recluse whose supernatural powers of magic can render him invisible. His emblem is the Yu Ku, a musical instrument shaped as a bamboo tube or drum with two mallets to beat it. The emperor Ming Huang wished to attract him into his Imperial court, but Chung Kuo refused to give up his wandering life. He disappeared and entered immortality, apparently without dying!

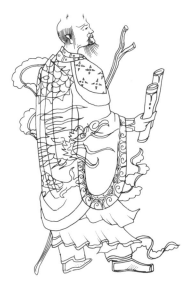

Chang Kuo Lao

Chung Li Chuan

CHUNG LI CHUAN

The Chief of the Eight Immortals lived in the Chou Dynasty and found the elixir of life. Generally shown as a fat man with an exposed tummy, sometimes holding a peach, and carrying his emblem: the fan used to bring the dead back to life.

Ho Hsien Ku

HAN HSIANG TZU The youngest of the Immortals has the power to make flowers grow and blossom instantly. He keeps a profusion of them in a sack that he carries on his back. His emblem is the flute, which he plays continuously as the patron saint of musicians. Animals, insects, and plants thrive in his presence. Those who love gardens will benefit from having his image in the home.

Lu Tung Pin

HO HSIEN KU Seventh-century daughter of a grocer, she ate the peach of immortality and turned into a fairy. Her diet of crushed mother of pearl and moonbeams produced immortality. She disappeared after being summoned to the Court of the Empress Wu of the Tang Dynasty. Her emblem is the lotus, which she carries in her left hand. She brings luck to housewives.

Li Tieh Kuai

LI TIEH KUAI The beggar who leans on his iron walking stick is extremely proficient in magic. In his hand he carries a pilgrim's gourd from which a scroll is escaping. This signifies his power to set spirits free from their bodies.

Lan Tsai Ho

LU TUNG PIN A scholar and recluse who learned the secrets of Taoism, he attained immortality at the age of fifty. He is the patron saint of barbers and is worshipped by the sick. His emblem is the flywhisk and a sword of supernatural powers is usually hung on his back. He travels the world slaying evil creatures. Displaying his image in the home provides protection from those who would harm you.

Han Hsiang Tzu

LAN TSAI HO Probably the strangest of the Immortals, she is usually drawn with one foot bare. Her emblem is the flower basket and she is the patron saint of flower sellers. She epitomizes the spirit of femininity. Place her image in the Southwest of your home to energize family and marriage luck.

Tsao Kuo Chiu

TSAO KUO CHIU The son of a military commander and brother of an empress of the Sung dynasty, he is depicted in court garments as an aristocrat. His emblem is a pair of castanets derived from court tablets authorizing access to the palace.

EIGHT MANSIONS

A powerful feng shui formula, based on year of birth and gender, which indicates personalized auspicious and unlucky directions. (*See* pp. 122–123 for more details. *See also* Kua Numbers, p. 251.)

EIGHT PRECIOUS OBJECTS

These eight treasures are extremely auspicious and consist of the parasol, the double fish, the vase, the lotus flower, the conch shell, the mystic knot, the banner of victory, and finally the dharma wheel.

Practitioners of symbolic feng shui usually display these eight treasures as embroidered fabric screens hung on doorways to attract good fortune. The fabric screens also make excellent shields to prevent areas with harmful chi from afflicting the rest of the household.

THE DOUBLE FISH symbol is often worn as an amulet to ward off evil intentions. Place it near the entrance of the home and anyone with bad intentions toward you will not succeed in staying for long. You can use a pair of brass carp for this purpose.

THE LOTUS brings every kind of good fortune. Grown at home it has the potency to turn bad luck into good luck.

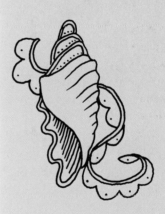

THE CONCH SHELL attracts auspicious travel luck. The best shells are those that are coiled and left turning. Seashells should be cleaned and soaked in salt water for at least a month, then can be placed in your living room. The cowrie shell is sometimes used as an amulet by travelers.

THE DHARMA WHEEL (or Wheel of Law) represents the power of heavenly energy. A representation of this wheel leads to positive spiritual development.

THE PRECIOUS VASE placed near the entrance of a home attracts peaceful chi. The Chinese word for vase is ping, which also means "peace." Keep vases empty if outside the house, but full when placed inside. Fill vases to the brim with seven varieties of semi-precious stones for good luck. Transform them into wealth vases to benefit the family. (*See* Wealth Vases, p. 281.)

THE PARASOL OR UMBRELLA is an excellent symbol of protection. It will ward off burglars when placed near the front of the home.

THE MYSTIC KNOT signifies a never-ending cycle of good luck turning into bad luck then into good luck again, like the cycle of birth and rebirth. In feng shui it is a popular symbol of never-ending affection and devotion—a cycle of love which continues until death. The mystic knot is an extremely powerful symbol to wear as it acts both as an amulet of protection as well as an energizer of relationship luck.

THE BANNER OF VICTORY symbolizes success in all of your endeavors. It is often depicted as a long flag similar to those that were used by ancient Chinese armies. The banner of victory is particularly auspicious for those who are in politics, the military, or the government, and will bring elevation in rank.

EIGHT TRIGRAMS

These are the principal symbols of feng shui analysis. Placed around the eight sides of the Pa Kua, the trigrams are three-lined combinations of broken and unbroken lines. The unbroken lines are yang lines while the broken lines are yin lines. The eight trigrams are Chien, Kun, Kan, Li, Ken, Chen, Tui, and Sun, and they make up the root of the 64 hexagrams that in turn comprise the I Ching. Understanding the significance of these trigrams and their placement around the Pa Kua unlocks the secrets of this octagonal symbol. (*See* pp. 88–89 for more details.)

ELEMENTS

(*See* Wu Xing, p. 282.)

ELEPHANT

The elephant is a precious animal symbolizing fertility, strength, and wealth. Its presence in the home benefits the family's descendants' luck.

The Chinese regard the elephant as one of four animals of power and energy, the other three being the tiger, the leopard, and the lion. The elephant is also one of the seven precious treasures of Buddhism and in Thailand is regarded as a most valuable creature. In China, the white elephant has been adopted as the national emblem. According to Hindu mythology, the world is supported on the back of an elephant standing on a tortoise and in the Hindu pantheon, the Lord Ganesh manifests in the form of an elephant God. In Mahayana Buddhism, the elephant is the "bearer of the wish-granting gem." Gigantic stone monoliths of elephants standing and kneeling can be seen on the avenue leading to the Ming Tombs in Beijing. (*See* p. 109 for more details.)

ELEVATED STRUCTURES

These should be examined to determine their effect on your outer doors.

Examples include tall buildings and multilevel roads which, if too close to the main door, can afflict both the door and the house. Trees can block such elevated structures from view. (*See* pp. 16–18 for more details.)

ENERGY

Feng shui is the study of environmental energy, which can be likened to the dragon's breath called chi. (*See also* Chi, p. 215.)

ENHANCERS

These are good fortune symbols, which are believed to attract and create good chi when correctly placed inside the home. All homes, temples, and palaces have their fair share of symbols that enhance good luck. Most feng shui techniques also use element methodology to energize the home to manifest good fortune. (*See* pp. 168–171 for more details.)

ENTRANCES

Entrances into buildings and homes are exceedingly important as they allow auspicious chi to enter. Entrances that suffer from feng shui afflictions will negatively affect the chi.

The entrance into the apartment complex is as important as the door to your apartment. At least one of these entrances should face a direction that is auspicious for you. For Flying Star natal chart analysis, use the facing orientation of the apartment complex.

The main door is defined as the one most frequently used. Entrances into homes can be protected in many ways, but the best method is to place a pair of lions beside the door with the male lion

on the right and female lion on the left. Lions are extremely powerful protectors, but you can also hang pictures of other fierce animals such as tigers, elephants, or panthers to create protective chi outside your home or office. (*See* p. 78 for more details.)

F
FACING DIRECTION

This term refers to the compass direction that a house faces. Generally, the facing direction of a house is the same as the main entrance, but this is not the case for all houses. Some masters advocate a view of the main road. Thus, if your house is oriented to the main road, but your door faces the side, then the facing direction is the side facing the road. Other masters maintain that the facing direction of a house has the most unencumbered view. So if you live in an apartment with a balcony overlooking a valley, then it is likely that that is the facing direction of your apartment. (*See* pp. 32–33 for more details.)

FAKE FLOWERS

Fake flowers can be as good as the real thing for purposes of feng shui, although fresh flowers are always a better enhancer of wood element chi. Flowers energize fresh yang energy in the home, especially in the living room. However, there is nothing worse than wilting or dried flowers. If you do not have time to replace fading flowers, fake flowers are just as effective. Silk flowers can be even better than real ones, if they look more vibrant and alive. (*See also* Flowers, p. 234.)

FAME LUCK

This is recognition luck that leads to success in the workplace and in politics. This luck also benefits those in the public eye, such as entertainers and politicians.

Fame luck can be activated and energized in the South corner of your home or office. Install bright lights in the South side of the home. A South-facing entrance is also conducive to obtaining a good name. (*See* pp. 57–59 for more details.)

FAMILY FENG SHUI

If you wish to enhance the harmony of relationships within the family, energize the center of the home by placing the family room or dining room in this area. Add a bright light to enhance and magnify the earth mother. Activity in the center of the home gives it life and precious yang energy.

If you find that family members are quarreling too much, or there are too many temper tantrums, place a big vase filled with yin or still water in this room to quiet things down a bit. (*See also* Center of the Home, p. 213.)

FAMILY PORTRAITS

An effective method for creating family closeness is hanging a family portrait in the living room or family room. Every member of the family should be included and, to symbolize happiness, all should be smiling.

A triangular arrangement with the breadwinner at the apex, is particularly effective when he or she is born in a fire or earth year. This arrangement creates the element of fire, signifying precious yang energy.

A wavy arrangement in which the family members' heads are not level creates the water element. It is a yin shape and is excellent when there is excessive yang energy in the house (e.g. more sons than daughters.

The rectangular arrangement suggests the wood element and is the most common arrangement. Here, all members pose so that their heads are level. This arrangement also suggests a balanced and regular shape and is suitable if the breadwinner was born in a wood or fire year.

A square arrangement is similar to the rectangle and is suitable for small families. This shape suggests the earth element, which also signifies the family. It is especially good if the head of the family was born in a metal year, since earth produces metal in the cycle of elements. (*See also* Portraits, p. 266.)

FAMILY ROOM

The family room in the center of the home fosters harmony. Family members will get along better, husband and wife will be on good terms, children will not become rebellious, and siblings will stay close to each other. This is because the house will be balanced with active, vibrant heart chi. (*See* p. 99 for more details.)

FAN

The humble hand-held fan is capable of protecting you from bad chi sent your way. In the old days, court officials were never without their fans, which had been blessed with special powers. Choose a sandalwood fan or one that is completely red in color to create a protective aura around you.

A golden fan will also serve as an excellent amulet.

Ceiling and electrical fans can be either protective or activating tools. When energy is stagnant, turning on the fan will do wonders in moving the chi. However, overhead ceiling fans are not good to sleep under. (*See* p. 187 for hand-held fans.)

FAT BUDDHA

The Fat Buddha, also known as the Happiness or Laughing Buddha, carries a huge bag to scoop up all your troubles.

The Fat Buddha is also known as the Happiness or Laughing Buddha. He brings good fortune into the home. His presence in any eating establishment is an excellent energizer of good fortune. (*See also* Buddha Statues, p. 211.)

FENG HUANG

(*See* Crimson Phoenix, p. 219.)

FENG SHUI

Feng shui means wind and water, and the luck conveyed by these two natural elements of the environment. Feng shui is the science of arranging the living space using correct orientations that reflect the patterns of chi energy in the environment. Its different methods and systems help create a harmonious interface between the heaven, earth, and humanity chi in any given space.

Feng shui brings harmony into the home by creating vibrations that attract wealth, health, and happiness. When a home is oriented to harmonize with surrounding landforms, good feng shui is welcomed and health, wealth, and prosperity ensue.

The key to feng shui is balancing the forces of yin and yang, and creating harmony between the five elements present in the space (*see* pp. 40–41). Feng shui coordinates time, placement, space, and energy to maximum effect, reflecting the interplay of chi between humanity and the universe.

Although it is one of the oldest known disciplines, feng shui's relevance to our health and happiness is gaining mainstream appeal today, reflecting a growing understanding and appreciation of the practice, as well as a belief in its potency. (*See also* Yin Yang Symbol, p. 283.)

FILES

Tape three Chinese coins tied with red string onto the cover or sides of important files, such as contracts and projects. The red string fires up precious yang energy for your work. Make sure your files never pile up directly in front of you on your desk. Files should be kept either behind you or at your left side. Piles of files are like mountains that create obstacles to advancement and preclude recognition of your hard work. (*See* pp. 52–53 for more details. *See also* Desks, p. 222.)

FIRE

Fire is one of the five elements that make up the Wu Xing, and is symbolized by the direction South. To energize the luck of opportunities and recognition, bright lights should be installed on South walls. The lights magnify fire energy and bring in the yang essence so vital for success luck to manifest. (*See* p. 40 for more details. *See also* Wu Xing, p. 282.)

FISH

The fish represents abundance because the Chinese word for fish—yu—also means abundance. Thus, many business people like to keep ornamental live fish both in the office and at home.

An aquarium is the easiest way to keep fish, and is best displayed near the front entrance or in the living room. Keep goldfish, carp, arrowana, guppies, or any other beautiful freshwater fish. Many swear by the arrowana (also called dragon fish) and just as many love the fabulous goldfish. Some prefer miniature ponds instead of aquariums, and these are perfect for interacting directly with koi, the colorful carp. In the garden, you can keep guppies in lotus and water lily pots, which are easily installed.

Neon-colored guppies are perpetually pregnant and invite wonderful growth chi. Flying Star Feng Shui will help you identify the places in the garden and inside the home where water features will attract the most wealth luck.

Always keep your fish healthy and clean. There is nothing worse than an ugly aquarium that is not properly maintained, or of diseased fish who look so miserable you can feel the sadness chi emanating from them!

If keeping live fish is difficult for your living situation, a figurine of a fish or two, or a vase or painting featuring fish, will be just as good. Never keep fish in the bedroom since water here is not a good sign. (*See also* Aquariums, p. 203.)

FISH PONDS

Ponds are excellent water features in the North, Southeast, and East, and also in the Southwest after February 4

2004, when Period 8 began. During this period, water features in the Southwest will be extremely auspicious, especially if your main entrance is also located in the Southwest of your home.

Fish are also effective for energizing special corners. Note that fishponds are particularly beneficial in the North (water) and Southeast or East (wood), as the element of water is compatible with both water and wood, which it nurtures. (*See* pp. 160–165 for more details about water features.)

FIVE (the number)

Five is an earth number and features as an earth star in all the compass formulas. It is generally regarded as inauspicious except under certain circumstances and during certain periods. (*See* pp. 64–67, 90, and 114–116 for more details.)

FIVE ELEMENTS

(*See* Wu Xing, p. 282.)

FIVE GHOSTS

Five Ghosts describes a type of bad luck in Eight Mansions Feng Shui. Advanced Flying Star Feng Shui identifies situations when Five Ghosts can be transformed into harbingers of good fortune but, in general, you should avoid this direction. Check your Kua number and note your Five Ghosts direction.

Kua 1	Northeast
Kua 2	Southeast
Kua 3	Northwest
Kua 4	Southwest
Kua 5	(male) Southeast
Kua 5	(female) North
Kua 6	East
Kua 7	South
Kua 8	North
Kua 9	West

(*See* pp. 119–121 for more details.

FIVE YELLOW

This annual time dimension affliction is a severe situation that must be corrected by hanging metal windchimes. The Five Yellow strikes different compass sectors in different years. Unless the effect of the Five Yellow is remedied, anyone sleeping in a room it occupies in any year may fall ill, lose money, or meet up with other misfortunes. (*See* pp. 152–153 for more details. *See also* Compass, p. 218, and Windchimes, p. 281.)

FLOOR PLANS

Your floor plan is very important, especially when practicing Compass Formula Feng Shui.

Always perform feng shui analysis with a floor plan on hand. This is the most efficient method of investigation, especially in Compass Formula Feng Shui, which requires intense concentration when demarcating the house into grids and compass sectors for analyzing chi distribution. (*See* pp. 42–43 for more details.)

FLOWER GARDENS

With Garden Feng Shui, you can design your flowerbeds and the choice of flowers to create harmony. Design your flowerbeds according to the shapes that are most conducive to different sections of your gardens and select flowers according to their colors.

In the Southeast, the North, and the East of your garden, use rectangular flowerbeds and plant blue flowers and leafy plants. The jade plant, also regarded as the money plant, is excellent in this part of your garden.

In the West and Northwest, select round or semi-circular flower containers and grow yellow or white flowers.

In the South, Southwest, and Northeast arrange square containers or flowerbeds and grow flowers in a riot of red, pink, yellow and orange. (*See also* Garden, p. 238.)

FLOWERS

Fresh flowers energize the home, especially benefiting the daughters. Remove thorns from roses before displaying them. Remember that wilting flowers create sick yin energy, so it is important to keep flowers fresh and to throw them away as soon as they start to fade. Dried flowers are also inauspicious.

Do not display flowers in the bedroom, as they bring too much yang energy into a place of rest. The only exception to flowers in the bedroom is if the inhabitant is sick or in a hospital, when the yang energy of flowers will help make the patient better. Avoid placing red flowers in the room of someone who is sick or recuperating from an illness. Red suggests the patient will not get better. (*See* p. 95 for more details of fresh flowers. *See also* Dried Flowers, p. 225, and Fake Flowers, p. 231.)

FLUTES

Long bamboo flutes are an excellent antidote for overhead beams. By hanging two flutes linked together by a red string and slanting toward each other like the letter A, you encourage the chi to rise through the hollows of the flutes and collect where the mouthpieces join. This causes auspicious Sheng Chi to form and dissipate the Shar Chi emitted by the overhead beam.

Flutes used in the same manner can also benefit your business. Hang the two flutes above your cash register, this time with the mouthpieces at the bottom. The chi will flow toward the cash register and settle there, symbolically causing it to "fill with money." (*See also* Beams, p. 207, and Sheng Chi, p. 273.)

FLYING STAR FENG SHUI

Flying Star Feng Shui deals with the time dimension. It comprises the casting of natal charts and is part of Three Period Feng Shui. This school of feng shui interprets the intangible influence of numbers believed to contain clues to the nature of chi in the environment and how these change over time.

Annual and monthly Flying Star charts reveal how luck changes yearly and monthly, indicating the orientations that are lucky and those that are afflicted from month to month and year to year. Knowing how to read Flying Star charts gives you an advantage in arranging the timing of all your major actions and decisions.

The Flying Star formula reveals the pattern of chi distribution in houses and buildings, thus making it possible to identify auspicious and inauspicious sectors of each. You will also know when to stay out of afflicted rooms or apply antidotes to them, thereby escaping misfortunes.

With Flying Star, the prosperity and luck of any residence or commercial building can be determined with great accuracy, but as it is an advanced formula, a beginner will need to be patient to learn its system. Those who want to use feng shui to improve their health and luck, should spend some time and money to learn Flying Star Feng Shui rather than hiring a consultant.

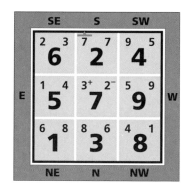

Here is a Flying Star natal chart of a house that faces South and was built after February 1984. The numbers inside each square reveal exciting information about the luck of different parts of the house. (*See* pp. 124–147 for more details.)

FORBIDDEN CITY

This is the Imperial Palace in Beijing, showcase of many feng shui features.

The Palaces of the Forbidden City are located in the heart of Beijing just south of Tiananmen Square. Built in 1420 by the third Ming emperor, Yong Le, many of the palaces, pavilions, gates, and halls of this complex remain beautifully intact and well preserved.

This distillation of several centuries of traditional Chinese palace construction is an almost-perfect showcase, not only of the arts and techniques of Chinese architecture, but also of the practice of feng shui at the highest imperial levels. The city demonstrates the application of important basic rules of feng shui. All the halls, rooms, and palaces are regular in shape, either rectangular or square, as are the pavilions and courtyards.

Ceiling designs in the public halls bear the protective eight-sided shape of the Pa Kua. Bricks used in the construction of the Palace complex are almost all square and roof shapes follow strict feng shui proportions and dimensions. Altogether there are nine different roof shapes used in the Forbidden City.

The City is laid out on a North-South axis. The entrance is the Meridian Gate, which faces South, at the time of building, an auspicious direction. The North-South central axis of the major buildings reflects the imperial nature of the residence. At the back in the North is Prospect Hill, an artificially created hillock that symbolizes the protective turtle hills.

The Forbidden City is sheltered by the Yan Shan Mountains in the North and the Bo Hai Sea in the East. The ground rises in the North and falls away in the South. In terms of ground level, it is higher in the North than the South by more than 3 feet (1 m).

The Golden River, so named to reflect its origination in the Northwest, is of the metal/gold element and was designed to create water in front of the palace complex. The origination, exit, and direction of flow of this river conform to environmental design. In the case of the Forbidden City, feng shui masters in the court of the Ming emperors determined that water should come from the direction of heaven, which is the Chien direction. (*See also* Pa Kua, p. 263.)

FORM SCHOOL

(*See* Landscape Feng Shui, p. 252.)

FORMULA FENG SHUI

These scientific methods of feng shui require accuracy of analysis and application. Formula Feng Shui covers a wide range of these methods that comprise the Compass School of Feng Shui. Broadly, these are sometimes categorized as Shuan Kong Feng Shui. Formula Feng Shui eliminates subjectivity and guesswork and work when applied and interpreted correctly. (*See also* Feng Shui, p. 233.)

FOUNTAINS

A fountain is a popular way of energizing to bring good luck, although fountains are more suitable for parks and shopping malls than for houses.

Fountains may cause imbalance in the home unless they are quite small. They are not as certain as other water features such as waterfalls and ponds, because the direction and flow of water in a fountain is haphazard: it can flow downward and outward or inward. Inside the house, you can use miniature fountains to activate water corners (North) or corners that benefit from water (East) to bring prosperity luck. (*See* pp. 160–164 for more details.)

FOUR AUSPICIOUS DIRECTIONS

In Eight Mansions Feng Shui, there are four auspicious directions described as:

❋ Sheng Chi, or growth direction.
❋ Tien Yi, or health direction.
❋ Nien Yen, or love direction.
❋ Fu Wei, or self development.

Based on the Kua formula, each person has four auspicious directions depending his or her number. (*See* pp. 114–116 for more details. *See also* Kua Numbers, p. 251.)

FOUR CELESTIAL CREATURES

(*See also* Celestial Creatures, p. 213.)

FOUR INAUSPICIOUS DIRECTIONS

In Eight Mansions Feng Shui, there are four inauspicious directions, as follows:

❋ Ho Hai, or Unlucky, Direction.
❋ Five Ghosts Direction.
❋ Six Killings Direction.
❋ Total Loss Direction.

Each person has four inauspicious directions based on their Kua number. (*See* pp. 120–121 for more details. *See also* Kua Numbers, p. 114.)

FOUR PILLARS OF DESTINY

This is one of the principle divinatory sciences of Chinese astrology.

Basically, the four pillars are the year, month, day and hour of birth. (*See* pp. 205, 209, and 236 for more details. *See also* Astrology, p. 205.)

FOYERS

Foyers should be brightly lit to attract Sheng Chi. Make sure the door opens to some space and that the entranceway is not cramped. If it is small, install a bright light to raise the chi. (*See* p. 15 for more details on lifting energy.)

FRIDGE

(*See* Refrigerator, p. 269.)

FROGS

Frogs and toads will bring auspicious luck and a family of frogs living in your backyard can protect you from any danger of bad luck coming your way. (*See* p. 169 for details of the Three-Legged Toad.)

FRONT DOOR

(*See* Entrances, p. 231.)

FU DOGS

These important guard dogs are traditionally used as protective symbols against every kind of bad luck.

Few Chinese homes are without a pair of Fu dogs. There are no rules as to what size Fu Dogs should be, but they should reflect the size of the home they are guarding. Fu Dogs should be placed high up on either side of the gate. They can be placed at table level, but should never be on the floor, so always use a table or stand.

Fu Dogs are quite easy to obtain from any authentic Chinese shop that sells statues and ceramics. Any color is suitable, but it is best to follow the element of the corner where you will place the Fu Dog. Let it be a controlling element. Thus, if your gate is located in the East, placing a pair of metal dogs will be effective, since gold controls wood, the element of the East. (*See* p. 183 for more details.)

FUK LUK SAU

These are the Three Star Gods of health, wealth, and happiness. The Three Star Gods are seldom worshipped, but they feature strongly in Chinese society and are displayed in many homes around the world. They are enormously popular since they symbolize just about everything that makes people happy and contented.

The best place for the Star Gods is the dining room in a suitably elevated position. Do not place them lower than the human beings in the room and do not place them in the bedroom. (*See* p. 171 for more details.)

Fuk   Luk   Sau

The Three Star Gods are popular gods that are displayed in homes around the world to encourage health, wealth, and happiness. Keep them in the dining room in an elevated position.

FURNITURE

Feng-shui-inspired furniture is particularly pleasing, because it holds little or no negative chi. Such furniture should be designed to fit tongue in groove and made without the use of nails. Beautiful antique Ming chairs, for instance, are highly prized because no nails were ever used in their construction. Secondly, these chairs are always nicely curved—absolutely no sharp edges or corners.

Modern furniture can imitate the concept and essence of this sort of furniture. Sofa sets should have sizeable back support and armrests. Tables and cupboards should have rounded edges. Bookshelves should have doors to shut out the negative chi of shelves.

Avoid furniture that has too much metal, as this exudes disharmonious chi. Steel chairs and tables are not a good idea, unless glass is used as a tabletop instead of wood. Also avoid furniture with sharp pointed edges or triangular shapes. (*See also* Chair, p. 214, and Desks, p. 222.)

G
GANZHI SYSTEM

Chinese astrology is based on the Ganzhi system calendar. Its cyclic symbols are associated with the Chinese Zodiac animals and the elements. Ganzhi comprises 22 characters grouped into two sets, 10 Heavenly (or Celestial) Stems and 12 Earthly (or Terrestrial) Branches. Each Heavenly Stem refers to one of the five elements, with a hard (yang) or a soft (yin) aspect. The Earthly Branches refer to earthly forces and are represented by the twelve animals of the Chinese Zodiac. They manifest in each hour, day, lunar month, and year. You can be born on a tiger day, in a rat month, at a snake hour and in an ox year. Each of these time periods also has manifest Heavenly Stems. Each hour, day, month and year comprise the Four Pillars. The combinations of all Four Pillars express eight characters, or Paht Chee. In astrology, these birth details generate these eight characters, which can be read like a map to reveals your destiny. (*See also* Almanac, p. 201, and Chinese Calendar, pp. 284–285.)

GARDEN

One of the most effective places for channeling healthy earth energy for the home is in the garden or yard. Install bright lights in a South-facing garden. Lights are also excellent for gardens that face Southwest or Northeast. Keep the lights turned on at night for at least three hours.

Fountains, waterfalls, fishponds, and birdbaths are great activators that attract good chi for the North-facing garden, as well as gardens facing East and Southeast.

Plant plenty of lush, leafy greenery in gardens that face East, South, and Southeast to emphasize the growth chi of the wood element. Strong plants attract good luck. If possible, include a bamboo plant for health and longevity. Always trim and clear old leaves. When plants are uncared for, yin energy sets in and chi will stagnate.

Metal ornaments like chimes and bells are excellent for gardens facing West and Northwest. North-facing gardens also benefit from metal energy

such as metal benches or steel pergolas for climbing plants.

Low brick walls, rock gardens, and ceramic urns bring excellent earth chi to the Northeast and Southwest corners. A long, hollow pole with a round light at the top encourages Sheng Chi to rise from deep in the earth, bringing up precious energy. (*See also* Flower Gardens, p. 234.)

GATES

The design and orientation of gates can attract good chi and abundance to the home. Ideally, gates should have two doors and open inward, with the center higher than the sides to symbolize the attainment of your goals. A center lower than the sides signifies bad career luck. Note that the front gate is not your main door, so place greater emphasis on the direction of the main door. The gate and door do not need to face the same direction. (*See also* Entrances, p. 231.)

GAZEBOS

Gazebos strengthen the chi of the main door when placed in a complementary location. Consider this feature if you have enough land. Ensure it strengthens rather than weakens the chi of the main door by following these guidelines:

✳ When the main door is in the East or SE, a gazebo in the North is excellent and supports the door. When the main door is in the West or NW the Gazebo should be in the SW or NE.

✳ TheWhen the main door is in the North, the gazebo should be in the West or NW. When the main door is in the South the gazebo should be placed in the East or Southeast

and when the main door is in the SW or NE the gazebo should be placed in the South. (*See also* Doors, p. 222.)

GEESE

While a pair of mandarin ducks symbolizes conjugal fidelity, a pair of geese soaring high together signifies the happy togetherness of the married state. Mandarin ducks are suitable for those aspiring toward marriage, but married couples should display a pair of geese as the promise of a gloriously happy marriage with no separation.

Newly married couples with work commitments that cause long separations should place the image of a pair of flying geese on the Southwest wall of the living room to help create togetherness chi and thus a happier relationship.

As migratory birds, geese embody the spirit of adventure, but they never fly alone–always in pairs. Geese pine for their mates when separated and are faithful creatures that do not mate a second time, thus, they symbolize undying love.

Geese also symbolize yang energy and are emblems of good fortune. (*See also* Mandarin Ducks, p. 257.)

GEM TREE

The gem tree is a variation of the money tree. With leaves made of semi-precious stones and stems made of gold, these small trees create wealth energy for the household.

The stones used should have good natural color and the stems of the tree should be solid and strong. A tree with plenty of branches and thick foliage will radiate a feeling of abundance. Spindly trees are not effective and will result in the opposite of abundance. Many of these gem trees simulate the jade plant—the succulent leaves of which resemble the precious jade stone Citrines and amethysts are excellent gem choices, as are rose quartz (good for activating relationship luck), aventurine, and coral. Hanging gold coins on the tree will makes the tree more potent. On New Year's Day, hang red packets with real money inside.

Keep a gem tree in the Northwest side of the living room to signify "wealth from heaven." It is also a good idea to keep one in the Southeast, which is the wealth corner. (*See* p. 171 for more details.)

GEMSTONES

Precious and semiprecious gemstones are Earth's vital treasures. Their intrinsic potency can enhance your personal and living spaces. Diamonds, crystals, quartz, and so on possess special qualities that can be harnessed to enhance feng shui. (*See also* Crystals, p. 220, and Quartz Crystals, p. 268.)

GINSENG ROOT

Ginseng is an herb, the root of which is used to enhance longevity (good health and long life). The Chinese believe that ginseng root has life extension attributes. Rumour has it that Chinese leaders have access to a magical ginseng potion, which accounts for their long lives. (*See also* Longevity, p. 256.)

GLOBE

The globe is a potent symbol of the earth element, especially when made of lapis lazuli, clear quartz, or jasper. Placed in the Northeast it attracts education luck. Placing such a globe in a college student's room will help him or her do well on exams.

The globe can also be used to stimulate higher export sales. Place it in the office of the Export Manager and spin it daily to enhance the world market penetration. (*See* p. 87 for crystal globes.)

GOD OF LONGEVITY

He is known as Sau Seng Kong and is regarded as the most auspicious symbol of longevity. This gentle deity brings good health, long life, and protection from unnatural, violent, and premature death.

Sau is always drawn carrying a ripe peach in his hand and accompanied by the crane and the deer, all of which symbolize longevity. In recent years Sau has also been drawn with children to signify descendants' luck.

Older renditions of Sau show him carrying a staff with a gourd (Wu Luo) containing the nectar of longevity. He is also shown with an extended forehead and domed head to symbolize his great wisdom. (*See* p. 172 for more details.)

GOD OF MARRIAGE

Chieh Lien, the Chinese God of Marriage, is none other than the man in the moon. He is reportedly in charge of all nuptials between mortals, and sanctions unions between potential couples by tying their feet together with an invisible red silk cord. This belief inspired the custom of the bride and groom sealing their marriage pledge to each other by drinking wine from two glasses tied together with red cord.

To activate romance luck in your home, display a painting of the full moon, which signifies yang in yin. The fifteenth day of each lunar calendar month is a good time for considering matters of the heart. (*See* pp. 72–73 for marriage rescue.)

GODS OF WEALTH

One of the most popular wealth gods is Tsai Shen Yeh, often shown sitting on a Tiger to symbolize his control over this animal. In the lunar years of the Tiger, displaying the God of Wealth is particularly good for protection. Invite this deity into your home as a symbolic gesture, generating prosperous energy.

Display a god of wealth on a table 30–33 inches (76–84 cm) high, directly facing the door, so he is the first thing you see upon entering your home. If this spot is already occupied by the family altar, you can place a wealth god diagonally opposite the front door, and again, facing toward it. Do not place your wealth god in the dining room or bedroom. (*See also* Tsai Shen Yeh, p. 279 for more details.)

One of the gods of wealth is invited into your home as a symbolic gesture. You do not need to pray to this deity. Placing him directly facing the front door symbolizes him greeting the chi entering your home.

GODDESS OF MERCY

The Goddess of Mercy, Kuan Yin, is the most popular Buddha deity in the Chinese pantheon. Her presence in the home creates an ambience of softness and love, which brings the rise of loving kindness and a good heart.

One legend describes Kuan Yin as the Princess Miao Shan who lived during the Zhou Dynasty. Buddhists often describe her as an emanation of the Hindu compassionate deity Avalokiteshvara; while in Tibetan Buddhism, she is portrayed as Chenrezig the Buddha of Compassion. In Japan, she is known as Canon. Kuan Yin is usually shown seated with the Buddha Amitabha or flanked by two other goddesses, Pu Hsien and Wen Shu. (*See also* Buddha statues, p. 211.)

GOLD

Gold symbolizes wealth, prosperity, and success. Different manifestations of gold inside the home will stimulate wealth luck.

Gold ingots are a traditional symbol of wealth, but creating gold stones or boulders to simulate a mountain of gold is also effective. A reader of mine uses gold leaf to gild stones, which she then arranges into small heaps of gold. Place "gold nuggets" such as these in your indoor garden, use them to enhance your table settings, or place them in bowls anywhere inside the home as wealth energizers. (*See* p. 171 for more details.)

You can also spray large boulders with gold paint for the same effect. Place them in front of the main entrance to invite wealth energy. (*See also* Entrances, p. 231 for more details.)

GOLDFISH

Goldfish are most auspicious when kept in aquariums in the North sector. Keep nine goldfish, eight gold and one black. The single black fish will absorb any bad luck that inadvertently enters the home. Keep the aquarium bubbling and well lighted. Goldfish bring the most luck when located in the North, East, or Southeast of the home. They should never be in the bedroom. (*See* pp. 104, 112, and 163 for more details.)

GOOD FORTUNE

Good fortune means attaining the Eight Aspirations by living in harmony with the environment and in your home. (*See* pp. 82–83 and 102–113 for more details. *See also* Eight Aspirations, p. 227.)

GOOD LUCK

Feng shui recognizes eight types of good luck and Chinese divination readings define luck as different types and grades of luck for each of these eight categories For example, money and wealth luck is subdivided into the luck of inheritance, gambling and speculation, and business success. In the language of feng shui luck has many different meanings. (*See* pp. 119–121 for more details.)

GRAND DUKE JUPITER

The Grand Duke Jupiter (known as Tai Sui) changes location every year. Knowledge of his location is vital because you must never incur the Grand Duke's wrath by facing or confronting him. If you do, you are certain to suffer defeat, demotion, and severe loss. You will lose any combative or competitive situation during the year.

Fortunately, the Grand Duke Jupiter occupies only 15 degrees of the compass, and his direction coincides exactly with the direction of the 12 Zodiac animals that are the earthly branch directions, so it is easy to avoid offending him.

The best protection to guard against offending the Grand Duke is the Pi Yao. In fact, it is a good idea to always have an image of this creature inside the home, as it is such a powerful protector. The Pi Yao is sometimes used synonymously with Pi Kan or Pi Xie.

The rules to observe regarding the Grand Duke are as follows:

RULE 1

Never sit in a position that is directly opposite to and thus facing the direction of the Grand Duke Jupiter. It is never worth confronting the Grand Duke because you will lose out every time.

RULE 2

Never disturb the Grand Duke Jupiter, or you might incur his wrath. If you are planning construction work, be sure to find out which sector of your home he is occupying in the year you are planning to renovate and don't do any work there. If you must perform digging or hammering in the grand Duke's sector, at least make sure you do not start (i.e., break ground) or end in his sector. This rule applies equally for land and buildings. (*See* p. 151 for more details about the Grand Duke.)

GRAVESITES

The good feng shui of gravesites and burial grounds can benefit surviving descendants. The orientation of gravesites is part of Yin Feng Shui practice, a difficult and potent branch that is not suitable for amateur practitioners. (*See also* Yin Energy, p. 283.)

GREEN DRAGON

The celestial Green Dragon of the East is the earth dragon and the ultimate symbol of good fortune. The Green Dragon makes his appearance as hills and mountains and is usually depicted embracing the White Tiger (*see* p. 281) to produce copious amounts of chi energy that bring abundance to those who can capture it.

Green Dragon images can be painted on porcelain or rendered as dragon replicas. Their powerful presence attracts prosperity. When placed near water features, dragons create potent feng shui inside the home. (*See* pp. 13–15 and 241 for more details. *See also* Celestial Creatures, p. 213, and Dragon, p. 223.)

GREENHOUSE

Greenhouses function like gazebos in strengthening or weakening the feng shui of the main door. (*See also* Gazebos, p. 238 and Entrances, p. 231.)

H

HAN HSIANG TZU

(*See also* Eight Immortals, p. 227.)

HANGING OBJECTS

Hanging object cures overcome various ills and afflictions caused by poison chi. Windchimes, bells, and flutes hung from beams and ceilings can counter sharp edges and straight lines.

These objects should be unobtrusive, so place them to one side of the room. Windchimes should never be hung directly above your head since this will cause negative energy. Similarly, when a door is afflicted, objects should not be hung directly above it, as this will affect those walking through the doorway. (*See* p. 91 for more details about windchimes.)

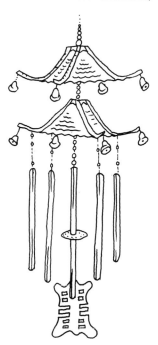

HARMONY

Harmony refers to the harmonious interaction of five elements in the living space. Elements in each part of the living space should be mutually enhancing rather than mutually destructive.

Harmony also refers to living in harmony with your natural environment and so requires working knowledge of the four celestial guardians that are part of Landscape Feng Shui. When you live in simpatico with the earth, hills, and water in your environment, a benevolent flow of chi will benefit you. (*See* pp. 16–18 for more details. *See also* Wu Xing, p. 282.)

HARVEST

Images of harvest time represent the fruit of the land and displaying them in your dining room brings prosperity to your family. Images of unploughed harvest are the luckiest of all food symbols. Paintings of matured cornfields, rice fields, and wheat fields are excellent for both home and office as they symbolize the crystallization of hard work.

Likewise, the season of summer represents the flowering and blooming of efforts and is considered a time of plenty, when there is a maximum amount of yang energy. Display fruits, freshly plucked from the tree, or beautiful paintings of luscious fresh fruit in the dining room to signify prosperity. (*See also* Art, p. 204.)

HEALTH BALLS

In a healthy body, the flow of chi is smooth without blockages. An excellent way to achieve this flow is by massaging the extremities of the body. Foot reflexology is another way. You can also use a pair yin and yang health balls to exercise the fingers. (*See also* Body Feng Shui, p. 210.)

HEALTH LUCK

Good health luck means enjoying a robust and vigorous life with the promise of living to a ripe old age.

Using the Eight Mansions Formula, it is possible to activate good health luck for every individual. One of the four auspicious personalized directions is the health direction and is called Tien Yi, the "doctor from heaven" direction. Sleeping with your head in your Tien Yi direction will enhance physical health.

Check your Kua number and note your Tien Yi direction.

Kua 1	East
Kua 2	West
Kua 3	North
Kua 4	South
Kua 5	(male) West
Kua 5	(female) Northwest
Kua 6	Northeast
Kua 7	Southwest
Kua 8	Northwest
Kua 9	Southeast

(*See* pp. 114–121 for more details.)

HEARTS

Western symbols for love can be used to energize for romance. Use heart-shaped decorations in romantic colors like red and pink. Display them in the Southwest sector or your personal romance corner to attract love luck. (*See also* Love, p. 257, and Romance Direction, p. 270.)

HEAVEN LUCK

Often called fate or karma—heaven luck exerts great influence over your destiny. You can make your heaven luck better by harnessing the powers of earth luck. Anyone who can successfully balance heaven with earth will have excellent feng shui. (*See also* Good Luck, p. 241.)

HEAVENLY KINGS

The Four Heavenly Kings are the celestial protectors of morality and ethics. They assist us in maintaining honorable attitudes in our pursuit of success.

These kings are supernatural Dharma Protectors or Deva Guardians. They guard the slopes of the sacred mountain paradise land of Mount Meru, where the gods live. The kings protect the world against evil spirits who cause havoc in households that do not have protection.

THE GUARDIAN OF THE EAST (MO LI CHING)

has a white face with a fierce countenance. He carries a spear and a magic sword engraved with the characters earth, fire, water, and wind. Each time he swipes his sword a black wind produces ten thousand spears to pierce the bodies of evil spirits and turn them to dust. The wind is followed by fire, which fills the air with ten thousand fiery serpents. Not one is able to escape.

Mo Li Hai

THE GUARDIAN OF THE WEST (MO LI HAI)

has a blue face and carries a four stringed guitar at the sound of which all creatures of the world and the abodes of his enemies catch fire. He guards all bad chi coming from the West and ensures that residents do not succumb to temptations associated with material gains.

Mo Li Hung

THE GUARDIAN OF THE SOUTH (MO LI HUNG)

has a red face and holds an umbrella. Each time the umbrella is opened, universal darkness descends. When the umbrella is overturned, terrible earthquakes and thunderstorms bring destruction to his enemies.

Mo Li Shou

THE GUARDIAN OF THE NORTH (MO LI SHOU)

has a black face. He carries two whips and a panther skin bag. Inside the skin bag is a fierce creature (often a snake) that devours men. He also carries a pearl that gives him control over all earthly creatures.
(*See* pp. 182–183 for more details of all the kings.)

HEAVENLY STEMS
(*See also* Ganzhi System, p. 237.)

HEDGES
Growing a hedge to block out unsightly structures in the neighborhood can dissolve bad chi from the Southwest or Northeast. Hedges can be as high as you wish, but they should not appear intimidating or threatening by being too close to the home. Select plants with small rounded leaves, as these are the most auspicious. (*See also* Garden, p. 238.)

HERB OF IMMORTALITY
It is not a widely known fact that the herb of immortality—also referred to as Ling Zhi—bestows not merely the promise of immortal life, but also rapid growth and success in careers such as politics and entertainment.

In appearance, the herb resembles water grass: long, oval, and pointed. The Ling Zhi is frequently included in paintings of the deer, the crane, and other symbols of longevity. When the image of this herb is carved onto family altars, residents will enjoy long and healthy lives. (*See also* Altar, p. 201.)

HEXAGRAM
The hexagrams are the 64 six-lined symbols that make up the I Ching. They are derived from the two fundamental elements of yang and yin forces—from light and dark, movement and stillness. This interaction of yin and yang gives rise to the trigrams, which in turn become the hexagrams.

The lines of the hexagrams are either at rest or in motion. When at rest, they build up the hexagram; when in motion, they transform the hexagram into a new hexagram. These two simple processes contain the secrets of the I Ching. The philosophy of the I Ching is that everything is in a state of flux, a state of change, and yet overall there is stillness.

When a line is broken, it represents the dark, the earth and the yielding; it signifies yin. When it is unbroken, it represents the light, heaven and the unyielding; it signifies yang. But the yin and yang lines can be at rest or in motion, reflecting all the nuances of a hexagram—inner, outer or secret. At the most obvious level, interpretation of the hexagrams is based on the relationship of the two trigrams (a set of three yin and/or yang three lines) that make up each one.

Upper

Lower

The I Ching is also the basis of feng shui technology. In it we see the interactions between yin and yang. The hexagrams and trigrams contain all the secrets of feng shui formulas, rituals, and magic. But there are layers of meaning shrouded within the symbolism of the trigrams in the way they are arranged and in the pervasive influence of the Tai Chi (the yin yang symbol) as well as the Wu Xing (the five elements). (*See* p. 42 for more details.)

HIGH-RISE BUILDINGS

The construction of any new building nearby affects your home's feng shui. If the new building blocks the main entrance, the effect is usually negative. If it rises behind your home, symbolizing solid support, the effect is positive. (*See also* Elevated Structures, p. 231.)

HILLS

Hills are natural undulations of the landscape where dragons dwell and are a sure sign of good feng shui potential. Hills are where the Green Dragon lives and breathes auspicious air.

Hills should be rolling with smooth, gentle slopes rather than sharp, craggy cliff faces. Where vegetation grows lush and green and there is a good balance of sunshine and shade, dragons and tigers are said to be present. If your neighborhood bears the scars of injured dragons—hills that have been haphazardly cut and ravaged—your luck may suffer.

There are five types of hill shapes, each one based on the five elements: fire, wood, earth, metal and water. It is useful to develop the ability to discern these differences, which offer clues as to their suitability for each individual. Understanding the element connotation of hill shapes will enable practitioners to judge the feng shui quality of a range of hills. (*See* pp. 12–18 for more details. *See also* Celestial Creatures, p. 213 and Mountains, p. 260.)

HO HAI

The Ho Hai is the least harmful of the four inauspicious directions. Translated literally, it means "accidents and mishaps." When you sit or sleep facing your Ho Hai direction it leads to bad luck; however, the misfortune is bearable.

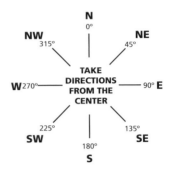

Check your Kua number and note your Ho Hai direction.

Kua 1	**West**
Kua 2	**East**
Kua 3	**Southwest**
Kua 4	**Northwest**
Kua 5	**(male) East**
Kua 5	**(female) South**
Kua 6	**Southeast**
Kua 7	**North**
Kua 8	**South**
Kua 9	**Northeast**

(*See* pp. 114–121 for more details.)

HO HSIEN KU

(*See also* Eight Immortals, p. 227.)

HO TU GRID

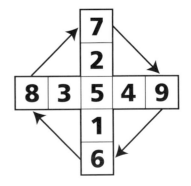

The Ho Tu diagram is associated with the Eight Trigrams of the Early Heaven arrangement. Chinese legend tells that Fu Hsi himself received a formation of numbers, brought to him on the back of a dragon horse that emerged out of the Yellow River (Hwang Ho).

This particular pattern of numbers is referred to as the Ho Tu, which means River Map. The numbers are arranged so that all the odd or all the even numbers add up to 20 (leaving out the central number 5).

The four Ho Tu number combinations of 1/6; 8/3; 7/2; and 4/9 are used in the Luo Pan. These four combinations of numbers are extremely auspicious for couples. When the Kua numbers of a couple reflect these four combinations of numbers, even if they belong to separate groups, one East and one West (as in 1/6 and 8/3), the couple is not only compatible but also very good for each other. (*See* pp. 64–66 for more details. *See also* Kua Numbers, p. 251, and Luo Pan, p. 256.)

HOME

Residential feng shui affects a person's luck the most. Even when the feng shui at work is poor, if you live in a home that has good feng shui, your overall luck will be quite good. Residential feng shui is especially important for families. The three major features to bring into balance are the main entrance (*see* p. 231), the bedroom (*see* p. 207), and the kitchen. (*see* p. 251). *See also* Center of the Home, p. 213.

HONG KONG

The thriving metropolis of Hong Kong has more feng shui believers and practitioners than any other city in the world. Once a barren rock, it is now a great financial center. There are many theories about its feng shui. Some say it is protected by its nine dragons. Others describe the harbor as a deep moneybag. Still others say its wealth lies in the clever harnessing of the waters around the city. The skyline of Hong Kong reflects many feng shui features and all tap the wealth of the harbor and the support and protection of Victoria Peak. (*See* p. 20 for more details.)

HOROSCOPES

(*See* Zodiac, p. 283.)

HORSE

The horse is a symbol of courage, speed, and perseverance. Hang a painting or picture of horses in the South side of the living room to capture the vital essence and fire element of the horse. Horse figurines that represent the tribute horse are exceptionally lucky. Placing horses in the Southwest will energize luck in social climbing, while placement in the Northeast brings luck in academic examinations. (*See* pp. 57–59 for more details.)

HORSESHOE

In the West, the horseshoe is an exceptionally lucky symbol and it is good to hang one in your work office. Be sure to hang it with the opening facing up so the good luck does not run out.

In Landscape Feng Shui, the horseshoe shape represents the ideal land formation. When three ranges of hills form a perfect horseshoe shape with the home in the center, (especially if overlooking flat land), feng shui luck will be excellent for at least five generations. (*See also* Good Luck, p. 240 for more details.)

HOSPITAL

Houses and buildings built near hospitals are too yin. The yin energies emanating from a hospital can be overwhelming, as they bear the negative chi of illness, despair, and death. Consequently, if your home is located on a site that previously housed a hospital, the place may remain too yin, often to a harmful extent. It is also better not to have a home too near a hospital. To deal with excessive yin energy, introduce healthy doses of yang energy into your home. (*See also* Yang Energy, p. 282, and Yin Energy, p. 283.)

HOSTILE STRUCTURES

Buildings, land features, outcroppings, elevated roads, and other large concrete structures can send intimidating chi toward your home. If there are such hostile structures near your home, study the text on poison arrows to see how you can overcome their harmful effects. (*See* pp. 22 and 27 for more details.)

HOUR PILLAR

The Hour Pillar comprises the Heavenly Stem and the Earthly Branch of the hour you took your first breath. The branch and stem each refer to one of the five elements. Combined with two elements each from the Year Pillar, the Month Pillar, and the Day Pillar, they make up the Eight Characters.

Those born in nighttime hours will have more yin in their time of birth, while those born in the daytime will have more yang. However, this is neither good nor bad. (*See also* Four Pillars of Destiny, p. 236, and Yin Yang Symbol, p. 283.)

HOUSE

Any abode in which you eat, sleep, and take shelter is defined as your house. No matter how short your stay, if the Feng Shui is good, it will benefit you. Treat college rooms and rented suites as home for as long as you are there. College students who have their own rooms "back home," will continue to be affected by the Feng Shui of that room as well. (*See* pp. 20–25 for more details.)

HSIA CALENDAR

(*See* Calendar, p. 212.)

HUMANKIND LUCK

This is the third kind of luck in what is termed the Trinity of luck–Tien is the luck from heaven, Ti the luck from the earth, and Ren the luck people create for themselves. Of the three, both earth luck and humankind luck are within our control. Earth luck is Feng Shui and humankind luck is what we create for ourselves. (*See also* Good Luck, p. 240.)

I

I CHING

The I Ching is the source book of most of China's cultural practices. Both Confucianism and Taoism have common roots in this ancient classic, known also as the Book of Changes. The I Ching alone, among all the Confucian classics, escaped the great burning of the books under emperor Chin Shih Huang Ti in 213 BCE.

The I Ching's hexagrams contain symbols and ideas from nature, society, and the individual and offer wisdom, warnings, and predictions of possible outcomes.

The hexagrams also advise on timing, behavior, and attitudes related to specific questions and, where applicable, counsel further preparation, advocate patience, or even reveal misfortune hidden in apparent good fortune and vice versa. (*See also* Hexagram, p. 243.)

ILLNESS

This is the most common manifestation of bad Feng Shui. When occupants of the same house repeatedly succumb to illness, this is an indication that the Feng Shui of the home can be improved.

Look for poison arrows harming the home. Check your main doors as well as doors into bedrooms for sharp edges of nearby structures, walls, or edges of furniture. Check for exposed overhead beams or a fan directly above a sleeping area. Determine whether any drains around the house are blocked and whether your plumbing and sewage are clear. Often a simple adjustment is sufficient to remove chi obstacles that cause illness. (*See* pp. 184–197 for more details.)

IMMORTALITY

This Taoist concept is part of the Seven Pillars of Tao, which implies the aspiration of attaining a state of no death, returning to the Source as a spiritual being living in a spiritual realm. The Taoists, however, regard the Eight Immortals as humans who have attained deity status.

Another definition of the Source is a goal so high that it transcends all other goals conceived by humans throughout time. Mere words cannot describe the bliss of attaining the Source, an experience so exalted–wisdom so divine–it transcends all existence. (*See also* Eight Immortals, p. 227.)

INCENSE

Incorporate regular space cleansing and purification rituals into your home with incense blocks or aroma sticks.

Every month, burn incense in each room of your home. Walk clockwise around the room and let the incense clear out corners with bad chi. Chant your favorite mantras or give thanks for your blessings as you move from room to room.

Use incense for purification whenever there has been a particularly loud quarrel between residents. This will clean out the anger energy in the room and restore harmony.

The practice of using incense to cleanse space is similar to the American Indian practice of smudging homes with smoke made from burning pine or sage branches. Of course, the marvelous herbal scent is wonderful for making energies crisp and clean.

Burning of incense creates ash, which simulates the creation of the Earth by fire energy. As fire produces earth in the Productive Cycle of the elements, the essence of fire energy expands earth chi.

Burning sandalwood incense is a ritual that has been recommended for centuries for scholars who study into

the night. You can also use a special herbal or pine incense to assist in meditation. (*See* pp. 192–193 for more details.)

INDOOR GARDENS

In this example, the garden has to be entered before entering the house, which can be auspicious.

If the open-air design of your home calls for indoor gardens, put them in the East, Southeast (*see* p. 112), or South sector of your home, not in the Southwest or Northeast of the home. In the Southwest, it will disrupt your family life and harm the marriage. In the Northeast, it can cause study luck to be destroyed, causing problems for your children. (*See also* Garden, p. 238.)

INFIDELITY

To guard against infidelity, avoid water features on the right-hand side of the main door (inside looking out) and avoid mirrors or other reflective surfaces in the bedroom that reflect the couple sleeping on the bed.

An amethyst geode tied with red ribbon is a powerful talisman against infidelity. It should be placed under the bed, on the side occupied by the female partner, ideally on the right hand side. The ends of the red ribbon should be attached to the foot of the bed.

The amethyst is also excellent for bringing errant husbands home. The male partner should sleep on the left side of the bed. (*See* p. 75 for more details. *See also* Amethyst, p. 201, and Mirrors, p. 258.)

INGOTS

Ingots are boat-shaped ancient Chinese currency fashioned out of gold or silver. These popular symbols of prosperity should be freely displayed, particularly during the lunar Chinese New Year. Displaying faux gold ingots in your home is auspicious as gold attracts good luck. Fill a bowl with ingots and place in the wealth corner to attract prosperity. (*See* p. 171 for more details.)

INK, SLAB, PAPER, AND PEN BRUSH

These are the Four Precious Treasures, displayed to attract educational success. Also referred to as the "invaluable gems of the literary domain," the four treasures are ink, paper, brush pen, and ink slab. These items signify the presence of learned scholars.

Display them at home and at least one of your children will gain the highest scholastic achievements. (*See* p. 84 for more details of scholarship luck.)

INSIGNIA

In Imperial China, court mandarins wore robes embroidered with insignia to signify their rank. Well-preserved antique robes with insignia intact can be hung in your home to produce an auspicious aura in which the cosmic currents will generate favorable luck. (*See also* Clothes, p. 217.)

IRREGULARLY SHAPED HOUSES

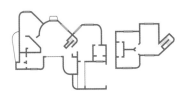

Irregularly shaped houses and apartments can result in missing corners, thereby creating imbalance in the energy of the home. Irregular shapes may also produce unnecessary corners, making it difficult to do Feng Shui analysis. Different views mean that a great deal of personal judgment is involved. Irregularly shaped floor plans can be misleading. In these cases, on-site investigation is crucial. (*See* p. 23 for more details.)

INTERIOR FENG SHUI

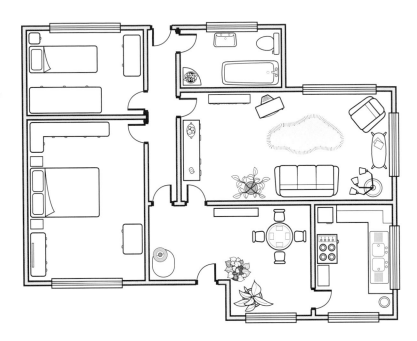

Home interiors must be planned to maximize good feng shui for everyone in the household. Rooms should be allocated according to feng shui guidelines and the choice of colors, lighting, and soft furnishings carefully considered.

Interior Feng Shui incorporates spatial guidelines and orientations into the placement and arrangement of furniture and doors to create harmonious vibrations in the home and ensure that negative chi is dissolved.

Interior Feng Shui also involves the design of the home and the allocation of rooms, as well as the selection of colors and patterns for curtains, carpets, and other soft furnishings. The ideal home offers an ambience of warmth where yang energy and auspicious chi flow freely from room to room. Bear in mind these tips to help create good Feng Shui:

✳ Use colors on walls that emphasize elements you wish to activate.

✳ Use blended colors with white added to signify the presence of yang energy.

✳ Let the layout of your interiors meander so that benevolent chi can accumulate.

✳ Camouflage all protruding corners with lush plants.

✳ Incorporate discreet lighting into all important areas and corners.

✳ Never hang art that seems hostile, scary, or disfigured, as it will attract negative energy.

✳ Incorporate auspicious symbols into your home to attract good fortune.

✳ Learn Flying Star Feng Shui to incorporate natal chart analysis in your efforts.

* Place water features to create wealth luck in correct corners. This is where Flying Star can be most helpful.
* Avoid inauspicious staircases.
* Do not place important things under staircases.
* Close all toilet seat covers and bathroom doors.
* Focus on the main door, the bedrooms, the dining room, the kitchen, and the living room, in that order, making certain that the flow of traffic in the home meanders.
* Avoid long narrow corridors inside your home.

Use a compass to determine the direction of the main door. Next, identify the different corners and which rooms are located in each corner. Systematically identify all poison arrows, note the flow of chi, and analyze the positioning and layout of furniture. Allocate rooms according to the Kua formula. Finally, energize each corner of every room. (*See* p. 23 for house shapes.)

INTERVIEWS

During job interviews, carry a small but reliable compass and discreetly check directions to make sure that you sit facing one of your auspicious directions during the interview.

The luck of good direction by itself does not offer protection against Shar Chi that may be caused by beams, pillars, and sharp edges. Be alert to the less obvious structures, features, and objects that may also be sending out poison arrows. For instance, paintings of guns or swords emit harmful and negative energy. (*See* pp. 52–59 and 76–83 for business success.)

J

JADE BELT WATER

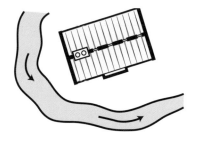

This is the name given to any "river" that embraces the front of a home like a belt, in a symbolic emblem of influence, authority, and wealth. Such a configuration is even better when there are also hills behind your home. The effect of the water is enhanced if it moves past your main door (from inside looking out) in the correct direction:

* For homes where the main door faces North, South, East, or West (one of the cardinal directions), drains should flow from left to right.
* For homes where the main door faces a secondary direction (Southeast, Southwest, Northeast or Northwest) the drain should flow from right to left.

(*See* pp. 160–165 for water empowering techniques.)

JADE PLANT

This "wealth plant" has succulent dark green leaves that resemble pieces of precious jade. These plants are best placed in the Southeast corner or in the display window of a retail shop to attract customers. (*See* p. 112 for prosperity luck in the Southeast.)

JAPANESE GARDEN

Japanese gardens are designed to suggest calm and serenity and are therefore excellent places for meditation. The layout and design of Japanese gardens are based on Zen principles considered optimal for silent and philosophical contemplation. They are not designed to attract good fortune chi; however, Japanese gardens offer creative ideas on the use of stones and pebbles, which can be incorporated into Southwest or Northeast facing Feng Shui gardens. (*See also* Garden, p. 238.)

JEWELRY

Good fortune jewelry or personalized amulets of protection provide excellent personal space Feng Shui.

Contemporary jewelry can ensure that luck-enhancing chi embraces the physical body, as did amulets and charms of long ago. Wedding and engagement rings incorporating the double-happiness symbol (*see* p. 223) bring excellent marriage luck, while coin jewelry energizes wealth.

Diamonds have greater power than crystals. While diamonds don't have to be large, they should be genuine, so the luck they attract is real, never fake. Real gold or platinum is more potent for the energizing of wealth luck than either steel or silver. Capture the symbolism of auspicious symbols in crystals before upgrading to diamonds. But as soon as is practical, wear diamonds.

A fun alternative is wearing colored stones for protection. Semiprecious stones that correspond to different vibrations and planets can attract good fortune and double as protectors.

Experiment with sapphires—blue, pink, and yellow; beryls—emeralds and rubies; star stones—star rubies and star moonstones; and corals—pink and red. Lapis lazuli is an excellent protector used to ward off illness. (*See also* Amulets, p. 201, and Crystals, p. 220.)

K

KAN TRIGRAM

This trigram is placed North; its element is water, and its season is winter. The image is that of a single strong yang line sandwiched by two yin lines. Kan usually signifies danger and reminds us that water is a double-edged sword. It can bring great wealth, but it can also get out of control. When you activate the North corner of your rooms with water, you are activating this trigram. Done correctly and moderately, it brings upward mobility in your career. (*See* pp. 104–105 for more details.)

KEN TRIGRAM

This trigram is placed Northeast, its element is earth, and it signifies the mountain—strong and solid with unknown treasures within. This trigram signifies preparation through silence, patience, and study. To activate the chi essence of this trigram, place an object of the earth element (crystals, globe, sand, boulders) in the Northeast. The wisdom chi is particularly helpful for students. (*See* p. 113 for more details.)

KHENG HUA

This rare white flower looks like the lotus and signifies good fortune when it blooms. The Kheng Hua is a rare type of succulent cactus that opens its petals at night, reaching its peak at midnight. The flower is completely white with yellow stamens and is both fragrant and beautiful.

Blooming on a full-moon night indicates illustrious marriages, great career and material success, and prominence in the world for the daughters and sons of the home. Blooming on a rainy night indicates the onset of tears and is not a good sign. In the past, grandmothers would tie the bud on rainy nights to ensure that it did not open. (*See also* Cactus, p. 212, and Lotus Flower, p. 256.)

KILLING BREATH

(*See* Shar Chi, p. 273.)

KING WEN

King Wen is one of the four men associated with the ultimate development of the I Ching. The sage Fu Hsi invented the Trigrams over four thousand years ago. King Wen took these Trigrams, combining each one with itself and the others in turn, making the 64 hexagrams. Later, each hexagram was given a meaning, textual explanation, and interpretation by the Duke of Chou. Even later, the sage Confucius gave commentaries that further enriched the book. (*See also* I Ching, p. 246.)

KITCHEN FENG SHUI

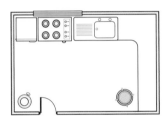

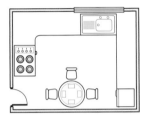

It is best if the stove and sink do not face each other in "confrontation." Avoid placing them close to each other.

The placement and orientation of the kitchen is vital. A general rule is that kitchens (especially the stove) should never be located in the Northwest. This is described as "fire at heaven's gate" and is enormously unfortunate. There is no permanent cure for this, but you can try placing an urn filled with yin water in the kitchen to minimize the effect. The kitchen is better placed to the right of the front door than the left when you enter the home. This ensures family harmony, especially between siblings.

The kitchen should be located more at the back than in front; to ensure that the family's assets are not easily lost. If you are familiar with the Kua formula, try to locate the kitchen in your worst Chueh Ming, or total loss, direction. Kitchens in this location will suppress your bad luck. Likewise, do not arrange the kitchen in any one of your personalized auspicious sectors, since this will suppress your good fortune. If kitchen is in this direction in the house, these are possible outcomes:

Sheng Chi	**Miscarriage, unpopularity, and no livelihood**
Tien Yi	**Illness, weakness, and fatigue**
Nien Yen	**Difficult to get married, many quarrels**
Fu Wei	**Poverty and a short life**
Chueh Ming	**Money, servants, and good health**
Six Killings	**A steady family life**
Five Ghosts	**Health and success**
Ho Hai	**Financial security and no serious illness**

Remember, while the kitchen should be located in your bad luck direction, the stoves, crockpots, and microwaves used to cook your food should be positioned so that the energy entering the appliance comes from your good direction.

Ensure that cooking appliances do not face one other in a confrontational mode, nor should they be next to each other. (*See* p. 123 for more details.)

KNIVES

Knives displayed pointing at where you are sitting act as poison arrows. If you display them in the home, be aware of the harmful energy they send out. This also applies to the display of spears, swords, or other weapons that can cause misfortunes involving bloodshed.

The curved knife; however, is used to cut away bad energy when you travel in an East or Southeast direction. If you receive a negative sign just before traveling, such as a lame dog, a car accident, or a funeral, then you should use a curved knife and swipe the air above you three times in a clockwise direction, facing the direction you are traveling, to protect your travel experience. (*See also* Curved Knife, p. 220.)

KUA NUMBERS

These personalized numbers reveal good and bad luck directions for individuals and are derived from the powerful Eight Mansions Formula.

To determine your personal directions, first calculate your personal Kua number using your lunar year of birth and gender. If you are born in January or February before the lunar New Year, subtract one year from your year of birth. The calculations are as follows:

THE FORMULA FOR MEN

Take the year of birth
Add the last two digits
Reduce to a single number
Deduct from 10.
Example: Year of birth 1936
$3 + 6 = 9$ and $10 - 9 = 1$
the Kua number is 1.

For boys born in the year 2000 and after, instead of deducting from 10, deduct from 9.

THE FORMULA FOR WOMEN

Take the year of birth
Add the last two digits
Reduce to a single number
Add 5.
Example: Year of birth 1945
$4 + 5 = 9$; $9 + 5 = 14$; $1 + 4 = 5$
the Kua number is 5
For girls born in the year 2000 and after, instead of adding 5, add 6.

• Those with Kua numbers 1, 3, 4, and 9 belong to the East group and auspicious directions are East, North, South, and Southeast.

• Those with Kua numbers 2, 5, 6, 7, and 8 belong to the West group and auspicious directions are West, Southwest, Northwest, and Northeast. (*See* pp. 64–65 for more details.)

KUAN KUNG

The general Kuan Ti, later known as Kwan Kung, is the most popular and famous general in Chinese history. Deified as the God of War, Kwan Kung eventually became known as a God of Wealth.

Displaying his image in the home facing the front door will chase away any Shar Chi. He is at his most powerful when placed in the Northwest corner of the house. At work, place the image behind where you sit at work so you will never lack powerful support from important people.

The best kind of Kuan Kong image is one showing him wearing a five-dragon robe and sitting on a horse. If you only keep one image of Kuan Kong in your home, it is best if it is heavy and made of good metals. Kuan Kong brings wealth and affords real protection. (*See* p. 180 for more details.)

KUN TRIGRAM

Kun is the ultimate yin Trigram. Kun means "The Receptive" and it is made up of three broken lines. Kun represents the dark, yielding, primal power of yin. The attribute of this important Trigram is the female maternal and its image is Big Earth. Kun symbolizes fertility and placing this trigram in the children's corner can assist couples in conceiving children. Placing Kun in the Southwest brings good luck in love, social life, family, and relationships. (*See* p. 110 for more details.)

L

LADY OF THE NINE HEAVENS

The Lady of the Nine Heavens brought the Luo Pan or Feng Shui compass to the Yellow Emperor who used it to defeat his enemies. (*See* p. 42 for more details about compass directions.)

LAKE

A lake is a form of big water in front of a house and it brings big wealth luck. A beautiful lake fronting the main door of your house is a source of precious Sheng Chi.

A lake to the North represents better fortune than a lake to the South of your front door, because North belongs to the water element while South is fire.

Make certain you can see the lake from inside your living room. Bring the chi of the lake into the home by installing a wall mirror in the living room to reflect the view of the lake. This signifies the arrival of wealth in your home. Do not build a home with a lake behind it. (*See* pp. 164–165 for more details about water flow.)

LAMPS

Lamps enhance romance luck as well as gaining the attention of powerful people. For romance, nothing beats a red lamp with the double happiness symbol painted in gold on the shade. The light activates the auspicious calligraphy! Recognition comes when you keep a bright red lamp shining continuously in the South corner of your home or living room.

Lamps simulate precious yang energy. Placing a lamp in the North corner, the place of the water element, does not spoil the Feng Shui since yang energy turns water into steam, creating the symbol of power. Lamps all over the home bring good energy, but balanced your use of this feature. Also, do not make lamps excessively bright. (*See* p. 57 for more details.)

LAND LEVELS

This refers to the topography surrounding your house, which provides important input into Feng Shui site investigation. Land that is completely flat is lacking in chi and inauspicious unless efforts are made to create variations of levels by introducing landscaping or buildings. Deserts have unexciting Feng Shui, but when buildings are introduced they create different levels that attract an auspicious flow of chi. (*See* p. 12–18 for more details. *See also* Celestial Creatures, p. 213, and Landscape Feng Shui, below.)

LANDSCAPE FENG SHUI

Landscape Feng Shui is the original classical school. All Feng Shui practitioners must be familiar with the principles of the Green Dragon and White Tiger.

Landscape Feng Shui is also known as Form School and, as the name suggests, it looks at the forms—the structures, shapes, topography, and levels—of the land to investigate the chi.

The environment is alive with chi and whether this is auspicious or not depends on how the winds and waters have shaped the landscape over time.

Exterior Feng Shui should always be assessed first. However, in modern times our control over the external environment is limited, so more emphasis has been placed on interior Feng Shui. (*See* pp. 12, 16–17, and 22 for more details.)

LATER HEAVEN ARRANGEMENT

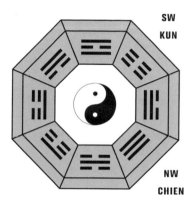

SW
KUN

NW
CHIEN

The Later Heaven arrangement is the pattern of trigrams arranged around the Yang Pa Kua (with the Kun in the Southwest and the Chien in the Northwest). This sequence was discovered after the Early Heaven sequence of trigrams was found inadequate for diagnosing the earthly realms for the abodes of the living. In the Later Heaven arrangement, the trigrams are taken out of their groupings in pairs of opposites and placed around the Pa Kua in a circular temporal progression. What are perceived then are cycles, such as the four seasons, or day and night. The cardinal points and the seasons are more closely related, and this arrangement is drastically different from the Early Heaven arrangement.

The sequence reflects the harmony and intrinsic balance of the year and illustrates a narration of life as reflected in nature. Its basic premise is closer to the attributes of life on earth than the afterlife in heaven. Most latter day practices of Chinese Feng Shui adopt this sequential representation of the Pa Kua. (*See* pp. 98–99 for more details.)

LEAF SHAPES

The shape of leaves determines the luck of plants placed near the home. Plants with thorns and prickly leaves emit negative energy. Round or succulent leaves are more auspicious than long knife-like leaves. (*See also* Cactus, p. 212, and Plants, p. 266.)

LEMON TREE

This is a powerful indicator of good fortune, especially when the plant is fully laden with fruits. When placed near the front part of the house during spring, it signifies the ripening of good fortune. A lemon plant made of jade is also an appropriate energizer. (*See also* Jade Plant, p. 249.)

LI TRIGRAM

This trigram is placed South in the Later Heaven or yang Pa Kua and it signifies the fire element. *Li* means clinging, and it is made up of one weak broken line between two strong unbroken yang lines.

Li is fire, the sun, brightness, lightning, heat, and warmth. Since the South is the corner of the Fire element, placing the trigram Li in the South is an effective way to activate the fame luck that the South sector can bring. The trigram Li also stands for the middle daughter. (*See* p. 102 for more details.)

LIGHTS

Like lamps, lights are excellent remedies for harmful Feng Shui. They can dissolve poison arrows and dissipate bad luck. Keeping the home well lighted at all times is good Feng Shui. Warm subdued light is better than glaring strong light.

Lights are one of the most versatile tools of Feng Shui practice. They correct a multitude of problems through their yang energy. They can resolve problems of missing corners, excessively yin corners, and land levels that are too low.

Lights attract Sheng Chi, bringing customers to restaurants and good fortune to corporations that keep their front entrances well lighted. They are particularly auspicious placed in the South and combined with crystals. Also make sure that the foyer into your home is always well lit. (*See* pp. 57 and 191 for more details.)

LILIES

Yellow lilies are much better than thorny red roses. White lilies especially are excellent for convalescing patients because they bring the pure healing energy of the West Trigram Tui, which stands for joyousness. Lilies generally signify good vibrations. (*See also* Flowers, p. 234.)

LIME FRUIT

The lime fruit absorbs all negative vibrations that cling to your body when you have been around people who wish you harm. Roll a fresh lime fruit clockwise in your right palm seven times to absorb the energy from your palm. Then either keep it in your pocket for a day or place it under your bed and after a full night's sleep wrap it up in paper and throw it away into fast moving water. This ritual gets rid of all negative vibes from your body in the same way as salt, but is less harmful to wandering spirits. (*See also* Lime Tree, below.)

LIME TREE

A lime tree symbolizes the ripening of prosperity. It is usually displayed near the door during the lunar New Year because lime is said to have the power to instantly absorb all bad chi. This makes for a very prosperous start to the New Year. An orange tree has the same effect. (*See also* Orange Tree, p. 263.)

LION DANCE

The main difference between the dragon dance and the lion dance is the length of the dragon. Smaller groups can perform the lion dance. This auspicious ritual makes such a din, all the bad spirits will run away! (*See also* Chinese New Year, p. 216, and Dragon Dance, p. 224.)

LIONS

A pair of lions standing guard on either side of the door is a classical feng shui feature. The use of these lions demonstrates the Chinese belief in symbolism. No practice of feng shui can be complete without the use of symbolic objects.

A pair of strong, heavy, and well-made lions at the entrance will protect your home and its residents from accidents, robbery, and premature death (*see* p. 78). The lions' size should be proportionate to your door. They need not be blessed. However, you may symbolically open their eyes on an auspicious day (first or fifteenth day of the month) between 9 and 11 A.M., or you can follow the auspicious times indicated in the Almanac, preferably while the sun shines brightly. (*See also* Almanac, p. 201.)

LIVING ROOMS

The living room is one of the best rooms in which to practice symbolic Feng Shui.

THE POWER CORNER

The most auspicious part of the living room is the furthest corner diagonal to the main entrance door. Place something of feng shui significance here to symbolize your major aspiration. Those desiring wealth should place wealth symbols in this corner. Those desiring love and romance should place symbols of love here.

THE LAYOUT

The living room furniture arrangement has many implications. Do not overcrowd the living room simplicity is best. Clean, neat rooms always have better feng shui than dirty or untidy rooms. Living rooms should be organized to let the flow of chi meander rather than move in a straight line.

Arrange sofas and chairs to allow gaps that let the chi flow through. Open rather than cramped spaces are preferred.

PLACEMENT OF FURNITURE

Arrange the furniture in a square or rectangular shape to ensure balance. Keep sofas in neutral but yang-dominated colors to ensure accumulation of yang chi.

Windows should be as large as possible. Make sure they bring in yang chi (sunlight). Hang crystals in the windows to create magical rainbows from the sunlight.

When the view outside is auspicious—lush plants, trees, flowers, landscaped gardens, or water—try to bring that view into the living room via windows, a balcony, or wall mirrors. Furniture should have support. Do not use chairs that look unstable or sofas with no backing.

TAPPING THE SMALL TAI CHI

All the formulas of compass feng shui that deal with orientations, directions, and corners can be reduced to the living room. Treat the living room like your universe and activate the different corners of the room in accordance with the Pa Kua attributes.

When you activate all eight corners of your living room, you can quickly feel the potency of the Eight Aspirations method. Keep wood chi in the Southeast for wealth, water chi in the North for career luck, earth chi in the Southwest for love and relationship luck…and so on.

HANGING AUSPICIOUS ART

Select auspicious art for your home. Avoid art that depicts tragic, sad, or hostile images. It is better to hang pictures that bring in sunshine and smiles and depict happy occasions. Try hanging powerful wealth and prosperity affirmations done in beautiful calligraphy. Remember that everything you display affects the feng shui of your home.living room. (See p. 99 for more details about Pa Kua in the living room.)

LO SHU SQUARE

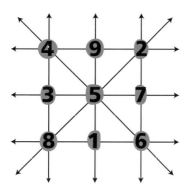

This is a magic square of nine numbers. It is one of the most vital symbols in compass Feng Shui.

The Lo Shu was brought to the attention of an emperor on the back of a tortoise rising from the River Lo. The arrangement of the numbers unlocks all the formulas of time dimension feng shui. It is the most important symbol in Flying Star Feng Shui.

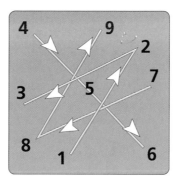

The significance lies in the arrangement of the numbers 1 to 9 in a nine-sector grid. The sum of any three numbers in any direction is 15. The number 15 is significant since this is the number of days for the new moon to become full. The number 15 expresses a cycle of lunar time. The Lo Shu grid offers clues to the fortunes of people and homes over a period of time. Lo Shu analysis centers around time-dimension Feng Shui.

The way the numbers are placed in the grid gives rise to a "flight pattern," which in turn creates another symbol known as the Sigil. The numbers "fly" around the grid.

The numbers move from one grid to the next from 5 to 6 (in the Northwest) and from there to 7 (in the West) and then to 8 (in the Northeast)…and so on. This forms double triangles with a line through the center symbol: the powerful sign of the Sigil. (See p. 48 for more details.)

LOGOS

A corporate logo should always be designed with its feng shui significance in mind. Companies have benefited from auspicious logos and suffered from unfortunate ones.

Follow these guidelines:

* Circular and curved designs are generally safer than designs with sharp edges and angles. Avoid triangles and zigzags. Companies that do well despite a logo with angular graphics and lines have these angles pointed outward—never toward the company name.

* Animals are incorporated to symbolize courage, strength, and resilience. Examples are the dragon, tiger, and lion. The dragon is best, especially if fat and prosperous and poised for upward flight, suggesting soaring ambitions. Be aware that fierce animals can turn against the company during inauspicious periods.

* A Pa Kua symbol is also not a good idea, especially if it is designed to look broken. In the retail business particularly, it is better not to use the Pa Kua symbol at all, for it generally repels customers.

* The use of flowers is good, although not as powerful as a living, moving creature. It is better to have buds than a flower in full bloom, for the first signifies a business about to take off, the second, a business about to wither. It is best to use spring colors (greens) rather than autumn ones (orange and brown).

* Mountains, hills, and rocks are good to incorporate as they signify strength, resilience, and support.

* Abstract shapes should be viewed with some care. In general, curved designs work better than angular ones. Be mindful of sharp edges always.

(See p. 78 for more details.)

LONGEVITY

This is the most important aspiration. Longevity always implies a healthy life where illness and sickness are kept at bay. Longevity also implies being safeguarded from death by accidents or unnatural causes. Longevity means one sees descendants succeed and bring honor to the family name.

The most important symbol of longevity is the God of Longevity, Sau Seng Kong. Other symbols are the pine tree, the bamboo, the peach, the crane, the deer, and the turtle. Any of them in the home will bring excellent luck. (*See also* God of Longevity, p. 239.)

LOTUS FLOWER

This flower is considered a symbol of enlightenment. A lotus pond is an excellent feature in any garden, and is extremely auspicious, but not from a material standpoint. Lotus ponds indicate a heightened sense of peace and mind transformation. They encourage spiritual development. (*See also* Eight Precious Objects, p. 229.)

LOTUS SEEDS

The presence of lotus seeds and pods in your garden signifies auspicious offspring luck. Displaying lotus seeds in the home hastens the arrival of grandchildren. Buddhists value prayer beads made of lotus seeds. (*See also* Garden, p. 238.)

LOVE

Feng Shui can bring love, romance, and serious marriage opportunities into anyone's life, but cannot guarantee the quality of the spouse or the relationship.

In feng shui, love is synonymous with marriage, so women who activate the Southwest corner or their Nien Yen direction will be activating for marriage as a first wife. For men, marriage means finding a woman able to produce children, work, and keep house. Not a very romantic view of love and certainly at odds with modern attitudes, but useful to understand.

To attract love, display a pair of mandarin ducks, which signify lovebirds that have a happy ending (*see* p. 75). They should not be confused with mallards, who are notoriously unfaithful. (*See also* Mandarin Ducks, p. 257.)

LUCKY NUMBERS

Display the address of your home or office building prominently if it is an auspicious number. Auspicious numbers end with any of the lucky numbers: 1, 6, 7, 8, and 9. The number eight is particularly lucky because it sounds like "Phat," which means prosperous growth. Nine is the premier number, because it signifies the fullness of heaven and earth.

The numbers 1, 6, and 8 together in any permutation are considered the luckiest of combinations. The number 8 is lucky because it represents this period (2003–2023).

If possible, choose house numbers, phone numbers, license plates, etc. with a lucky combination. If you cannot influence the number, play it down by displaying it small.

The number 4 was considered the death number because phonetically, it sounds like sey or "die" in Chinese. For many people, however, the number four has brought fabulously good luck!

The combination of 2s and 3s together is inauspicious. It often leads to misunderstandings, quarrels, and other problems. The worst number is 5. When this number appears, it brings with it severe difficulties and problems. (*See* p. 135 for more details.)

LUNAR CALENDAR

The Chinese lunar calendar is divided into twelve months of 29½ days each. Every 2½ years, an extra month is added to adjust the calendar, and this extra month is consecutively interposed between the second and the eleventh months of the lunar year. An auspicious day of the lunar calendar is the "first day of spring," or Lap Chun. Some years have double Lap Chuns (considered auspicious); others have no Lap Chun at all (considered bad luck for births and marriages). (*See also* Almanac, p. 201, and Chinese Calendar, pp. 284–285.)

LUO PAN

Luo Pan is the Chinese geomancer's compass, which usually contains secret codes and formulas. It is elaborately complex, comprising 24 concentric rings drawn round a small magnetic compass. The inner rings show the eight trigrams and orientations. The rings that follow display the Heavenly Stems and the Earthly Branches. (These terms are used in the Ganzhi system.)

The Luo Pan can be confusing. It does not require deep knowledge of

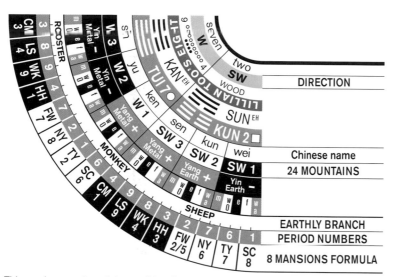

	DIRECTION
	Chinese name
	24 MOUNTAINS
	EARTHLY BRANCH
	PERIOD NUMBERS
	8 MANSIONS FORMULA

This modern version of the traditional Chinese Luo Pan, the geomancer's compass, is an advanced feng shui tool.

feng shui, but does require knowledge of the formulas of feng shui. Formula Feng Shui is based on fundamentals: the trigrams and their attributes, the numbers and their attributes, and the yin and yang manifestations of their combinations. It is easier to work from preformulated tables simplified by the masters and placed on the compass. (*See* pp. 42–43 for more details.)

M

MAGIC

Feng shui magic was once regarded as "Taoist magic" since many Taoist magic rituals also made use of the nine-sector Lo Shu grid, a principle tool of feng shui analysis. Although not truly magic, the results of using feng shui are sometimes so spectacular one can be forgiven for thinking of it as magic. (*See also* Lo Shu Square, p. 255.)

MAGNOLIA

Magnolia is a good flowering shrub to grow on the West side of your home or in a West-oriented garden. The magnolia is a symbol of feminine sweetness and beauty. (*See also* Garden, p. 238.)

MANDARIN DUCKS

These wonderful representatives of conjugal happiness symbolize a young couple in love. Displaying a pair of mandarin ducks in the Southwest

corner attracts the luck of romance and love. Ducks made of wood are not as effective as ducks made of the semi-precious stone jasper. (*See* pp. 69, 75, and 103 for more details.)

MAO TSE TUNG

Communist "emperor" of China best known for his little red book and the cultural revolution he unleashed in the mid-twentieth century.

The rise of this legendary leader was reportedly due to the special and rare feng shui of his grandfather's grave. Said to nestle "in the palm of the moon goddess," it signified that a descendant would ascend the Dragon throne.

After Mao became the most powerful man in China, he was obsessed with the rise and fall of past dynasties. Mao never stepped foot into the Forbidden City because he believed that the North-South alignment would hurt his personal feng shui. Indeed, he was born in a Snake year and belonged to the West group! (*See also* Forbidden City, p. 235.)

MARRIAGE

To energize good fortune in marriage, activate the earth elements of the Southwest. The ruling element of this corner is big earth, thus objects that simulate or produce this element, such as lights and crystals, are excellent energizers. (*See* p. 110 for more details. *See also* Love, opposite.)

MASTERS

Authentic feng shui masters who are genuinely skilled are a rare breed indeed and worth their weight in gold.

Usually such masters are humble and rarely reveal the depths of their knowledge. If you have the patience to slowly entice the knowledge out of them, you will begin to appreciate their great worth. Be wary of those who protest their superiority.

As with other esoteric and holistic practices, feng shui must be practiced in the context of contemporary living. Practitioners may not always call themselves masters, but results are the ultimate criteria we should use to appraise them. (*See* p. 19 for more details.)

MATTRESSES
One big mattress in a conjugal bed is better than two separate single-bed mattresses, which could cause a rift between husband and wife. It is less harmful to have two separate beds, or even separate rooms, than to have two mattresses on one bed. (*See* pp. 62 and 73 for more details.)

MEASUREMENTS
Feng shui measurements are especially potent when used to "make" a feng shui desk or bed. The four sets of auspicious and inauspicious directions can be measured using a special tape measure. The four levels of good fortune are:
* Chai (General Good Fortune)
* Yi (Patronage Luck)
* Kwan (Influence and Power)
* Pun (Wealth and Assets)
(*See* p. 49 for more details.)

MEETINGS
At important meetings, always sit facing one of your four auspicious directions

based on the Eight Mansions formula To ensure that luck is on your side. But you must be accurate. Directions Feng Shui

cannot be based on guesswork, so carry a compass and know your auspicious directions by heart (*see* p. 121). Never face one of your four bad directions. Once you know your Kua number, you can determine whether you are East or West and thus determine your auspicious directions. (*See also* Kua Numbers, p. 251.)

MENTOR (PATRON) LUCK
Powerful support and assistance from influential people is gained by activating the Northwest of your home, or your living room, if you spend a great deal of time there. Create the essence of metal energy to activate this area by hanging a six-rod windchime or placing six auspicious gold coins in the Northwest. (*See* p. 111 for more details.)

METAL ELEMENT
Metal or gold is one of the five elements and is associated with the West and Northwest. The word metal in Chinese is synonymous with the word for gold. The presence of earth energizes metal, since earth produces gold. Thus, a symbolic earth element in the metal corner of your home brings success and wealth.

Metal is destroyed by the element of fire, so bright lights in metal corners are not auspicious. Keep the lighting here dim and place your metallic appliances such as stereos and computers in these corners. (*See* p. 40 for more details about the elements.)

MIRRORS
Wall mirrors are excellent for bringing in good Sheng Chi from outside. They are also excellent in correcting cramped spaces and narrow corridors. Mirrors can be used to correct missing corners and columns. They can also be used to double auspicious symbols and counter poison arrows.

When using wall mirrors, make sure they are placed neither too low (thus "cutting off" heads) nor too high above the ground (thus "cutting off" feet). Mirrors should never reflect staircases, doors, toilets, or unsightly views.

In addition to wall mirrors, you can also use small mirrors made from gold or other metals and fashioned with auspicious symbols for protection. These small mirrors can also be used to harness the energy of both the sun and the moon to improve relationships and bring love into your life. (*See also* Doubling, p. 223.)

MISSING CORNERS
(*See* Corners, p. 218.)

MOBILES
Hang a mobile where the baby can see it, but never place anything directly above his or her head, as it will become symbolic suppressing the infant's growth. (*See* pp. 84–85 for details to help a child's growth.)

MONEY LUCK

Money luck can be created with symbols and water feng shui, and in the practice of the water dragon classic. Symbols of money include coins and the wealth deities. Energizing the Southeast sector of the home with luscious plants or a water feature is also a popular method of activating money luck. (*See* p. 112 for more details.)

MONEY PLANT

These creeper plants symbolize successful enhancement of income. Found in the tropics, the money plant has heart-shaped leaves that are yellow and green in color. (*See also* Money Luck, above.)

MONGOOSE

The mongoose symbolizes wealth and is usually depicted spouting coins from its mouth. This symbol is usually especially powerful when displayed alongside an image of the Dzambhalas, Tibetan gods of wealth. (*See* p. 169 for more details.)

MONKEY ON A HORSE

The monkey on a horse signifies instant promotion and is especially auspicious for those in large corporations, the military, and politics. (*See* pp. 52–59 for more details on career success.)

If you are ready for promotion, place this image in the Northwest corner of your office for career luck.

MOON GATE

A circular entranceway is considered an auspicious balance of yin and yang energies and was popular long ago. (*See also* Yin Yang Symbol, p. 283.)

MOTHER EARTH

The trigram Kun that rules the Southwest symbolizes "Mother Earth" (big earth). It is the ultimate yin trigram and signifies the female in every one of us. Enhance relationship luck by doubling this trigram (three broken lines) into the hexagram Kun (six broken lines), and hanging it in the Southwest sector. Mother Earth can also be energized by a large globe or map of the world placed in the Southwest. (*See* p. 110 for more details.)

MOU TAN FLOWER

(*See* Peonies, p. 265.)

MOUNTAIN STAR

Mountain stars indicate good fortune in the area of relationships for those living where its number is auspicious. The mountain star is also known as the Chor Sin, or "sitting star."

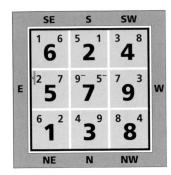

In the Flying Star natal chart shown, the Mountain Stars are the small numbers on the left of each large number. (*See* pp. 186–189 for more details.)

MOUNTAINS

Mountains are vital for good feng shui in the environment and signify the source of heaven luck. Mountains low enough to have vegetation usually harbor the benevolent Green Dragon. They also provide stunning support and backing, anchoring you firmly and preventing you from being swept away by misfortune, bad luck, or betrayal.

Completely flat land without elevated landforms cannot sustain the dragon's lair and are inauspicious. Where there are no mountains, you can simulate their presence with the picture of a mountain. Mountain shapes are categorized into the five elements and mountain orientations are classified as one of the Celestial Creatures. In cities, tall buildings are viewed as mountains. (*See* pp. 12–15 for more details.)

MULTI-LEVEL HOMES

Homes with multiple floor levels tend to suffer from unbalanced fortunes, so you should favor spacious rooms with the same level of flooring. (*See* pp. 22–25 for more details.)

MUSIC

Music in the home brings precious yang energy, causing the chi to become benevolent and is especially effective in homes where both husband and wife are at work the entire day. Keep radios and television sets turned on to simulate the presence of energy so that chi does not get stale or stagnate. It has actually been found that productivity increases when music is piped into factories. The feng shui benefit of doing this is self-evident. Chi in the space becomes lighter and more auspicious. (*See also* Sheng Chi, p. 273, and Stereo Systems, p. 275.)

MYSTIC KNOT

There are many variations of the mystic knot, which stands for undying love, neverending success, and riches. Wearing the mystic knot on your body as fine jewelry made of gold and diamonds is a great way of activating romantic luck. The mystic knot rivals the Longevity sign in popularity. (*See* p. 173 for more details.)

N
NARCISSUS

A bulb plant with white fragrant flowers, the narcissus brings excellent career luck if it blooms during the first fifteen days of the New Year. The faster these bulbs grow and bloom during the New Year, the faster your career will rise. Display a narcissus in your office to symbolize the manifestation of your latent talents, leading to recognition and promotion. (*See* pp. 52–59 for career success. *See also* Flowers, p. 234.)

NATAL CHARTS

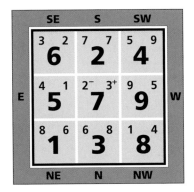

These feng shui charts reveal the lucky "nine palaces" of the home, as well as encapsulating a great deal of information in the code of numbers placed around the Lo Shu grid. Natal charts are best read in conjunction with annual Flying Star charts. (*See also* Flying Star Feng Shui, p. 235.)

NATURAL CONTOURS

These natural hills and valleys of the land simulate the four celestial creatures, including the dragon and the tiger. The forms of water flows indicate good or bad chi. Generally speaking, undulating land is luckier than flat land.

However, do note that wherever natural landforms (e.g. mountains) and buildings occur together the impact (of both good and bad luck) of the natural mountain is much stronger since the chi of the mountain is millions of years old while the chi of buildings is only as old as the building. (*See* pp. 12–15 for more details. *See also* Landscape Feng Shui, p. 252.)

NEW HOUSE

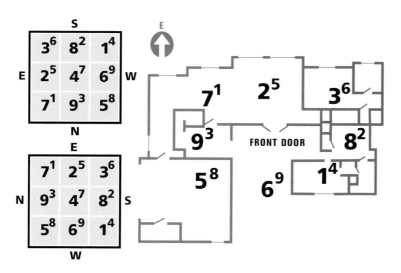

This plan for a West-facing Chen house (see p. 117) is based on a feng shui chart (top left) that has been turned for easier analysis (bottom left).

When you move into a new house, select an auspicious date for moving in. When you build a new house, be sure to design it with feng shui input. Prevention of bad luck starts with the first brick laid and enhancing good luck begins from the day the house plans are drawn up. It is worthwhile to factor in usage of rooms and placement of toilets, kitchens, and bedrooms.

Design your home according to feng shui using the charts and analysis. Focus your feng shui according to your own needs and aspirations. (*See* Chapters 14 and 15 for more details.)

NEW YEAR

(*See* Chinese New Year, p. 216.)

NIEN YEN

Nien Yen is one of the four auspicious directions allocated to each Kua number in the Eight Mansions formula. Nien Yen is the best direction to energize for matters relating to love, marriage, and the family. Activating your Nien Yen corner helps to attract the chi of love that leads to marriage. (*See* p. 119 for more details.)

NINE (THE NUMBER)

The number nine is a full and complete number. Some say because of this it is even luckier than eight. But the number nine also has the ability to enhance bad luck brought by unlucky numbers, so it must be used with care. It is best when it appears unjoined to any number other than eight.

Nine multiplied any number of times will always come back to nine. Try it: $9 \times 3 = 27$ and $2 + 7 = 9$. Check this with all the numbers multiplied by nine and you will realize why this number is most powerful when by itself. (*See* p. 135 for more details.)

NINE STAR KI ASTROLOGY

This Japanese hybrid system of feng shui was first popularized by a Japanese prisoner of war. Nine Star Ki was studied and researched in the West. Nine Star Ki enables predictions on a yearly, monthly, and daily basis. This system uses the trigrams of the I Ching to define its eight principal "stars," then relates the Five Elements to the I Ching to work out which family member they belong to. (*See also* I Ching, p. 246, and Wu Xing, p. 282.)

NOISE

Noise manifests intense yang energy and in the past featured prominently in all New Year celebrations, often in the form of fireworks. In modern times, noise levels have been brought down substantially due to proximity of homes in most suburban and city areas and fireworks can be dangerous if improperly used. Loud and happy Chinese New Year music, complete with cymbals and drums, can have a similar effect. Hanging a fake firecracker simulates the creation of yang energy. (*See also* Chinese New Year, p. 216.)

NORTH

This direction is symbolized by the Kan Trigram, which belongs to the element of water. North is also the place of the tortoise. The feng shui attributes of the North sector of any home are energized with the presence of water, so a water feature here is most beneficial.

The best water feature is a fishpond. If you cannot place a real water feature, a painting of a water scene is a good way to simulate water. Placing metal here is also recommended. Since metal produces water. The number of North in the Later Heaven arrangement is one (1). (*See also* Kan Trigram, p. 250.)

NORTHEAST

This compass sector is represented by the trigram Ken, which stands for the mountain, signifying small earth element. This direction also activates for education and scholarship success. It is represented by the number eight, and is a yang direction. Display earth element objects, e.g., crystals, porcelain, and clay decorative objects in the Northeast. (*See also* Ken Trigram, p. 250.)

NORTHWEST

This compass sector is signified by the trigram Chien. This yang direction is the most important corner of any home since its energy comes from heaven. Always keep the energies of this sector activated and fresh: clean, bright, and airy.

The Northwest is the place of big metal and placing earth or metal objects here will create excellent energy. Metal objects can be anything made of brass, cloisonné, or gold.

Never place open fire in this corner, including fire element objects like lamps and other lights, since in the cycle of elements fire destroys metal. (*See also* Chien Trigram, p. 215.)

NUMBERS

The numbers one through nine have a multitude of good and bad feng shui connotations. One interpretation is based on the phonetic sounds of the numbers, which would indicate that three and eight are excellent, while the number four is to be abhorred. However, Chinese numerology goes far beyond the "sound" of numbers, and although four sounds like "to die," it is a good number in Flying Star. While three sounds like "to grow," in Flying Star it means hostility and quarrels. In this analysis, the numbers five and two are the villains while the numbers one, six, and eight are considered excellent. The number nine is thought to be powerfully lucky. The number eight has universal appeal and indicates great prosperity under all systems of analysis. (*See* p. 135 for more details.)

O
OFFICE BUILDING

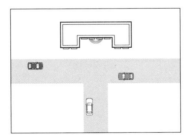

Above: Inauspicious site at a T-junction may adversely affect wealth luck.

Below: Auspicious entrance faces a wide road and an open park space.

The back of your office building should be supported either by hills or by a higher building so that all the businesses conducted within have good support. Tall buildings directly in front of your building block opportunity and luck, unless there is a wide road between that allows energy to flow smoothly. Traffic in front of the building should be slow rather than fast. Traffic moving two ways is not as good as traffic moving one way, although whether or not the direction of traffic flow is good or bad depends on the facing direction of the building.

A view of water in front of the building is always auspicious. Be careful of placing a sculpture in front of the building as you could unwittingly harm your door or front entrance.

Feng shui implications in the use of reflective glass, colors, and shapes are incorporated into building design. The most important aspect is that the entrance must be properly planned; a business should never have multiple entrances, as they make orientation difficult, or have a main entrance resembling a "deep hole," which means the building is lacking in something. (*See* pp. 26–31 for more details.)

OFFICE DESKS
(*See* Desks, p. 222.)

OFFICE FENG SHUI

The same principles apply to feng shui at work as at home, except that in the office the priorities focus on energizing wealth and staff cooperation. The directions that benefit everyone are those in accordance with individual birth dates and Kua numbers, while overall luck of the office depends on the Kua number of the most senior person. To ensure company protection against negative periods of the business cycle, the prosperity corner of the office should always be energized by the presence of a healthy fresh plant in the Southeast. (*See also* Flying Star Feng Shui, p. 235.)

OFFICE INTERIORS

Corporate feng shui is becoming increasingly popular and many CEOs in the UK and the US are using feng shui to create a better image and attract better results for their companies. It is important to select a feng shui consultant carefully. Unless you use someone who also knows about management and is familiar with the different methods of feng shui, it could end up being an exercise in futility. Always do sufficient research when using feng shui consultants. (*See* p. 19 for more details.)

OPEN SHELVES

(*See* Bookshelves, p. 210.)

ORANGE TREE

Another favorite way to activate the symbolism of orange gold is by placing orange plants in the home. Fruit-bearing orange plants displayed during the Lunar New Year symbolize wealth luck. If you wish to plant an orange tree in your garden, plant it in the Southeast corner. (*See also* Lime Tree, p. 254.)

ORANGES

In Chinese, the word for orange—kum— phonetically sounds like "gold" and thus signifies gold. You can display bowls of oranges to symbolize "gold" during the New Year holidays. (*See also* Lime Fruit, p. 253.)

ORCHIDS

In selecting plants for the garden, if your climate permits, the growing of orchids signifies strength and courage as well as longevity of tenure in your career. Orchids are long-lasting flowers that bring healthy chi to the home. (*See also* Flower Gardens, p. 234.)

ORIENTATIONS

These refer to the directions of doors, as well as sitting, facing, and sleeping directions. Orientations are an important aspect of correct feng shui practice and must be accurately implemented according to various feng shui formula and guidelines. Orientation also means the correct placement of the home with regard to the surrounding environment including rivers, lakes, hills, and fields. (*See* pp. 42–43 for more details.)

OVERHEAD BEAMS

(*See* Beams, p. 207.)

OX

The Ox is the second sign of the Chinese Zodiac and its intrinsic element is earth. The hour of the Ox is between 1:00 A.M. and 3:00 A.M.; anyone born between those hours is born in the hour of the Ox. The compass direction of the Ox is North-Northeast, and this sector can be enhanced with crystal figurines of the wish-fulfilling cow, the raging bull, or a metal box filled with jewels. (*See also* Zodiac, p. 283.)

P

PA KUA

This eight-sided pictogram contains the symbols, directions, and numbers required for basic feng shui analysis. There are two types of Pa Kuas, yin and yang.

The yang Pa Kua is used for analyzing the feng shui of houses, apartments, and buildings. The yang Pa Kua is based on the Later Heaven arrangement of the trigrams.

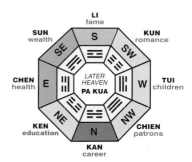

In the Yang Pa Kua, the placement of the eight trigrams shows Kun in the Southwest and Chien in the Northwest. Each of the compass sectors stands for the kind of luck that can be activated in the corresponding corners on the ground. This simple method of feng shui is known as Pa Kua Eight Aspirations Feng Shui.

The Yin Pa Kua shows a different placement of the trigrams around the sides and this difference is crucial. The Yin Pa Kua is used for protection against poison arrows and evil chi caused by hostile structures in the environment. The Yin Pa Kua has the power to deflect and dissolve bad energy; however, in doing this it also repels and harms everything in its direct path. Use the Yin Pa Kua only as a last resort because it does hurt people.

The Yin Pa Kua is also used in conjunction with the Yang Pa Kua in advanced feng shui work involving both yin and yang houses. It is especially useful for analyzing the effects of surrounding roads and mountains on your house.

In this Yin Pa Kua, the placement of the all-important Chien is placed on top in the South and opposite Kun so that ultimate yang faces ultimate yin, the father faces the mother, heaven faces earth. Water is in the West, directly facing fire, which is placed East. The trigram Kan faces the trigram Li. (*See* pp. 98–99 for more details.)

PA KUA MIRROR

This symbol for the Yin Pa Kua used to deflect poison arrows in the environment is usually painted with a red background to create vital yang energy. The trigrams are placed in Later Heaven arrangement. In the center is the mirror that absorbs all the hostile energy coming in its direction. The Pa Kua mirror is a popular defensive tool; however, since it has the power to harm people with its burning rays, use plants, trees, walls, and hedges instead of the Yin Pa Kua to block the path of poison arrows. (*See also* Pa Kua, p. 263.)

PAINTINGS

Paintings can cause misfortunes or they can be lucky, depending on the colors, textures, and subject matter. Assess figures with care once you know what constitutes auspicious or inauspicious symbolism. Avoid sharp lines and angular structures that may send out little slivers of poison arrows. Choose rounded or circular shapes instead. (*See also* Art, p. 204.)

PARK

When located in front of your main door, a park or any empty space creates the bright hall effect, which attracts precious yang chi. The chi is able to settle and accumulate before entering your home. When selecting homes to buy or rent, look for those with an empty space or park in front of them. (*See* pp. 12–18 for more details. *See also* Bright Hall, p. 211.)

PATHWAYS

Winding pathways are better than straight pathways, and any kind of walkway, driveway, or even corridor is less harmful if not straight and long. In the garden, a winding pathway causes chi to meander, slowing it down and allowing it to accumulate. An office pathway that meanders to simulate the dragon, with all desks and workstations designed around it, will ensure that bad chi does not stay long in the office.

It is also a good idea to create a wavy effect when building water features, since a meandering border causes the chi to become benevolent. (*See also* Paving Stones, below.)

PATIO

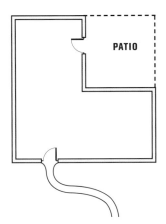

Patios can solve the problem of missing corners. Depending on the direction of the patio, you can also enhance it with element energizers. For example, a patio located in the North will benefit from a water feature. One in the South can be the barbecue area, and so forth. Patios must also be considered as part of your house for purposes of superimposing the Lo Shu chart onto the floorplan. (*See also* Lo Shu Square, p. 255.)

PAVING STONES

A winding pathway of paving stones brings good chi flow toward the house and is excellent in the earth corners of your garden (i.e. in the Northeast or Southwest). (*See also* Pathways, left.)

PEACH

Peaches are the fruit of longevity. Displaying a jade creation of a peach branch will enhance longevity. Paintings or porcelain decorated with peach plants, peach fruits as decorations, or a peach tree in the garden signify not only longevity but also a good life. Displaying the peach in the center of the home is excellent for the family's health.

Peaches make a meaningful birthday gift for your parents and grandparents. Decorations, foods, and gifts that incorporate peaches wish your parents many more years of happy and healthy life. (*See* p. 93 for more details.)

PEACOCK

This beautiful bird with extraordinary plumage signifies dignity and beauty, supremacy and victory. If you are engaged in competition with someone, placing a peacock image nearby will benefit you enormously. Try to get one in cloisonné.

For centuries, the stunning hues of the peacock's tail feathers have made them popular emblems of official rank, and fans made of peacock tail feathers are often used as decorations for the home. The peacock can be used as a substitute for the Phoenix *See also* Phoenix, right.)

PEONIES

The peony is the king of flowers, excellent for creating good romance luck. The peony is associated with beautiful women. The legendary Yang Kwei Fei, one of the most beautiful women in Chinese history and concubine to the emperor, decorated her bedchamber with magnificent

peonies all year round. The emperor, who could deny her nothing, had to arrange for these flowers to be brought to her all the way from the South.

The peony is also called the Mou Tan flower, and is the principal flower symbol for love and marriage. Displaying it in the home brings marriage luck to unmarried members of the family. Silk paintings of peonies in the bedroom of young daughters are most beneficial.

Do not display peonies in the bedroom of an older couple, since this might cause the husband to develop a relationship with a younger woman outside the marriage. (*See also* Love, p. 256, and Marriage, p. 257.)

PERIOD EIGHT

Period Eight began on February 4, 2004, and will end twenty years later on February 3, 2023. Period Eight symbolizes the mountain. It is an earth period represented by the trigram Ken. During this Period, there will be much introspection and a rise in interests having to do with meditation and scholastic research.

Those who use Flying Star Feng Shui should begin to change their homes into Period Eight homes, since Period Seven houses will lose energy as their chi weakens. A fairly in-depth knowledge of Flying Star will help effect this change in a graceful manner. (*See* pp. 44–45 for more details.)

PERIOD SEVEN

Period Seven, the previous twenty years, was known as the Joyous, or Tui, Period, signifying young women and joyousness. Tui also means "lake" and "mouth" and so represents wealth and communications. During this period, which ended on February 3, 2004, we saw a rise in the influence of women and the importance of the media, as well as a great accumulation of wealth. (*See* pp. 44–45 for more details.)

PHOENIX

For career luck, a phoenix symbolizes new opportunities. To activate work luck, a phoenix without a dragon is best. With the dragon, the phoenix is a yin creature; without the dragon, it becomes a yang creature, bringing financial success and prosperity.

In Landscape Feng Shui, the phoenix is represented by slightly elevated land in the South or at the front of the home. If you do not have this feature facing your front door, you can artificially create one to energize the luck of the sector.

If you cannot find a suitable phoenix symbol to use, other well-plumaged birds such as the rooster or peacock can be used to represent the phoenix. (*See also* Crimson Phoenix, p. 219 and Dragon and Phoenix, p. 224.)

PHOTOGRAPHS

Never keep photographs in the bathroom, under a bed, or under the staircase, as family albums are not to be "stepped on." Apply the same logic to all important books, files, and notes. Anything that you step on suffers from the negative effect and often materializes bad luck associated with those items. (*See also* Portraits, right, and Family Portraits, p. 232.)

PI YAO

A symbol of good fortune, in the form of a heavenly creature with one horn, lion-dog face, hoofs, wing, and tail, who offers protection from evil spirits. Pi Yao has the power to counteract and overcome bad luck caused by the Grand Duke Jupiter after you renovate your home or move into a new one. (*See* p. 15 for more details.)

PILLARS

(*See* Columns, p. 218.)

PINE TREES

Pine trees are stunning symbols of longevity and strength in adversity. Plant at least one pine in your yard or garden. The needles of the pine tree possess excellent qualities for clearing the home of negative energy. (*See also* Trees, p. 279.)

PLANTS

Plants signify the growth essence of the wood element. Many growing plants around your home, especially in the East and Southeast, will greatly enhance your feng shui. It is important to keep them under control by cutting back and trimming regularly. Dying plants should be discarded immediately. (*See also* Flower Gardens, p. 234.)

PLUM BLOSSOM

Hang a picture of a plum blossom for a long, happy life. The plum, the peony, the lotus, and the chrysanthemum are the four auspicious flowers. They also represent the four seasons. The plum signifies winter and symbolizes longevity owing to the fact that the flowers appear on the leafless and apparently lifeless branches of the tree until it reaches an advanced age. For this reason, during the lunar New Year, many households display the plum. In Malaysia, instead of the plum, pussy willow branches are imported from China. The meaning of the pussy willow is the same. From dead-looking branches come leaves and flowers, signs of renewal and rejuvenation. (*See also* Flowers, p. 234.)

POISON ARROWS

These harmful hostile structures in the environment send out harmful Shar Chi. Develop the ability to spot them and learn how to deflect, dissolve, and block them. Ensure that your front door is not afflicted by an arrow.

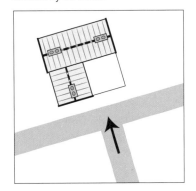

A poison arrow T-junction.

Examples of poison arrow structures that can harm your home include:

* A long straight road, seeming to point at your main door, as in a T-junction.
* The triangular roof line of a neighboring house.
* A transmission or building tower, or a crane.
* A tall, imposing building or pointed facades on a nearby building.
* Rocky outcroppings or sharp sculptures.

(*See also* Shar Chi, p. 273.)

POMEGRANATE

The many seeds of the pomegranate fruit make it an emblem of fertility. Many families advise the young newlywed generation to display a pomegranate fruit painting or sculpture in the conjugal bedroom to create the luck of having many healthy grandchildren. (*See* p. 109 for more details.)

PONDS

Small ponds are best placed in the North, Southeast, and East. Aerate the pond with moving or flowing water. Keep life in the pond: fish, terrapins, or plants. These bring good chi into the home. But remember you must not dig a hole in the ground inside the home. If you want to have a water feature inside the house, use a standing urn or a water feature placed above ground. The only way to have a pond inside the house is to build around an existing pond in the yard or garden, as this will expand the house to embrace the water. (*See* pp. 180–185 for more details.)

PORTRAITS

Family portraits hung inside the home or office should not face personal inauspicious directions. Calculate the Kua number of the person whose picture is being displayed. If there are several people in the picture, let it face the auspicious direction of the eldest person in the picture. Make sure the portrait is not hit by poison arrows such as sharp edges, and is not facing a staircase or a toilet. Install two bright lights shining day and night at the portrait to stay healthy and inundated with yang energy. (*See also* Art, p. 204.)

PRICKLY PLANTS

(*See* Cactus, p. 212.)

PRODUCTIVE CYCLE

(*See* Cycles of Chi, pp. 221.)

PROTRUDING CORNERS

(*See* Corners, p. 218.)

PURPLE

The color purple signifies water but is more auspicious than blue. Purple is particularly lucky when teamed with chrome or silver. The two colors together—Ngan chee—mean "money" in Cantonese. (*See* pp. 28–29 for colors of buildings.)

PURPLE STAR ASTROLOGY

Purple Star astrology, or Tzi Wei Dou Shu, is one of the most revered systems of destiny analysis in the world. This highly complex system converges on fourteen major stars and twenty-six supporting stars, which create more than one hundred fifty thousand combinations.

According to ancient texts, more than eighty stars can be found in a destiny analysis chart, although in actual practice, half of the "fictitious" stars can be ignored without affecting the accuracy of the reading. Tzi Wei Dou Shu was written during the Tang Dynasty and made popular during the Sung Dynasty. During the past decade, Tzi Wei Dou Shu has become a popular system of astrology.

The Purple Star astrology reading is based on twelve palaces of destiny, each of which describes a significant aspect of a person's life. A complete chart is plotted according to the particulars of a person's birth (year, month, day, time, sex, and place) converted to the Lunar Calendar.

1 The Life Palace is the most important palace and is concerned with a person's outlook, inborn capabilities, achievement, and character. It governs development, and wealth.

2 The Brothers and Sisters Palace is about relationship with siblings. It also describes relationships with colleagues.

3 The Spouse and Marital Palace reveals whether a marriage will be happy and fruitful. It also explains why some people marry many times while others stay unmarried.

4 The Children Palace indicates the number of children and describes the relationship between parents and children. Sometimes this palace refers to your subordinates and students.

5 The Wealth Palace describes income level, wealth, and general financial situation. This palace also indicates success or failure in getting rich.

6 The Health Palace describes physical and mental health, as well as the possibility of injuries, accidents, or illness you may be prone to contracting.

7 The Travel Palace advises for or against travel to incur career luck. It also describes whether or not a place of residence is suitable.

8 The Friends Palace reveals whether friends and subordinates are loyal. This palace also indicates luck with respect to business partners.

9 The Career Palace contains advice on career and whether you are suited to work for a company or set up a business. It indicates what career to pursue and what level of achievement to expect.

10 The Property Palace governs living environment and how much property, investment capital, or inheritance you are likely to acquire. It also describes lifestyle.

11 The Fortune or Happiness Palace reveals attitude and behavior, describes mental state of happiness, and indicates life span.

12 The Parents Palace describes relationships with parents and superiors (teachers and bosses). It sometimes indicates whether parents are separated or not.

Tzi Wei Dou Shu reveals time dimension in the analysis. The reading can be divided into blocks of ten years, one year, or one month. This calculation is used to map out the cycle of your life path. (*See also* Astrology, p. 205.)

Q

QUA

This red ceremonial dress decorated with beautiful embroidery and beadwork is the traditional Chinese wedding dress for brides. It is considered auspicious for brides to wear the qua and historically only the first or principal wife was allowed this honor.

The qua can be a long dress with a high collar or it can comprise a skirt and a blouse. Crystals and precious stones are used depending on the status and wealth of the bride's family. The embroidery usually depicts the dragon and phoenix with peonies and other symbols of good fortune. The mother of the bride often wears a red top and black skirt, but there is likewise a great deal of colorful embroidery.

Chinese brides, no matter how modern, should get married in a qua since it is most auspicious to do so. If you do not want a qua, at least get married in red. Do not wear black as it is much too yin for such a yang occasion. The bride must not change into black for her own wedding party. Guests should also not wear black to a wedding as this is deemed to be very unkind. They may, however, wear red since this heightens the yang energy.

The bride and groom should drink a mixture of wine and honey from glasses tied with red ribbon, exchanging goblets and drinking again. This seals their commitment to each other. At this point, the bride can change out of her ceremonial wedding dress into a more comfortable evening cheongsam, which should also be red. (*See* pp. 168–171 for symbols of good fortune.)

QUARTZ CRYSTALS

Quartz crystals are wonderful conductors of energy. Natural crystal clusters are excellent earth element activators for the Southwest and Northeast. These two corners are of interest to the younger generation since the Southwest represents love and social life and the Northeast signifies education luck.

It is possible to energize living rooms with beautiful crystals fashioned into wealth chests filled with fake precious jewels. They look beautiful and also bring in plenty of yang energy.

Crystals are the treasures of the earth and signify the precious fruit of the earth, so use them to create earth chi or energy. Hang a faceted lead crystal in a window to catch the direct sunlight shining along any wall. The crystal will break up the sunlight and create beautiful rainbows in your home, bathing it in precious yang energy and creating harmony and a feeling of optimism. (*See also* Yang Energy, p. 282.)

QUEEN (PRECIOUS)

The Precious Queen symbolizes the essence of the Matriarch and is a powerful symbol. Hanging pictures of any Queen familiar to you creates good energy for the mother and female members of the family.

The Precious Queen is part of the Buddhist Mandala offering and, in this context, can be viewed as the matriarchal equivalent of the emperor. Activate the Southwest sector, since this is the place of the trigram Kun, which signifies the essence of the matriarchal spirit. (*See also* Kun Trigram, p. 252.)

QUEEN MOTHER OF HEAVEN

Legendary Taoist Queen of Heaven is the patron Goddess of sailors and sea-going men. She is believed to ensure good weather and safe conduct for their journey on the high seas. She is known as Ma Tsu Po. (*See also* Gods and Goddesses, pp. 239–240.)

QUEEN MOTHER OF THE WEST

References to the Queen can also refer to the Queen Mother of the West, Hsi Wang Mu (or Xi Wang Mu). Her image in the home is said to bring enormous good fortune. This Queen is the legendary lady believed to reside in the paradise realm located high in the Kun Lun Mountains. She is shown seated on a phoenix and accompanied by two handmaidens. One waves a large magic fan and the other carries a tray filled with peaches of immortality that grow in her gardens. This image brings good fortune for many years. (*See also* Fan, p. 232, and Peach, p. 265.)

QUIET AREAS

The bedroom of the house should be a place of relative quiet. This is when yin chi is to be preferred over too much yang chi. However, when the whole house is excessively quiet then luck stagnates. Never allow house energy to turn yin or get stale—the energy will depress you. (*See also* Yin Yang Symbol, p. 283.)

R
REAL ESTATE

Real estate is symbolic of the earth element. Any business involving property and development will benefit from the energizing of the earth element. Crystals, urns, terracotta pots, and decorative stones can be used as good fortune symbols. Work them into the décor of the office and make sure they are placed in the earth sectors (in the Southwest or Northeast). (*See* pp. 52–59 for success in business.)

RED

Red is the ultimate yang color. It stands for the trigram Li and represents the fire element. Red strengthens and energizes whoever is adorned in it and is usually worn at all happy, upbeat occasions. It is important in winter when yang energy is on the wane.

But red can also cause serious problems in excess. Fire, if not kept under control, can burn and destroy. So keep red under control and let it serve you. (*See also* Yang Energy, p. 282.)

RED STRING

Most symbolic objects of good fortune benefit from being tied with red string to signify yang energy and make the object "come alive." When placing coins and other good fortune objects, tie with red thread to animate the chi. (*See* pp. 168–171 for symbols of good fortune.)

REFRIGERATOR

Placement of the refrigerator in the kitchen should take into account placement of the stove because water (represented by the refrigerator, dishwasher, and sink) and fire (stove, oven, and crockpots) are clashing elements and should not mix. These two elements should neither be placed beside nor opposite one another. The latter arrangement is more harmful than the first, although both are bad. (*See also* Kitchen Feng Shui, p. 250.)

RICE URN

The rice urn symbolizes the rise and fall of family fortunes since rice, is the staple food of the Chinese.

When passed from generation to generation rice urns are usually well-preserved to ensure that a family will remain wealthy even through turbulent times. The family rice urn, like the symbolic wealth vase, should be kept hidden, signifying the family's fortune being safely hidden away. Embedded under the rice is usually a carefully wrapped red packet containing gold coins to signify money. This money gets renewed every lunar new year, which ensures continuity of good fortune from year to year. If the previous year was prosperous, one of the old coins is kept, but new ones should be added each year to symbolize wealth steadily growing. (*See also* Wealth Vases, p. 281.)

RIVERS

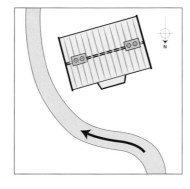

The presence of a slow-moving river visible from your home is an auspicious feng shui feature. Rivers are purveyors of good chi, especially when the water is meandering and clean. Polluted rivers tend to be afflicted with poisonous breath.

✳ For homes where the main door faces North, South, East, or West (one of the cardinal directions), it is auspicious if the river flows from left to right (when facing the river from inside the house.)

✳ For homes where the main door faces a secondary direction (Southeast, Southwest, Northeast or Northwest) it is auspicious if the river flows from right to left. (*See* pp. 164–165 for more details.)

ROADS

Roads have good or bad feng shui depending on their levels (whether lower or higher than your house) and their moving directions. Roads that aim directly at the home (especially its main door) usually bring bad feng shui in the form of a poison arrow.

Modern feng shui masters use guidelines that historically applied to rivers, to analyze the impact of modern roads and highways. In the Form School, however, a visual analysis is often sufficient for an experienced master to tell whether the roads in front of and around any building are potentially harmful or not. (*See* pp. 18–24 for more details.)

ROCKS

Rocks tied with red string are an effective antidote for bathrooms located in the North part of the home, where they can cause bad career luck.

Rocks can energize for good luck in the Northeast and Southwest areas of the garden. They simulate earth energy, which is auspicious for relationships. (*See also* Boulders, p. 210, and Earth Luck, p. 226.)

ROMANCE DIRECTION

There are two major compass directions, which anyone can use to activate heightened quantities of love luck. The first is the general direction, which indicates that romance luck depends on the Southwest of any space. If you have a bathroom, storeroom, or kitchen in the Southwest of your house, romance can be washed away. Activate the Southwest with good earth energy and the symbols of love, marriage, and family, to bring romance into your life.

The second romance direction is the personalized direction known as your Nien Yen direction, which brings love and family luck. This personalized romance direction is based on your Kua number, which in turn is calculated according to your year of birth and your gender. To tap your Nien Yen chi, you should sit facing your personalized direction whenever possible and sleep with your head toward your Nien Yen.

Kua 1	South
Kua 2	Northwest
Kua 3	Southeast
Kua 4	East
Kua 5	(male) Northwest
Kua 5	(female) West
Kua 6	Southwest
Kua 7	Northeast
Kua 8	West
Kua 9	North

(*See* pp. 119–121 for more details.)

ROMANCE LUCK

The Southwest is the romance sector of any house. Symbols that signify romance, love, and togetherness, include mandarin ducks, the double

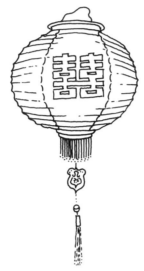

happiness symbol, and crystal clusters. Other objects that encourage romance chi are the peony flower and red lanterns with the double happiness symbol. These red lanterns are powerful, inexpensive, and romantic. You can also keep a double happiness sign close to your heart and let it attract romance into your life.

For those who have lost a loved one either through separation, divorce, or death, and are looking for a new love interest, place a pair of symbolic magpies in the bedroom. These birds spell renewal and fresh beginnings in love. As for colors the best for attracting love luck is yellow, not red, so wear yellow and put on a bright smile. (*See* pp. 68–69 for more details.)

ROOFS

The shape and size of roofs can influence residents as well as neighbors. It is always a good policy to do feng shui with an eye for its effect on your neighbor. Poison arrows such as sharp edges or pointed features will send Shar Chi toward your neighbor. Note whether your roof affects your neighbor as well as yourself.

Roofs are best when they simulate earth or wood hills. They tend to become dangerous when they signify the fire or water. Roofs should not be too pointed. Undulating rooflines that suggest gentle slopes are best.

It is not a good idea to have a big water element on the rooftop. If you happen to have a rooftop garden and wish to energize the north corner with a small fish bowl, make sure it is not too large. You must definitely not have a swimming pool on the rooftop. Another harmful feature is a blue roof, since this signifies "water above mountain" and spells danger. (*See also* Blue Roof Tiles, p. 210.)

ROOMS

Each room in the home or office building can be regarded as a small universe where all the rules and formulas apply. Feng shui for yang dwellings can be approached on a room-by-room basis and this implies the application of the Small Tai Chi principle.

Space that seems to flow from one room to another without too many walls is exceptionally good. Good chi in one room spills over to the next room.

Allocate room use in accordance with the attributes of the trigrams placed around a Pa Kua, so rooms located in different parts of the home can be allocated according to their orientations. Use the Pa Kua arrangement of trigrams to guide you in the allocation of rooms for the children. (*See* pp. 84–87 for more details.)

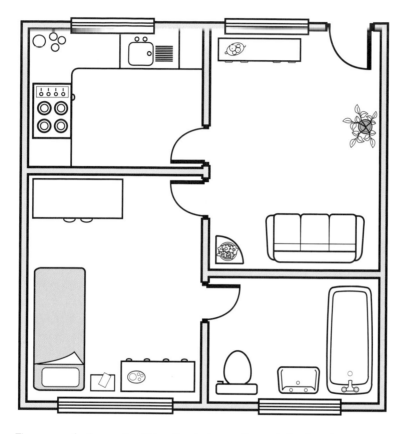

The rooms of a house should be allocated according to their orientations.

ROUND

This shape represents the metal element and is auspicious in the West, Northwest, and North, and it is also great for those with Kua numbers six and seven. The round shape can also represent gold. Round shapes can be incorporated into structures and designs used in these corners of the house or garden. Round tables made of metal and glass are excellent for the West corner and better still if the glass table top has etchings of auspicious objects such as the double fish, the five bats, or the longevity symbol. (*See* pp. 168–171 for symbols of good fortune. *See also* Longevity, p. 256.)

S

SAILING SHIP

The sailing ship brings wealth from the wind and water. Fill the ship with faux "gold" or with crystals cut to resemble diamonds. Position it in your best Kua direction, no higher than a coffee table to prevent the symbolism of flooding. Few things are as auspicious as a ship filled with diamonds.

You can have several ships in your home or office. Having more than one ship symbolizes different sources of income. You can even arrange to have an entire fleet of ships bearing gold coming into your harbor. However, one

sailing ship is usually sufficient to bring in good business luck. (*See* pp. 82, and 168–169 for more details.)

SCIENCE

It is much better if feng shui is practiced as a science. Evidence as to the potency of feng shui is generally anecdotal. Approaching it as science stresses the point that feng shui is neither completely folk magic nor completely spiritual. It is not religious, as it does not require faith in its efficacy for it to work.

It is important to differentiate between historical and modern feng shui practice. A great deal of feng shui knowledge has been uncovered and revealed to the world. At the same time this knowledge is more accessible. Those skeptical of feng shui should look on it as they would the study of geography or physics. Feng shui science is based on the I Ching's trigrams, the Five Elements, and the theory of yin and yang. (*See* pp. 6–9 for more details.)

SCULPTURES

Sculptures can create either beneficial or harmful chi depending on whether they appear hostile or friendly.

In the garden, sculptures bring good fortune when placed in harmonizing corners. Sculptures made of stone, granite, marble, or ceramic are suitable for the earth corners—Southwest and Northeast—while metallic sculptures are suitable for the West and Northwest. Avoid sculptures that have sharp points and angles or that depict wild animals. (*See also* Art, p. 204.)

SEASONS

In feng shui each of the four seasons has a corresponding element. Winter belongs to the water element. Spring is the wood element. Summer is the fire element while autumn is the metal element. When arranging your home décor and colors, be influenced also by the seasons. In winter it is cold and your home requires warmth, so fire energy is needed.

Creating fire energy (fireplace, wearing red, and burning brighter lights) will improve the chi of the home. In summer there is an excess of fire, so water to put out some of the fire, or earth and metal to exhaust the fire energy are useful. In these ways you can improve your home during all seasons of the year. (*See also* Wu Xing, p. 282.)

SELLING YOUR HOUSE

If you are having a hard time selling your house there are three different rituals you can try.

First, shine a bright light at the back of the house. Place the light high up on the back wall of the house and keep it on continuously until you have sold the house.

Second, place a "For Sale" sign just outside the front door with a picture of a bird carrying the sign in its beak. This symbolizes the bird carrying your wish to find new people to live in the house.

The third ritual is to write the address of the house on a piece of paper and fold it. Throw the piece of paper into a slow-moving river and walk away without looking back. (*See also* House, p. 246.)

SHADE

Shade is as important as sunlight as it influences the balance of yin and yang. In any garden or environment there should be both shade and sunshine. Shady patches balance the sunlight but too much shade becomes excessively yin. (*See also* Sunlight, p. 275.)

SHAPES

In Form School Feng Shui, shapes signify the five elements and can add to or detract from the harmony of elements in any corner of the home. Bear this in mind when arranging and decorating your rooms. The shapes of the five elements are as follows: round is metal; square is earth; triangular is fire; wavy is water; and rectangular is wood.

AUSPICIOUS SHAPES

Regular shapes are always preferred to irregular shapes. Thus squares, circles and rectangles are auspicious, while triangles, L-shapes and other irregular shapes are inauspicious. Regular shapes connote balance. The perfect shape for buildings is square.

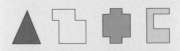

UNLUCKY SHAPES

Irregularly shaped houses usually have missing corners. Add yang energy to missing corners by using bright lights or adding more space.

Recently the pyramid shape has become popular. It is a yin shape. To live or work under it can lead to loss, illness, or worse. Companies with pyramids on their buildings may suffer financial losses. (*See* pp. 28–29.)

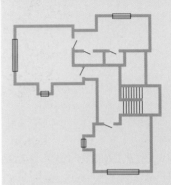

The first floor (above) and ground floor (below) of an L-shaped house. Regularize the shape through an extension or plant the missing corner with flowers and install bright garden lights as a remedy.

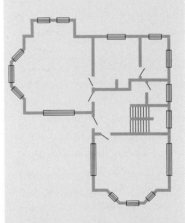

(*See* pp. 22–23 and 28–29 for more details.)

SHAR CHI

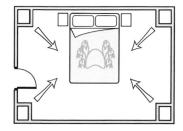

Avoid sharp edges pointing at the bed.

Shar Chi is Chinese for killing energy, which may be caused by poison arrows, discord of yin and yang, or the passage of time. This is the antithesis of the good growth energy, the Sheng Chi that feng shui seeks to attract. Shar Chi brings grave misfortune. Dissolve, destroy, or deflect any coming your way. Poison arrows, fading plants, rotten food, and a location near buildings associated with death, violence, or unhappiness create Shar Chi. Take action to counter it using the color red, bright lights, mirrors, and deflectors. (*See* pp. 30–31 for more details. *See also* Poison Arrows, p. 266.)

SHARP EDGES

The sharp edges of corners and buildings create one of the most severe forms of Shar Chi. If your building entrance is hit by the sharp edge of another building it will send bad Shar Chi that you should try to block from view. The most effective way is to plant trees. If this is not possible, using a yin Pa Kua mirror might help temporarily. If the edge of the building is too large it is simply not possible to escape its killing energy. (*See also* Pa Kua Mirror, p. 264.)

SHELVES

(*See* Bookshelves, p. 210.)

SHENG CHI

Sheng Chi is beneficial and benevolent energy that brings good fortune. These characters connote success and advancement. Houses with plenty of Sheng Chi (*see* pp. 38–39) enjoy auspicious feng shui and bring residents success, peace, and health, harmony, and happiness. The configuration of the surrounding landscape creates Sheng Chi (*see* pp. 16–17), but the application of feng shui formulas are also very effective in creating spaces that are awash in Sheng Chi.

Sheng Chi is also the best direction in your Kua formula of auspicious directions. Check your Kua number and note your Sheng Chi direction.

Kua 1	**Southeast**
Kua 2	**South**
Kua 3	**South**
Kua 4	**North**
Kua 5	**(male) Northeast**
Kua 5	**(female) Southwest**
Kua 6	**West**
Kua 7	**Northwest**
Kua 8	**Southwest**
Kua 9	**East**

(*See* pp. 118–121 for more details.)

SILVER

As a color, silver is especially auspicious when combined with purple. In feng shui silver belongs to the element of metal and is symbolic of the West and Northwest. (*See also* Purple, p. 267.)

SINGING BOWL

Use the singing bowl to clear space that is filled with negative energy. With a specially made singing bowl, move clockwise around any room to absorb all the negative energy at the end of each day.

Strike the edge of the bowl three times with a wooden mallet and place the bowl on a cloth cushion while walking round the room. Fresh new energy energizes the space instantly so everyone feels better.

Singing bowls are made from seven types of metals. The best singing bowls are made by Buddhist monks living in Kathmandu monasteries. (*See* pp. 194–197 for more details.)

SITTING DIRECTION

This is the opposite of the facing direction. (*See* pp. 28–29 for more details.)

SIX KILLINGS

Lui Shar, or "Six Killings" is an unlucky direction based on the Kua Formula. Take note of your Six Killings direction and avoid sitting or sleeping in it. This direction is based on your Kua number:

Check your Kua number and note your Six Killings direction.

Kua 1	**Northwest**
Kua 2	**South**
Kua 3	**Northeast**

Kua 4	West
Kua 5	(male) South
Kua 5	(female) East
Kua 6	North
Kua 7	Southeast
Kua 8	East
Kua 9	Southwest

(*See* pp. 118–121 for more details.)

SLEEPING POSITIONS

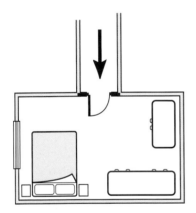

Sleep in an auspicious direction.

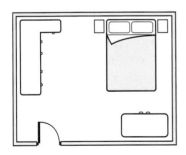

Beds should be positioned diagonal to the door.

Your Kua number determines your four best and worst directions. Always sleep with your head toward one of your good directions. (*See* pp. 64–65 for more details. *See also* Bed Position, p. 207, and Bedroom, p. 207.)

SLOPES

It is preferable to live at the mid-levels of a slope. Being at the very top exposes the home to the elements while being at the very bottom cause auspicious chi to sink. (*See* pp. 12–18 for more details.)

SMALL WATER

In feng shui this refers to the flow of water in drains around the home or artificially created water features that are not part of the natural landscape. Small water is just as effective as big water in attracting good feng shui when correctly oriented. (*See* pp. 160–165 for more details.)

SOCIAL LIFE

Your social life can be improved with feng shui. The best way to create the luck that brings an active social life is to use bright lights to give a boost of yang energy to the Southwest corner of your home. (*See also* Yang Energy, p. 282.)

SOUTH

The trigram of the South is Li, which indicates fire. As the season of summer, the South is one of the happy directions of the compass. If you site your house with a South facing orientation it will bring you good feng shui. Keep the South part of your living room brightly lit. The South is the place of the phoenix, so an image of any kind of winged creature—rooster or peacock—here is auspicious. (*See* pp. 102–103 for more details.)

SOUTHEAST

The Southeast is the place of the Sun trigram and also the place of the eldest daughter. This is the universal wealth corner. If you want to increase your income level, place a water feature in the Southeast. Plants and fish make the water come alive with yang energy so add these features as well. (*See* p. 112 for more details.)

SOUTHERN HEMISPHERE

The North referred to in feng shui is the same North irrespective of whether your country is in the North or South hemisphere. Residents of countries in the Southern hemisphere need not attempt to change compass directions when applying and using compass school formulas.

Chinese feng shui masters consider the placement of the trigrams around the Pa Kua as the arbiter of the element assigned to each compass direction. Thus, in the North the trigram placed there according to the Later Heaven sequence is the trigram Kan, which stands for water. In the South, the trigram is Li, which is symbolic of fire. Thus the element here is fire. (*See also* Li Trigram, p. 253.)

SOUTHWEST

This is the corner of the matriarchal energy. It is completely yin energy, and it is the place where relationship luck is enhanced or reduced. (*See* p. 110 for more details.)

SPRING

This is the most auspicious season as it signifies a time of growth. It is a good time to start a new business, but base the exact date on the Chinese Almanac. (*See also* Almanac, p. 201, and Seasons, p. 272.)

STAFF TURNOVER

If you want your company to grow and prosper, make sure your staff stay happy, motivated, and keen. Stress is often the result of overwork and poor feng shui. Systematically eliminate sources of bad chi. Place water features to encourage the chi to circulate. Nurture the energy of the staff by placing a large crystal or boulder in the corner where the Mountain Star Eight is located in your office. Be sure to position employees in accordance with their personal auspicious directions. Happy employees are your best assets. (*See* pp. 52–59 to help manifest business success.)

STAIRCASES

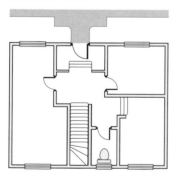

Staircases are conduits of chi.

The feng shui of internal staircases is extremely important since these are conduits of chi that lead the energy from one level to another. Staircases should be wide and curving to encourage the benevolent flow of chi.

Metal staircases are best in the West and Northwest. Wooden staircases are best in the East, Southeast, and South. Select according to the element of the corner where the staircase is located.

Staircases should be at the side of the building. They should neither start nor end directly facing a door, a toilet, a mirror, or the bedroom. (*See* pp. 38–39 for chi flow.)

STATUES

Statues carved of stone create excellent feng shui if placed in the Southwest or Northeast. (*See also* Sculptures, p. 271.)

STEPS

There are two main guidelines for steps in the garden. The level of the back of the house should be higher than the front and land on the left hand side should be higher than land on the right hand side. Steps leading up to your front door are auspicious features. (*See also* Landscape Feng Shui, p. 252.)

STEREO SYSTEMS

Stereo or hi-fi equipment is of the metal element and should be placed in the West sector. Stereos are excellent purveyors of yang energy, so keep them on to bring the yang energy of music into the home. This is particularly good feng shui when the house is otherwise silent. (*See also* Music, p. 260.)

STOVE

(*See* Kitchen Feng Shui, p. 250.)

STREAMS

Streams with slow-moving fresh water represent excellent feng shui. (*See* pp. 160–165 for more details.)

STUDY

If you work from home, pay special attention to the feng shui of your home office as this affects your livelihood and professional reputation. Energize your office with relevant good fortune symbols and continue to observe all the taboos and recommendations for office feng shui. (*See also* Office Feng Shui, p. 262.)

SUCCULENTS

Succulent plants and fruits are auspicious because they look ripe with goodness. They contain enough water to stay alive and healthy. Succulent cacti are excellent replicas of the precious stone, jade. (*See also* Cactus, p. 212.)

SUNLIGHT

Few things can beat natural sunlight for bringing yang energy into a room. Design your windows and doors in such a way that they capture the sunlight. Have your windows on walls that face the sunlight. (*See* p. 189 for more details.)

SWIMMING POOLS

Pools must be placed strategically, on the left side of the entrance door (inside looking out). Pools should be a regular shape with rounded edges that do not harm the home. Rectangular pools are fine as long as the corners are not pointed directly at any doorways. (*See* p. 160 for more details.)

SYMBOLS

Placing good fortune symbols around the home activates auspicious chi. Learning to place them correctly and in the correct sectors of the home is part of symbolic feng shui. (*See* pp. 168–171 for symbols of good fortune.)

T

T-INTERSECTIONS

T-intersections are the ultimate poison arrow. If your house is on a hill, a road pointing at it will not cause problems. The hill serves as a mountain that stops the road. When the oncoming road is slightly curved, it is no longer a poison arrow. Only straight roads can hurt.

A cure for T-intersections makes use of the intersection itself to capture fast moving chi, slow it down, and turn it into benevolent chi.

This cure involves welcoming the chi from the oncoming road by building a wall with windows that opens into the courtyard on the other side. The inner courtyard will capture chi through the windows and force it to slow down enough to be transformed into benevolent chi. (*See* pp. 22–25 for more details.)

TAI CHI

This slow, graceful exercise is based on energizing the flow of chi inside the body. It looks like slow motion dancing, but the precise series of exercises that make up Tai Chi practice slowly exercise and warm up every part of the physical body. Like feng shui, Tai Chi has attracted and benefited millions of practitioners worldwide. (*See also* Body Feng Shui, p. 210.)

TAOIST LEGENDS

Much of feng shui "magic" can be traced to Taoist tales of the Eight Immortals. These tell of their clairvoyance and ability to be in several places at the same time. Dragon battles and disappearing sages reinforced belief in Taoist magic and in Immortal figures, many of whom were deified over the years. Today, images of the Eight Immortals attract powerful chi associated with their magical powers. (*See also* Eight Immortals, p. 227.)

TEA CEREMONY

A Chinese marriage is not complete without the traditional tea ceremony in which newly married couples dressed in their wedding finery kneel in front of their respective parents and offer each of them a small cup of tea. After the offering, the parents bless them and give them a red packet filled with money.

Offering tea signifies respect for the parents and expresses filial gratitude. The parents of the bride often also present gold to their daughter after the ceremony. Tea is also offered to every member of the family—one generation older than the couple—to indicate respect for the family elders. (*See also* Marriage, p. 257.)

TEN DIRECTIONS

In addition to the eight compass directions are the direction from above and the direction from below. Good and bad luck come from ten directions: eight from the material world and two from heavenly realms. (*See also* Compass, p. 218.)

TEN DYNASTY COINS

It is excellent feng shui to hang ten dynasty coins in the office. Place them behind where you sit or on your left side to simulate the dragon. Coins taken from each of ten emperors' reigns tied together with red string symbolize wealth. The coins can be genuine antique coins or copies. Antique coins carry the chi of their period, so if the period was auspicious then the chi is beneficial. (*See* p. 169 for more details.)

TERRAPINS

Terrapins are popular domesticated turtles. They can be kept in shallow ponds in the North to bring good fortune to the household. Build a small waterfall falling into a circular pond about three feet in diameter for keeping live terrapins.

Soon they will learn to recognize you. They bring great chi to your home, ensuring long life, excellent children, and safeguard from disease. They also bring wealth, prosperity, and protection to the home. (*See* p. 172 for more details. *See also* Black Tortoise, p. 209.)

THORNS

Thorns are slivers of poison arrows, so flowers and plants with thorns do not bring good feng shui. Do not send red roses to your loved ones unless the thorns have been removed. Cactus plants are also not advised. Over time they will cause problems and difficulties. (*See also* Cactus, p. 212, and Poison Arrows, p. 266.)

THREE (THE NUMBER)

Three is the number of the trinity of Heaven, Earth, and Man. The number three can also sound like "growth" and therefore is considered auspicious. Its color is dark green and its element is wood.

It is auspicious to tie three I Ching coins with red string and place in your wallet, purse or handbag, or attach to your phone, computer, and files.

However, in Flying Star Feng Shui, the meaning of three is associated with the Jade Star Three, which is regarded as an evil star of disputes and quarrels. This star should be avoided, although it can sometimes bring good fortune when it successfully interacts with the elements of the space it occupies. (*See also* Three Killings, p. 277.)

THREE FEELING WATER

This describes three orientations of water that bring good fortune to the home. These "good feeling" waters bring prosperity and success.

1 Generally speaking, water is excellent if it comes toward you wide and leaves narrow.
2 Water is auspicious when two or three small branches flow into a main river and then the river passes your home.
3 A third auspicious flow of water is when it embraces your home like jade belt.

Water should never flow away from your home in full view of the front door. This always signifies wealth flowing out. (*See* pp. 180–185 for more details. *See also* Jade Belt Water, p. 249.)

THREE KILLINGS

The Three Killings, or Sarm Saat, is an inauspicious annual Flying Star feature. The Three Killings occupies one of the four cardinal directions each year and occupies 45 degrees. These are the guidelines on handling the Three Killings.

✳ Never allow the Sarm Saat to be behind you.
✳ Face it directly, as confronting the Three Killings will not harm you.
✳ Do not do home repairs or construction in the sector that houses the Three Killings for the year.

The location of the Three Killings during the years as described by the Zodiac are as follows:
Ox, Rooster and Snake—East
Sheep, Rabbit, and Boar—West
Monkey, Rat, and Dragon—South
Dog, Horse, and Tiger—North
(*See* pp. 154–155 for more details.)

THREE-LEGGED TOAD

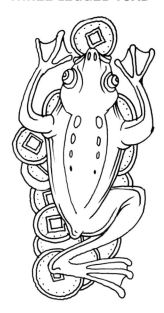

The three-legged toad is probably the most auspicious symbol of moneymaking. This creature is most frequently depicted sitting on a bed of coins and ingots, holding three coins in its mouth. The three-legged toad will attract gold to your home.

Place the toad fairly low, diagonally across from the front door, looking at the door as though expecting to greet wealth chi coming in. The frog should not appear ready to hop out, so it is best if it is not directly in front of the door.

You may keep up to nine toads in your house. They can be kept in the public areas of the home like the living room, dining room, and garden, but never in bedrooms, kitchens, or bathrooms. You can also wear jewelry formed into three-legged toad images to enhance career luck. (*See* p. 169 for more details.)

THREE STAR GODS
(*See* Fuk Luk Sau, p. 237.)

TIEN YI

Tien Yi is the direction that taps good health. It is personalized direction based on the Eight Mansions formula. Look up your Kua number and then check your personalized health direction. Sleep with your head to this direction for good health or if you are convalescing after a long illness.

Check your Kua number and note your Tien Yi direction.

1	**East**
2	**West**
3	**North**
4	**South**
5	**West (for men)**
	Northwest (for women)
6	**Northeast**
7	**Southwest**
8	**Northwest**
9	**Southeast**

(*See* pp. 118–121 for more details.)

TIEN TI RIEN

This refers to the trinity of luck—heaven, earth, and humanity—that governs fortunes and misfortunes. Heaven luck is what you are born with while humankind luck is self-created. Earth luck and humankind luck are within our control while heaven luck is beyond our control.

It is generally accepted that heaven luck reflects past karma. Good heaven luck often leads to good feng shui, automatically getting your orientations correct and displaying all the correct symbols of good fortune. Earth luck must supplement heaven luck just as it must be supplemented by good humankind luck. (*See also* Earth Luck, p. 226, and Heaven Luck, p. 242.)

TIGER

The Tiger is the third sign of the Chinese Zodiac, and its intrinsic element is wood. The hour of the Tiger is between 3:00 A.M. and 5:00 A.M. The compass direction of the Tiger is between 37.5 and 67.5 degrees, East-Northeast. This sector of the house is a lucky location for people born in Tiger years, and can be energized with images of the tiger in wood element materials. Wooden carvings or sculptures as well as paintings of a tiger are good in this sector. (*See also* Art, p. 204, and Sculptures, p. 271.)

TIGER HILLS

According to Form School Feng Shui, land on the right hand side of your home (the direction taken from inside the home looking out), represents dragon hills irrespective of the actual compass direction. According to compass school, however, the West side of the home represents tiger hills. (*See* pp. 12–15 for more details.)

TIGER'S EYE

This popular stone comes in a variety of colors, ranging from gold to cream to brown to reddish-black. It gives out vibrations of dynamism and stability, and promotes orderliness in projects and new ventures. When worn, tiger's eye promotes clear thinking and confidence in the wearer. It is said to be effective in the treatment of various maladies such as headaches and disorders of the throat, eye, reproductive system, and bones.

Tiger's eye is also considered to be protective. (*See also* Illness, p. 278.)

TIME DIMENSION IN FENG SHUI

Time complements the space perspective of feng shui philosophy and determines whether a building and its residents will enjoy prosperity.

Time is divided into cycles of 180 years, each of which has three 60-year periods, called upper, middle, and lower. In each period are three ages of 20 years' duration, so there are a total of nine ages for each 180-year cycle. (*See* pp. 44–45 for more details.)

TOILETS

Toilets are considered harmful feng shui. Decorating the toilet with fittings, flowers, and fancy adornments does not enhance it. In fact, it magnifies the bad luck and worsens its ill effect.

Toilets should be as small as possible, with minimal decoration. Always keep the bathroom door closed and auspicious objects away from it. (*See* pp. 61 and 73 for more details.)

TORTOISE

(*See* p. 172 for more details. *See also* Black Tortoise, p. 209, and Terrapins, p. 276.)

TOTAL LOSS

The Chueh Ming, or total loss, direction is the most harmful of the four unlucky directions. It means complete loss of wealth and of descendants. Facing your Chueh Ming direction or sleeping in a Chueh Ming location leads to severe bad luck. Your Cheuh Ming direction is based on your Kua number as follows:

Check your Kua number and note your Chueh Ming:

1	**Southwest**
2	**North**
3	**West**
4	**Northeast**
5	**North (for men)**
	Southeast (for women)
6	**South**
7	**East**
8	**Southwest**
9	**Northwest**

(*See* pp. 181–121 for more details.)

TRAFFIC FLOW

In modern cities, roads are interpreted in the same way as rivers, thus fast-moving traffic creates Shar Chi while slow moving traffic creates Sheng Chi. Traffic lights and speedbumps in the vicinity of your office or home are thus excellent since they force the traffic to slow down. However, traffic jams are simply bad feng shui since they signify blocks in the flow. (*See* pp. 12–18 for more details.)

TREES

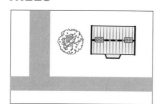

Trees block bad chi (above) and give support (below).

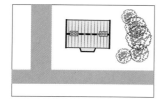

Broad-leafed trees not only block poison arrows, but also form an effective visual "wall" that can double as back support for your home. Green trees with good foliage are excellent energizers for the East and the Southeast. Trim trees regularly so that fresh shoots are always discernible. These signify continuous growth and generate auspicious chi. Avoid palm trees due to their prominent long trunks. Trees standing alone are like columns and emit harmful Shar Chi. (*See also* Shar Chi, p. 273.)

TRIANGLE SHAPE

The triangular shape can harm a home when any of its three points are aimed at the entrance. The triangle is often regarded as a protective symbol and is considered excellent when placed in the South, because it is the symbol of the fire element. (*See* pp. 28–29 for more details. *See also* Fire, p. 233, and Wu Xing, p. 282.)

TRIBUTE HORSE

The tribute horse is traditionally a white horse. The tradition began during the Sung Dynasty and since then high-level mandarins have decorated their homes with images of the horse laden with gold, precious stones, gifts and all the symbols of prosperity.

In the Horse year, the tribute horse is an excellent image to display. It is even better if the horse is being led into the house by the Wealth God. Place this image at the foyer near the front door for respect and honor, or place a tribute horse in the South sector for recognition. (*See* p. 170 for more details.)

TRIGRAMS

(*See* Eight Trigrams, p. 230.)

TSAI SHEN YEH

This powerful God of Wealth often has a fierce countenance and is usually shown dressed in dragon robes and seated on a tiger. Tsai Shen Yeh often carries a symbolic ingot of gold as well as coins tied with red string in his right hand and a staff adorned with precious symbols in his left. If he is leading a tribute horse, even better! (*See* p. 82 for more details. *See also* Gods of Wealth, p. 239.)

T'UNG SHU

(*See* Almanac, p. 201.)

U
UMBRELLA

The umbrella, or parasol, symbolizes shelter and protection from bad chi. The parasol is one of the eight precious objects of Buddhism and the modern umbrella is a variation of this symbol. The umbrella should never be opened indoors as this brings bad luck. (*See also* Eight Precious Objects, p. 229.)

UNICORN

The unicorn, also known as the dragon horse, is said to possess gentleness, goodwill, and benevolence toward all other living creatures. It is an animal of solace and appears only when a particularly benevolent leader sits on the throne, or when a wise sage is born. *See also* Chi Lin, p. 215.)

URNS

These receptacles have many feng shui uses. The motifs painted on them give these urns auspicious significance. When placed strategically, urns signify longevity and wealth. Use them for plants and flowers or place a pair on either side of the entrance door inside the house. You can also fill urns with yin water to neutralize feng shui afflictions, such as quarreling or bad neighbors. (*See also* Ponds, p. 266.)

V

VASES

The word for vase—ping—means "peace." Vases are best known for being transformed into wealth receptacles to attract good fortune and can be made into wealth vases. (*See* pp. 174–175 for more details.)

VERANDAS

The verandas of the home are considered to be part of the home for undertaking feng shui analysis; however, the veranda space becomes wasted unless you spend time there. Verandas are good places to hang windchimes since their tinkling sounds in the Northwest and West bring excellent good chi into the home. (*See also* Windchimes, p. 281.)

W

WALLS

The walls of your home can be painted in colors that enhance the element of their location. You can also hang paintings and display auspicious objects to energize specific types of good fortune. (*See also* Art, p. 204, and Color, p. 217.)

WATER

Water signifies wealth and correctly placed water causes the cash to keep rolling in. Too much water, however, can also be a source of potential danger and according to the I Ching it should be treated with respect. Through the year 2043, water is auspicious when placed in the North, East, Southeast, and Southwest. The North and East are the best locations for a water feature, either in your garden or in your home. (*See* pp. 161–165 for more details.)

WATER DRAGON

The water dragon is the best configuration of water flow around the home. This is part of the feng shui Compass School on water flows. (*See* pp. 161–165 for more details.)

WATER LILIES

Water lilies are excellent substitutes for the lotus and, like the lotus, they symbolize purity. If you have an outdoor water feature but birds are attacking your fish, consider planting some water lilies. Lilies are auspicious plants to have in your garden. (*See also* Lotus Flower, p. 256.)

WATERFALLS

When clean water appears to flow toward your home entrance or window, it brings great good fortune. Building a waterfall on the North corner of your land is excellent. Ensure the waterfall is proportional to the size of your house. Make sure the sound of the falling water is a soft rhythmic sound rather than a loud booming sound. If you are using a pump opt for the less powerful pump. Remember that slow-moving water is superior to fast moving water. (*See* pp. 161–165 for more details.)

WAVY LINES

Wavy, undulating lines incorporated into a design motif suggest the water element and are suitable for the North, East, or Southeast of your home or room. (*See also* Design, p. 221.)

WEALTH DIRECTION

Your personalized wealth direction (Sheng Chi direction) is based on your Kua number. Your wealth direction brings you success, growth, and prosperity—all the manifestations and byproducts of wealth. Sit facing your Sheng Chi direction. When you sleep, orientate your head to Sheng Chi. Your main entrance should also face your Sheng Chi direction.

Check your Kua number and note your Sheng Chi direction:

1	**Southeast**
2	**Northeast**
3	**South**
4	**North**
5	**Northeast (for men)**
	Southwest (for women)
6	**West**
7	**Northwest**
8	**Southwest**
9	**East**

(*See* pp. 118–121 for more details.)

WEALTH LUCK

Wealth luck is one of the eight major types of luck that feng shui can create for you and your family.

Prosperity is one of the most exciting and welcome manifestations of correct feng shui practice. Wealth-enhancing techniques always require knowledge of symbolic feng shui.

You can energize for wealth by displaying the three-legged toad or Chinese coins to attract money chi. Also energize the Southeast with plants or build a water feature in the North. (*See* pp. 160–163 for more details.)

WEALTH VASES

Usually made of gold or porcelain, wealth vases are to be filled with precious gold, money, pearls, and diamonds.

A personal wealth vase is an excellent way to create wealth chi in the home. Your vase can be made of earth or metal elements. Fill your vase with "precious" gems (semiprecious stones) such as crystal, malachite, amethysts, citrines, and so on. You can also keep jewelry in the vase. Hide your vase,

perhaps in a bureau in your bedroom, but never facing your front door as this represents your wealth draining away. (*See* pp. 174–175 for more details.)

WEST

If you wish to create good descendants' luck in your home to benefit the next generation, energize the metal chi of the West sector of your home. You can use white colors, metallic display items, and objects such as bells and singing bowls. An authentic singing bowl will create a clear sound that attracts auspicious chi when you strike the bowl three times with a special wooden mallet. (*See* pp. 196–197 for more details.)

WEST GROUP Everyone benefits from either the West or the East group of directions, depending on their Kua number. Kua numbers 2, 5, 6, 7, and 8 belong to the West group. The West group's auspicious directions are West, Northwest, Southwest, and Northeast.

West group people should use West group directions. They should avoid using the East group directions, which are inauspicious for them. (*See* pp. 64–65 for more details. *See also* Kua Numbers, p. 251.)

WESTERN SUNLIGHT

Temper the intensity of the afternoon sun by hanging small faceted crystals to disperse the sunlight into a rainbow of lights. This not only softens the severity of intense yang energy but also re-establishes the cosmic balance. Rainbows inside the home create happiness for the family. (*See* p. 189 for more details.)

WHITE TIGER

This celestial creature of the West complements the Green Dragon. The White Tiger is the creature that protects the abode. Without the tiger, the dragon is not a genuine dragon.

Always keep the tiger under control by making sure the West does not dominate. Do not allow the West or tiger side of any home to be higher or larger than the East side. (*See* pp. 13–15 and 181 for more details.)

WIND

The landscape is carved by wind and water. In some cultures, the wind is regarded as one of the elements. In feng shui, the wind can bring wonderful luck or it can turn malevolent.

Avoid places where excessive winds blow. When winds take on too much intensity, they turn malevolent. Protect your home against harsh winds whether warm or cold. (*See* pp. 12–18 for more details about locations.)

WINDCHIMES

Hang bamboo windchimes in the East and Southeast. Metal windchimes are to be hung in the West and Northwest, while ceramic windchimes can be hung in the Southwest and Northeast.

Windchimes can energize good chi and correct bad vibes. If you use the windchime to suppress bad luck or to deflect Shar Chi caused by a poison arrow, hang a 5- or a 6-rod metallic windchime. Note that 6-rod wind chimes are more potent, so choose the number of rods to vary the intensity of your cure or energizer.

Make sure the rods are hollow. Windchimes with a small pagoda feature at the top also work well for trapping Shar Chi. (*See* p. 91 for more details about hanging windchimes.)

WINDOWS
Windows complement doors as places where chi flows in and out of any building. They are best placed on walls on either side of the entrance door rather than opposite the door. Homes without windows lack openings for the good Sheng Chi to flow in. But there should not be too many windows in any home. The ideal ratio of windows to doors is three to one. Placing a gem tree outside your window "sweetens" the chi before it enters the home. (*See also* Sheng Chi, p. 273.)

WOOD ELEMENT
Wood is one of the five elements—the only one with intrinsic life energy. Thus wood element signifies growth, and it is excellent to have this yang element in all corners of the home.

The directions that correspond to wood are East and Southeast and the trigrams are Chen and Sun. The best energizer of wood is a healthy growing garden with lush plants and flowers. (*See also* Flower Gardens, p. 234.)

WU LUO
The Wu Luo gourd is a symbol of good health and contains the elixir of immortality. When placed by the bedside or worn on the body, the Wu Luo brings good health and long life.

Many Taoist deities and some of the immortals are depicted carring the Wu Luo. Sometimes the Goddess of Mercy, the beautiful and compassionate Kuan Yin, is depicted holding the Wu Luo as

a container of amrita, the precious nectar that symbolizes her blessings.

A jade Wu Luo can be worn as a symbol of good health or an amulet for protection. (*See* p. 92 for more details about the gourd container.)

WU XING
Wu Xing is the Chinese name for the Five Elements: wood, water, fire, metal, and earth. The word "Wu" means "five" and "Xing" is the short form for "five types of chi dominating at different times," which has been shortened to mean "elements." The Chinese believe that everything in the universe is inherently one of these elements, which form the basis for their esoteric sciences.

Water is the element of winter, wood of spring, fire of summer, and metal of autumn. Between all the seasons, the months are said to be of earth element. The names—water, wood, fire, metal, and earth—refer to substances whose properties contain the essence of the chi. The elements aid us in understanding the attributes

of the five types of chi. Water chi flows downward and there is always danger of overflow. Wood chi grows upward and is an excellent representation of life and growth. (This is the only element that has life.) Fire chi spreads in all directions, radiant, hot, and likely to get out of control. Metal chi is piercing inward, sharp, and can be deadly and powerful.

Earth chi attracts and nourishes, and is stable, caring, and protective. (*See* p. 40 for more details.)

Y
YANG ENERGY
This is the intrinsic nature of life energy, brightness, daylight, sunlight, movement, and activity. Yang is the life half of the yin and yang Tai Chi symbol of the universe. Yang energy is vital for the presence of good feng shui.

But yang energy should never be present in such excessive quantities that yin is obliterated completely. When yin is absent, yang also ceases to exist. Yang and yin together form the Tai Chi and are the fundamental basis of all life. (*See also* Canopy, p. 213, and Yin Energy, p. 283.)

YELLOW
Yellow is regarded as auspicious and as yang as the color red. Historically, yellow was an imperial color and commoners could not use yellow in their garments or home decoration. Red became the universal favorite symbol of good fortune. Yellow bouquets are lucky as are yellow packets of money and yellow curtains and interior décor. (*See also* Red, p. 269.)

YIN ENERGY

Yin energy is the diametric opposite of yang energy, but they do not conflict; instead they complement each other. Yin energies are more suitable for houses of the dead, including gravesites, burial grounds and cemeteries. Yin is darkness and total silence, which makes it excellent for places of rest such as the bedroom. (*See* p. 41 for more details.)

YIN YANG SYMBOL

This symbol eloquently describes how the two opposing yet non-conflicting energies complement each other. This symbol shows the ebb and flow of the energy and also signifies that there is always a little of the other present. Yin always gives rise to yang and vice versa. Together, these energies shape the universe and form a balanced whole known as the Tao–or "the Way"–the eternal principle of heaven and earth in harmony. (*See* p. 41 for more details about yin and yang.)

YONG LE

Yong Le was the third Ming Emperor; he started construction of the new capital at Beijing that evolved into the Forbidden City. Yong Le completed the palaces in 1419, but shortly after their completion the palaces burned to the ground. (*See also* Forbidden City, p. 235.)

Z

ZHONG KUEI (CHONG KWEI)

The most famous of Chinese heroes for overcoming black magic spells, Zhong Kuei is sometimes considered a deity. He is also an exorcist of the highest ability as he reportedly has 84,000 demon spirits under his command.

His image in the home offers excellent protection against evil spirits and black magic. The best time to invite him into the home (that is, to hang up his picture) is the fifth day of the lunar fifth month.

He is best placed near the front door so that he can see everyone coming into the home. Or, if you wish, you can place him on the wall at the foot of the stairs to protect the upstairs bedrooms from being affected by the Five Yellow and by evil spirits.

Zhong Kuei is frequently depicted as having an ugly black face. He is sometimes shown surrounded by urns of wine as he is said to be almost always drunk. (*See* p. 183 for more details. *See also* Five Yellow, p. 234.)

ZODIAC

The twelve animals of the Chinese zodiac symbolize the twelve Earthly Branches of the lunar calendar. Together with the ten Heavenly Stems, they make up the Chinese horoscope. The animals are: the Rat, Ox, Tiger, Rabbit, Dragon, Snake, Horse, Sheep, Monkey, Rooster, Dog, and Boar.

Each animal has a corresponding compass direction, which features in Compass Formula Feng Shui. Experienced practitioners can foresee trends of environmental destiny according to the yin and yang energy and the compatibility or conflict aspects of these signs. (*See* p. 63 for more details. *See also* Chinese Calendar, pp. 284–285.)

CHINESE CALENDAR

ANIMAL (ELEMENT)	CHINESE NEW YEAR DATES	EARTHLY BRANCH	HEAVENLY STEM
Rat (Water)	Feb 5, 1924 – Jan 23, 1925	Water	Wood
Ox (Earth)	Jan 24, 1925 – Feb 12, 1926	Earth	Wood
Tiger (Wood)	Feb 13, 1926 – Feb 1, 1927	Wood	Fire
Rabbit (Wood)	Feb 2, 1927 – Jan 22, 1928	Wood	Fire
Dragon (Earth)	Jan 23, 1928 – Feb 9, 1929	Earth	Earth
Snake (Fire)	Feb 10, 1929 – Jan 29, 1930	Fire	Earth
Horse (Fire)	Jan 30, 1930 – Feb 16 1931	Fire	Metal
Sheep (Earth)	Feb 17, 1931 – Feb 5, 1932	Earth	Metal
Monkey (Metal)	Feb 6, 1932 – Jan 25, 1933	Metal	Water
Rooster (Metal)	Jan 26, 1933 – Feb 13, 1934	Metal	Water
Dog (Earth)	Feb 14, 1934 – Feb 3, 1935	Earth	Wood
Boar (Water)	Feb 4, 1935 – Jan 23, 1936	Water	Wood
Rat (Water)	Jan 24, 1936 – Feb 10, 1937	Water	Fire
Ox (Earth)	Feb 11, 1937 – Jan 30, 1938	Earth	Fire
Tiger (Wood)	Jan 31, 1938 – Feb 18, 1939	Wood	Earth
Rabbit (Wood)	Feb 19, 1939 – Feb 7, 1940	Wood	Earth
Dragon (Earth)	Feb 8, 1940 – Jan 26, 1941	Earth	Metal
Snake (Fire)	Jan 27, 1941 – Feb 14, 1942	Fire	Metal
Horse (Fire)	Feb 15, 1942 – Feb 4, 1943	Fire	Water
Sheep (Earth)	Feb 5, 1943 – Jan 24, 1944	Earth	Water
Monkey (Metal)	Jan 25, 1944 – Feb 12 1945	Metal	Wood
Rooster (Metal)	Feb 13, 1945 – Feb 1, 1946	Metal	Wood
Dog (Earth)	Feb 2, 1946 – Jan 21, 1947	Earth	Fire
Boar (Water)	Jan 22, 1947 – Feb 9, 1948	Water	Fire
Rat (Water)	Feb 10, 1948 – Jan 28, 1949	Water	Earth
Ox (Earth)	Jan 29, 1949 – Feb 16, 1950	Earth	Earth
Tiger (Wood)	Feb 17, 1950 – Feb 5, 1951	Wood	Metal
Rabbit (Wood)	Feb 6, 1951 – Jan 26 1952	Wood	Metal
Dragon (Earth)	Jan 27, 1952 – Feb 13, 1953	Earth	Water
Snake (Fire)	Feb 14, 1953 – Feb 2, 1954	Fire	Water
Horse (Fire)	Feb 3, 1954 – Jan 23, 1955	Fire	Wood
Sheep (Earth)	Jan 24, 1955 – Feb 11, 1956	Earth	Wood
Monkey (Metal)	Feb 12, 1956 – Jan 30, 1957	Metal	Fire
Rooster (Metal)	Jan 31, 1957 – Feb 17, 1958	Metal	Fire
Dog (Earth)	Feb 18, 1958 – Feb 7, 1959	Earth	Earth
Boar (Water)	Feb 8, 1959 – Jan 27, 1960	Water	Earth
Rat (Water)	Jan 28, 1960 – Feb 14, 1961	Water	Metal
Ox (Earth)	Feb 15, 1961 – Feb 4, 1962	Earth	Metal
Tiger (Wood)	Feb 5, 1962 – Jan 24, 1963	Wood	Water
Rabbit (Wood)	Jan 25, 1963 – Feb 12 1964	Wood	Water
Dragon (Earth)	Feb 13, 1964 – Feb 1, 1965	Earth	Wood
Snake (Fire)	Feb 2, 1965 – Jan 20, 1966	Fire	Wood
Horse (Fire)	Jan 21, 1966 – Feb 8, 1967	Fire	Fire
Sheep (Earth)	Feb 9, 1967 – Jan 29, 1968	Earth	Fire
Monkey (Metal)	Jan 30, 1968 – Feb 16 1969	Metal	Earth
Rooster (metal)	Feb 17, 1969 – Feb 5, 1970	Metal	Earth
Dog (Earth)	Feb 6, 1970 – Jan 26, 1971	Earth	Metal
Boar (Water)	Jan 27, 1971 – Feb 14, 1972	Water	Metal
Rat (Water)	Feb 15, 1972 – Feb 2, 1973	Water	Water
Ox (Earth)	Feb 3, 1973 – Jan 22 1974	Earth	Water
Tiger (Wood)	Jan 23, 1974 – Feb 10, 1975	Wood	Wood
Rabbit (Wood)	Feb 11, 1975 – Jan 30, 1976	Wood	Wood
Dragon (Earth)	Jan 31, 1976 – Feb 17, 1977	Earth	Fire

ANIMAL	CHINESE NEW YEAR DATES	EARTHLY BRANCH	HEAVENLY STEM
Snake (Fire)	Feb 18, 1977 – Feb 6, 1978	Fire	Fire
Horse (Fire)	Feb 7, 1978 – Jan 27 1979	Fire	Earth
Sheep (Earth)	Jan 28, 1979 – Feb 15, 1980	Earth	Earth
Monkey (Metal)	Feb 16, 1980 – Feb 4, 1981	Metal	Metal
Rooster (Metal)	Feb 5, 1981 – Jan 24, 1982	Metal	Metal
Dog (Earth)	Jan 25, 1982 – Feb12, 1983	Earth	Water
Boar (Water)	Feb 13, 1983 – Feb 1 1984	Water	Water
Rat (Water)	Feb 2, 1984 – Feb 19, 1985	Water	Wood
Ox (Earth)	Feb 20, 1985 – Feb 8, 1986	Earth	Wood
Tiger (Wood)	Feb 9, 1986 – Jan 28, 1987	Wood	Fire
Rabbit (Wood)	Jan 29, 1987 – Feb 16, 1988	Wood	Fire
Dragon (Earth)	Feb 17, 1988 – Feb 5 1989	Earth	Earth
Snake (Fire)	Feb 6, 1989 – Jan 26, 1990	Fire	Earth
Horse (Fire)	Jan 27, 1990 – Feb 14, 1991	Fire	Metal
Sheep (Earth)	Feb 15, 1991 – Feb 3, 1992	Earth	Metal
Monkey (Metal)	Feb 4, 1992 – Jan 22, 1993	Metal	Water
Rooster (Metal)	Jan 23, 1993 – Feb 9, 1994	Metal	Water
Dog (Earth)	Feb 10, 1994 – Jan 30, 1995	Earth	Wood
Boar (Water)	Jan 31, 1995 – Feb 18, 1996	Water	Wood
Rat (Water)	Feb 19, 1996 – Feb 6, 1997	Water	Fire
Ox (Earth)	Feb 7, 1997 – Jan 27, 1998	Earth	Fire
Tiger (Wood)	Jan 28, 1998 – Feb 15, 1999	Wood	Earth
Rabbit (Wood)	Feb 16, 1999 – Feb 4, 2000	Wood	Earth
Dragon (Earth)	Feb 5, 2000 – Jan 23, 2001	Earth	Metal
Snake (Fire)	Jan 24, 2001 – Feb 11, 2002	Fire	Metal
Horse (Fire)	Feb 12, 2002 – Jan 31, 2003	Fire	Water
Sheep (Earth)	Feb 1, 2003 – Jan 21, 2004	Earth	Water
Monkey (Metal)	Jan 22, 2004 – Feb 8, 2005	Metal	Wood
Rooster (Metal)	Feb 9, 2005 – Jan 28, 2006	Metal	Wood
Dog (Earth)	Jan 29, 2006 – Feb 17, 2007	Earth	Fire
Boar (Water)	Feb 18, 2007 – Feb 6, 2008	Water	Fire
Rat (Water)	Feb 7, 2008 – Jan 25, 2009	Water	Earth
Ox (Earth)	Jan 26, 2009 – Feb 13, 2010	Earth	Earth
Tiger (Wood)	Feb 14, 2010 – Feb 2, 2011	Wood	Metal
Rabbit (Wood)	Feb 3, 2011 – Jan 22, 2012	Wood	Metal
Dragon (Earth)	Jan 23, 2012 – Feb 9, 2013	Earth	Water
Snake (Fire)	Feb 10, 2013 – Jan 30, 2014	Fire	Water
Horse (Fire)	Jan 31, 2014 – Feb 18, 2015	Fire	Wood
Sheep (Earth)	Feb 19, 2015 – Feb 7, 2016	Earth	Wood
Monkey (Metal)	Feb 8, 2016 – Jan 27, 2017	Metal	Fire
Rooster (Metal)	Jan 28, 2017 – Feb 15, 2018	Metal	Fire
Dog (Earth)	Feb 16, 2018 – Feb 4, 2019	Earth	Earth
Boar (Water)	Feb 5, 2019 – Jan 24, 2020	Water	Earth
Rat (Water)	Jan 25, 2020 – Feb 11, 2021	Water	Metal
Ox (Earth)	Feb 12, 2021 – Jan 31, 2022	Earth	Metal
Tiger (Wood)	Feb 1, 2022 – Jan 21, 2023	Wood	Water
Rabbit (Wood)	Jan 22, 2023 – Feb 9, 2024	Wood	Water
Dragon (Earth)	Feb 10, 2024 – Jan 28, 2025	Earth	Wood

INDEX

Lillian Too

For more information about feng shui, visit Lillian's personal website or the World of Feng Shui website or contact her by email:

Websites:
www.wofs.com; www.lillian-too.com

Email:
ltoo@wofs.com